THEORY AND INTERPRETATION OF NARRATIVE
JAMES PHELAN AND PETER J. RABINOWITZ, SERIES EDITORS

Techniques for Living

FICTION AND THEORY IN THE WORK OF
CHRISTINE BROOKE-ROSE

KAREN R. LAWRENCE

THE OHIO STATE UNIVERSITY PRESS
COLUMBUS

Copyright © 2010 by The Ohio State University.
All rights reserved.

Library of Congress Cataloging-in-Publication Data
Lawrence, Karen, 1949–
  Techniques for living : fiction and theory in the work of Christine Brooke-Rose / Karen R. Lawrence.
      p. cm. — (Theory and interpretation of narrative)
  Includes bibliographical references and index.
  ISBN-13: 978-0-8142-1123-6 (cloth : alk. paper)
  ISBN-10: 0-8142-1123-2 (cloth : alk. paper)
  ISBN-13: 978-0-8142-9221-1 (cd-rom)
  1. Brooke-Rose, Christine, 1923– -Criticism and interpretation. I. Title. II. Series: Theory and interpretation of narrative series.
  PR6003.R412Z75 2010
  823'.914—dc22
                                    2009034038

This book is available in the following editions:
Cloth (ISBN 978-0-8142-1123-6)
CD-ROM (ISBN 978-0-8142-9221-1)
Paper (ISBN: 978-0-8142-5661-9)
Cover design by Jason Moore
Type set by Juliet Williams in Adobe Palatino

CONTENTS

Acknowledgments		vii
The Unbearable Lightness of Being: A Preface		1
CHAPTER ONE	The Specter as Sign: Ghost Stories	7
CHAPTER TWO	Dead White Males: *Out* and *Such*	24
CHAPTER THREE	*Between:* A New Vessel of Conception	56
CHAPTER FOUR	*Thru:* "Corpus Crysis"	78
CHAPTER FIVE	*Amalgamemnon:* Pre-dicting the Future	98
CHAPTER SIX	An "Endjoke": Floating-point Real and Fixed-point Real in *Xorandor*	117
CHAPTER SEVEN	Saving the Text: Cultural Crisis in *Textermination*	137
CHAPTER EIGHT	Inscriptions of Life: *Subscript*	150
CHAPTER NINE	The Art of Losing: *Remake, Invisible Author,* and *Life, End Of*	174
CHAPTER TEN	Conclusion	190
A Discussion with Christine Brooke-Rose		193
Notes		217
Bibliography		232
Index		243

ACKNOWLEDGMENTS

THIS BOOK HAS BEEN long in coming—over fifteen years in the making. Although my passionate interest in Christine Brooke-Rose's work never flagged over that time, the period coincided with my assuming greater administrative responsibilities: chairing the English Department at the University of Utah; serving as Dean of Humanities at the University of California, Irvine; and moving in 2007 to Sarah Lawrence College to become president of the College. My various computers charted my slow pace and the shrinking calendar for my own research: chapter 1 was dated August 1993, chapter 2, August 1994, chapter 3, August 1995 and so on, with some lean years when, although my reading and study continued (I needed to keep up with Brooke-Rose's own productivity), the writing lagged behind. Finally, upon assuming my exciting new duties at Sarah Lawrence, I realized it was now or never.

I first discovered Christine Brooke-Rose's work when my colleague at the University of Utah, Robert Caserio, introduced me to the novel *Between*, as I was writing my book on women and travel, *Penelope Voyages: Women and Travel in the British Literary Tradition*. I fell in love with that work and decided that my final chapter would focus on Brooke-Rose's novel. Robert Caserio has continued to be an invaluable interlocutor for discussion of the significance of Brooke-Rose's work. I have also greatly profited from conversations with Barry Weller, another former colleague at the University of Utah.

It is appropriate that this book be published in the Theory and Interpretation of Narrative Series at The Ohio State University Press, the home also of the International Society for the Study of Narrative, as I first met Brooke-Rose when she delivered a plenary address at the Society's annual narrative conference, which was held in Park City, Utah in 1995. Thus began a friendship that included three trips to visit Christine in her home near Avignon, where, in the summer of 2004, we conducted the discussion recounted at the end of this book. My knowledge of Christine Brooke-Rose deepened as well by virtue of trips to the Harry Ransom Humanities Research Center at the University of Texas at Austin, home now to her papers. Tom Staley, friend, fellow Joycean, and director of the Ransom, first informed me of the library's acquisition of her papers; the librarians at the Ransom expertly guided me to the papers and manuscripts I needed, even early on before some of the work had been fully catalogued.

Both the University of Utah and the University of California, Irvine supported my research, for which I am extremely grateful. Doctoral students at both universities eagerly responded to Brooke-Rose's work in seminar, helping to mine the richness of her texts. Paul Lin, my research assistant at UCI, graciously put up with the fits and starts of my research schedule and continued to help me after I moved to New York, where I appreciated UCI's continued support of the final stages of the project. I had the pleasure of guest teaching *Out* and *Between* to the wonderfully curious and creative undergraduates at Sarah Lawrence in Stefanie Sobelle's course on postmodernism.

My deepest gratitude goes to my husband, Peter. Despite his own incredibly busy and productive life as an academic vascular surgeon, he has taken pleasure in my career as an author. From the time Christine discussed the physiology of phantom limbs with him (many years after she wrote "The Foot"), to our last visit with her at her home, he never ceased to champion this project. Finally, my son, Jeff, a doctoral student in comparative literature, read and discussed parts of the manuscript with me. His astute comments give me confidence that generations of readers will continue to appreciate the techniques for living in the work of Christine Brooke-Rose.

I gratefully acknowledge permission from the publishers to reprint, in revised form, portions of the following previously published material:

"Postmodern Vessels of Conception: Brooke-Rose and Brophy," in *Penelope Voyages: Women and Travel in the British Literary Tradition* (Ithaca: Cornell University Press, 1994), 207–36.

"Saving the Text: Cultural Crisis in *Textermination* and *Materpiece Theatre*," *Narrative* 5 (January 1997): 108–16.

"'Who Could Have Read the Signs?'" Politics and Prediction in Gertrude Stein's *Mrs. Reynolds* and Christine Brooke-Rose's *Amalgamemnon*," *Western Humanities Review* (Fall 1995): 18–38.

"Dialogizing Theory in Brooke-Rose's *Thru*," *Western Humanities Review* (Winter/Spring 1997): 352–58.

This book is dedicated to Christine.

The Unbearable Lightness of Being

A PREFACE

IN INTERVIEWS AND ESSAYS on her status as a writer, Christine Brooke-Rose describes herself as having "little or no existence." In *Stories, Theories and Things*, where she considers her dual career as experimental writer and literary theorist, she says ruefully: "outside the canon no interpretation, rather as one (now abandoned) dogma had it: outside the Church no Salvation. Fish [Stanley] would add: therefore no existence" (Brooke-Rose, *Stories, Theories and Things* 4). She notes that although her work has been reviewed, she lacks existence at the "critical level":

> I am one of the many authors who have a brief existence at what Hirsch (1967), as opposed to Fish, calls the interpretation level (the 'meaning' or simple reading of the text as syntax, for instance by reviewers), but who have little or no existence at what Hirsch calls the critical level (the 'significance' or what others call interpretation, that links the text to other things/realms of thought: the world, that is, other stories, other texts). This can only begin to happen, for better or for worse,

when an author enters a canon, however shifting, and I have a knack of somehow escaping most would-be canonic networks and labels: I have been called *'nouveau roman* in English' and *nouveau nouveau*, I have been called Postmodern, I have been called Experimental, I have been included in the SF Encyclopaedia, I automatically come under Women Writers (British, Contemporary), I sometimes interest the Feminists, but I am fairly regularly omitted from the 'canonic' surveys (chapters, articles, books) that come under those or indeed other labels. On the whole I regard this as a good sign. (Brooke-Rose, *Stories, Theories and Things* 4)

"On the whole," she considers this neglect "a good sign," but there is the distinct note of complaint in this description. The predicament of the "I" here is worth noting, for this predicament of invisibility or omission is ubiquitous in both Brooke-Rose's fictions and her critical writings. The author, Christine Brooke-Rose, is a specter, a being of "little existence." Like the shades that inhabit the underworld in *The Odyssey*, like the ghost of King Hamlet intoning "remember me," the author's existence depends upon the ear of the other. Only within the "Church" of the canon is a literary afterlife (Salvation) possible. Beyond the hint of petulance is a serious point about the ontology of authorship: the "I" of the author is simultaneously established in writing (on the page) and yet always aware of the persistent threat of its "textermination" at the hands (or deaf ears) of others. The proper name, "Christine Brooke-Rose," is a signifier for the life of the author; the author's existence is a function of intertextuality, which is another word for a living on by virtue of a haunting of other texts.

Now past eighty and living a relatively reclusive life in the south of France after her retirement from her teaching post at the University of Paris, Vincennes, Brooke-Rose desires to haunt the theories and fictions of critics and novelists with an interest in narrative experiment. She desires to be read. Although she has courted difficulty, like the modernists before her, and refused to pander to more popular tastes, she is reaching the end of her life with the desire she fictionalized in her novel *Textermination*: a desire to be given existence through her words. Her most recent books are overtly valedictory, *Invisible Author: Last Essays* (2002), a collection of essays in which she returns to the themes of *Stories, Theories and Things* to further ponder the ontologies of authorship, and *Life, End Of*, a memoir (2006). Like Italo Suevo's chapter in *The Confessions of Zeno*, "The Last Cigarette," these "last essays" are both a rehearsal of and protest against the death of the author.

In *Stories, Theories and Things* (published in 1991) and *Invisible Author: Last Essays*, Brooke-Rose conducts a kind of self-interview in which she makes a claim on the ear of the other by offering notes on her "intentions." The word is, of course, anachronistic in a poststructuralist, postmodernist context, the context in which we must discuss Brooke-Rose. Indeed, she has consistently derided the biographical approach to fiction in which the life is meant to explain the work. Yet in the genre of self-examination in her essays, Brooke-Rose reconnects the umbilicus between the author's being and her words, as if to add weight to her unbearable lightness. In commenting on her dual roles as critic and writer, she describes a "double paradox, that despite the long taboo on author intention . . . writers are constantly invited to talk about their work (first paradox), though the taboo survives in that they are not supposed to *write* about it (second paradox)" (Brooke-Rose, *Stories, Theories and Things* 5). Ironically, the "taboo" that Brooke-Rose notes is a form of logocentrism, a privileging of the author's speech in articulating her "intention." Indeed, the fate of Brooke-Rose's writings in being both ignored and misunderstood enacts an extreme case of the predicament of all texts, according to poststructuralist theory, a predicament that Derrida has explored, that is, as the fragility and tenacity of the connection between language and being (*Cinders*). This is a predicament that Brooke-Rose investigates in her fiction and criticism. She fictionalizes the orphaning of the text from the author, what Derrida describes in "Signature Event Context" and elsewhere as "writing . . . cut off from all absolute responsibility, from *consciousness* as the ultimate authority, orphaned and separated at birth from the assistance of its father" (Derrida, "Signature Event Context" 181). With nuance and, sometimes, pathos, Brooke-Rose's fiction theorizes this central poststructuralist perception of the "death of the author" and the spectrality of all language cut off from its source in being.[1]

Deconstructing the metaphysics of presence occurs on the level of character as well as author. The "unbearable lightness of being" afflicts the characters in Brooke-Rose's fiction as it afflicts Brooke-Rose, the author. It is most clearly narrativized in her metanovel *Textermination*, in which literary characters assemble at a convention to hold a "Prayer for Being" to the Implied Reader, hoping, the narrator tells us, to "recover, after an unimaginable journey, to savour what remains of international ritual for the revival of the fittest" (*Textermination* 8). The characters are "ghosts" (*Textermination* 19), languishing from "lack of involved attention" (*Textermination* 2) in an age of popular culture. In this comic, apocalyptic novel, we are reminded of fiction's link with death. *Texter-

mination brings literature to the brink of extinction, thematizing, and, ironically, bringing to life the various "deaths" that have become such critical commonplaces—of the author, of character, of the novel. And, although the postmodern condition has forced us to confront this situation, exacerbated as it is by the technological developments that produce competing claims on the attentions of would-be readers, Brooke-Rose's novel makes us understand that *all* fiction in some sense theorizes its own potential demise. Not only postmodern fiction, but realist fiction as well constructs phantoms of the imagination who demand the reader's faith. In a meeting between Milan Kundera's Tomas and Austen's Emma Woodhouse, Brooke-Rose even stages an acknowledgment that reality and unreality are wed in *both* realism and antirealism, nineteenth- and twentieth-century fiction. Emma thinks: "Being seems to trouble him for some reason, and he calls it unbearably light. And to her astonishment she finds herself agreeing. She has never thought of it in that way, and it somehow relieves her of the oppressive feeling she has had ever since she arrived, that her certitudes are uncertain, that she no longer quite exists in them, no longer quite coincides with herself" (*Textermination* 109). Specters and speculation go together in the textual world Brooke-Rose has created as she tests and tries out the endurances and vulnerabilities of fiction and its elements. In the thought experiments of Brooke-Rose's fiction, criticism, character, and theory converge as points of speculation.[2]

In Brooke-Rose's oeuvre narrative and theory are chiasmic; she demonstrates how theories tell stories and stories tell theory. Theories themselves are metastories told about language and fiction in particular; conversely, fictions are theories that take narrative form; they embody abstractions as they create a fictional 'world.' In *Stories, Theories and Things* and *Invisible Author*, Brooke-Rose attempts to add weight to the unbearable lightness of fiction's being and to the kind of speculation we call narrative theory.

This chiasmus of theory and fiction might seem to confine us within a closed circle of postmodern theory and practice that includes new techniques, but not the "techniques for living" promised in my title. For Brooke-Rose, however, new fictional techniques are needed to represent the cultural narratives of the twentieth and twenty-first centuries, narratives that must capture heightened constraint and loss. In *A Rhetoric of the Unreal*, she describes this cultural narrative:

> Never before have the meaning-making means at our disposal (linguistic, economic, political, scientific) appeared so inadequate, not only to

cope with the enormity of the problems we continue to create . . . but simply to explain the world. This seems to be the century which, despite or because of the pace of technological advance, has taken the longest, relative to that pace, to emerge from the mental habits of the previous century. We know that all the old secure values have gone, that a radical change is occurring which man must undergo or perish, yet we somehow go on *as if*, ensconced still in relics of nineteenth-century ideologies, in a way which other times in parallel situations apparently did not. (*Rhetoric of the Unreal* 6)

Brooke-Rose associates the last fifty years with a painful loss of our ability to differentiate reality from what she calls "the unreal." Her novels mime the absence of certain reality, or of some crucial analog for what we used to take as indubitably real. Obsolescence and extinction—even the loss of the human archive—haunt her texts. As they rupture "the relics of nineteenth-century ideologies," her fictional experiments are performed for the sake of finding new ways to theorize life and formulate conduct in a new world order. The revival meeting at the heart of *Textermination*, meant to staunch the extinction of its attendees, presages the grand narrative of evolution told in her last novel, *Subscript*, which begins 4500 million years ago with a chemical reaction and ends with humans on the earth about eleven thousand years ago. In *Subscript*, constraints on language, mirroring constraints on biological life, turn out to be glorious modes of engendering evolution and survival. Every one of Brooke-Rose's fictions is a rehearsal for living under the constraints of a new world, one that is as much a matter of shrinking possibilities as it is of a renewed expansion. Yet, contrary to any melancholy implied by Brooke-Rose's vision, her fiction draws creative vitality and moral inspiration out of the limitations it evokes.

In this book I make three claims about Brooke-Rose's fictions: (1) Despite their playful experiments with language, they are not insouciant about the pain underlying the "corpus crysis" (*Thru* 736) and "direlogue[s]" (*Amalgamemnon* 29) of the twentieth and twenty-first centuries; (2) They explore opportunities to convert pain, through discipline, into fictional power; and (3) They trust theory to emerge fictionally. Her novels produce significant experiments in writing and theorizing the novel tradition that fictionally "diagnose" the unreality of twentieth-century life, the conditions that much contemporary theory seeks to analyze and demystify. Kenneth Burke said that literature provides "equipment for living." Brooke-Rose's texts and techniques offer us just such instruments.

CHAPTER 1

The Specter as Sign

GHOST STORIES

THE MOST FITTING PLACE to start an examination of "the unbearable lightness" in Brooke-Rose's writing is with her ghost stories. In *Go When You See the Green Man Walking*, a short story collection published in 1970, for example, narrative speculation begins with the specter. Many stories are told from the position of the already dead: a seraph who greets people at the "Point of No Return" ("George and the Seraph") or a suicide who takes on bodily existence for one more time to demand that her unfaithful ex-lover give her away in marriage to death ("On Terms"). In the latter story, the "terms" of the title play off of the "on no terms" that mark the failed relationship between narrator and ex-lover. Jealousy feeds the narrator's fantasy of assembling her bodily atoms one more time to require her ex-lover's presence at her marriage to death ("But the being not on terms is the driving force which impels me to invent new terms, for of course we are on terms even if only those of agreeing to give me away" ["On Terms" 26]). Protesting her premature obsolescence in their relationship, she forces him to acknowledge his role in her suicide.

In these stories, the work of fantasy is equated with the physical energy needed to sustain an illusion, to prop up a ghost and make her function. The gothicism of these stories underlines the gothicism of *all* fiction. The ghosts perform the metacritical function of reminding us of fiction's task of conjuring and the energy it takes—atom by atom—to create the "semblance of a temporal body" ("On Terms" 18) out of words. The difficulty of sustaining this temporal body is emphasized in the truncated form of the short story itself. The fruitful play on the phrases "on terms," "not on terms," and "new terms" couples the terms of the love bond with the narrative bond between an "I" narrator and the reader. Out of the literally dead-ended relationship between lovers, the "new terms" of posthumous fiction combine the gothic with black comedy. The postmortem conducted thus leads to new techniques for fiction, with fantasy providing new inspiration, new life. It is no surprise, then, that "On Terms" was first published in a collection called *The Fourth Ghost Book. Go When You See the Green Man Walking* also included the republication of a rich and emblematic story called "The Foot," that first appeared in *The Unlikely Ghosts*. In this story, the most fascinating in the collection, Brooke-Rose allegorizes the spectrality of narrative.

As with "On Terms," the brevity of the story encapsulates the precariousness of fiction's conjuring act. Like the other ghost stories in the collection, this story is told from a posthumous position. Composed roughly at the same time as her novel *Out* (1964) but published later, this important early story is narrated by a phantom limb. Specifically, the first-person narrator is the phantom limb of a beautiful woman whose leg has been amputated following an automobile accident. The narrative "I," then, derives his existence from his ability to "haunt" his "victim" with sensations of pain from her already severed foot. The story begins: "The victim to be haunted is female. And beautiful. This makes a difference" ("The Foot" 43). The victim is also intelligent, which, according to the narrator, also makes a difference. The "highly intelligent undoubtedly suffer more than the plethoric unimaginative" ("The Foot" 46). In other words, their active imaginations goad them to feel the phantom pain through "imitation neurones" ("The Foot" 49), even though they realize that the limb is gone. Like Beckett characters or Scheherazade, narrators who must continue talking or risk extinction, this spectral voice speaks in order to affirm his ghostly existence and maintain his hold on the patient. The narrator is not the amputated limb but its image, a phantom subject to banishment if the patient, lying disconsolate in a hospital bed, is "cured" by the suave doctor, Mr. Poole. Like the narrative "I" in the story "On Terms," the jealous lover who is threatened with replacement in the beloved's and the reader's attention, the phantom limb guards its existence through narrative. He inflicts pain in order to reassert his connection to the place of the limb's origin, the body of the female victim.[1] Indeed, the patient's pain consummates the phantom foot's existence:

> She cries much more than quietly now, she shouts, she sobs, she yells, she gasps. I find it very exciting. The imitation neurones I am composed of agitate their dendrites like mad ganglia that arborise the system as the cell bodies dance along the axis cylinder within the fibres of the foot that isn't there, move backwards now, tugging away from the interlaced antennae as if trying to wrench themselves from some submicroscopic umbilical tie anchored into soft tissue, caught into bone, straining, straining to freedom birth and terror of time and space as the impulses race down the fibrils and create me, shape me and I ache strongly, I swell to huge existence that possesses her wholly and loves her loves her loves and hurts her unendurably until the cortical area can only respond by switching off the supply of blood along the nerves going out of the spinal cord so that she faints. ("The Foot" 49–50)

The metaphors suggest that the narrator is both orphan, cut off from the body of the mother, and castrated phallus ("I do not mind however at present being thus wound round cut off castrated as a phantom limb for I have temporarily spent my energy in possessing her so hugely hurtfully and I must rest recuperate my atoms . . . ["The Foot" 51]). This phallic "I' swells to its phantom existence in writing, yet he recognizes that his power is a sham, a magic puff subject to dissipation. We are made to see the enormous energy necessary to sustaining the narrative's conjuring act ("the impulses race down the fibrils and create me, shape me), in this case identified as a phallic energy. Tumescence and detumescence are the underlying rhythms in the narrative—as the desire to be felt swells into existence and ebbs after satisfaction. This "lover's discourse," a heterosexual plot of longing and abjection, splits the subject, the "I" of narration, into self-confronting parts. The narrator speaks from the point of view of the abjected part, severed from the bodily whole. One could say that his is a synecdochic desire, the desire of the part for the whole that animates the story itself.

"The Foot" is doubly a narrative of abjection: a story of a phantom lover who longs to return to the body of the mother/lover and jealously guards his companionship through pain and a metacritical tale about writing cut off from presence. The story emblematizes the divorce of narrative utterance from its "lived" context and writing from being. One thinks again of deconstruction's seminal recognition that "writing [is] an iterative structure, cut off from all absolute responsibility, from *consciousness* as the ultimate authority" (Derrida, "Signature Event Context" 181). In Brooke-Rose's version of this "cut," the prelapsarian body is a female body, its origin haunting a male narrator, as he, in turn, haunts it. The phantom limb, which derives its power by successfully mimicking a lost connection to the body, fears it will be exposed as a fraud. "The Foot" is a narrative *of and as* fetish, a substitute phallus whose potency is a sham. Like the Wizard of Oz, the narrative "I" fears discovery behind the magic curtain. The short story is a kind of foot fetish, enacting an erotics of longing and substitution.

The potency of the narrator vies with the potency of science, represented by the English doctor healer, Mr. Poole. In the context of the plot, the jealousy of the speaker stems from his fear that his own mimetic powers will be no match for the potent treatment of the doctor. The doctor is a disenchanter, the scientist who tries to convince the patient that her pain is only phantom. Yet this male rivalry between the narrator's potency and the doctor's scientific disenchantment is only a screen. For the narrator comes to acknowledge that the patient herself creates his existence. It is SHE who mourns the loss of her bodily image, in the process giving him his paradoxical phenomenality. "And now she thinks about me, giving me strength, existence, and creating my shape, her slim phantom foot, her unendurable phantom pain" ("The Foot" 47–48). He realizes that through her act of mourning, it is she who ontologizes his remains. Although the titles of the short story collections refer to ghosts, these posthumous hangers-on in Brooke-Rose's fiction have a sensuous materiality to them, more specters than ghostly spirits. These specters figure memory as a palpable reminder and remainder of event and relationship.

By the end of the story, it is the writing of the young woman that itself presents the greatest threat of extinction for the narrator, as the technology of writing becomes a prosthetic tool that will allow her to control her own pain. The story circles back on itself. When Mr. Poole asks his patient what she plans to do when she leaves the hospital, she replies that she has been thinking of writing. "Love stories?" ("The Foot" 59) he asks in his characteristically flirtatious and patronizing tone, and she says no. At this point the narrator, who has already told us that he is not "partial to words, they can be enemies too" ("The Foot" 46), recognizes that the young woman wants to write about him so as to exorcise the phantom pain ("She is thinking of me to write about in order to get me out of her system as they call it not sympathetic or parasympathetic autonomous but cerebrospinal out of her midbrain on to paper instead of aching there fifty-three and a half centimetres away from her stump" ("The Foot" 59). "I shall not let her get rid of me with words that recreate my shape my galvanising atoms of agony on mere paper to be read by careless unsuffering millions vicariously and thus dispersed" ("The Foot" 60). Her words "recreate" his shape, creating her own prosthesis in language. Disperse him is what she attempts to do, for as she writes, she encircles his narrative, the one that began "the victim to be haunted is female": "and she opens meanwhile the small exercise book and in thin impersonal strokes she writes the words she hears like white sun swamping all other receptors in the brain so that the white page slowly engraves itself with the victim to be haunted is female. And beautiful. This makes a difference" ("The Foot" 61).

The white page engraves itself with the beginning of the story, the "I" of the phantom foot now subsumed in the young woman's act of authorship. The grammatical and narrative tables are turned: It is she who is the subject and he who is the object; his effect is already her creation, her cause. She objectifies her pain and mourns her narrative into existence: "à la recherche du pied perdu" ("The Foot" 61), the narrator jokes near the end of the story, but unlike Proust, Brooke-Rose restricts herself to the ephemeral present tense in representing the search of the lost object. Emily Dickinson wrote, "Power is only Pain—/Stranded, thro' Discipline."[2] Through the discipline of her gothic writing, the young woman "strands" her pain and usurps the phantom authority of the phantom limb. Writing functions as her prosthesis, extending the life and limits of the body. Brooke-Rose generates narrative, rather than lyric, out of this self-stranding; the discipline of language counteracts loss.

In her meditation on the nature of narrative and loss, *On Longing, Narratives of the Miniature, the Gigantic, the Souvenir, the Collection*, Susan Stewart helps to shed light on the erotics of narrative, its relation to the body and to fetish. Her description of narrative as a structure of desire is helpful in discussing Brooke-Rose's fiction. In chapters on the souvenir and the collection, Stewart interprets the souvenir as "emblematic of the nostalgia that all narrative reveals—the longing for its place of origin" (Stewart xii). "It is this very desire of part for whole which both animates narrative and, in fact, creates the illusion of the real" (Stewart xii). But as Stewart makes clear, the longing for the whole body is marked by a play "between the present and an imagined, prelapsarian experience" (139). In Brooke-Rose's case, the beautiful women, the "model," functions as this platonic body image of wholeness. In "The Foot," the narrative returns to this archetypal female image, the body of the mother/lover figured as source both of life and death, womb and tomb:

> Eyes open can bring beauty alive with awareness of pain terror despair or anger, not to mention desire and liquid tenderness or even the alluring invitation down the pathways to the womb the tomb the cavern the ebb and flow of time linked to the sun-devouring moon the monster chasm of death and timelessness that draws man like a magnet from the moment he is conscious of a fall a wrench of umbilical tissue rough manhandling tumbling lying in soft cloud sucking at heaven severed weight of body on stumbling legs and fall, fall through the days and minutes. Eyes open can bring archetypes alive . . . ("The Foot" 43–44)

Stewart describes her title, "On Longing," as itself "a kind of ache," a perfect reference for capturing both the erotic longing and sense of loss that underwrite narrative. It aptly describes the combination of mourning and erotic desire that makes up the particular "lover's discourse" of "The Foot." As I will show, this metaleptic lover's discourse is replayed in much of Brooke-Rose's fiction, with its apotheosis in her most metacritical narrative, *Thru*: "'You are the sentence I write I am the paragraph, generating each other cutting off each other's word.'"[3] Roland Barthes explored these erotics in terms of the relationship between writer and reader, the "I" and the "you" of the text, in *A Lover's Discourse* and *The Pleasure of the Text*. Famously announcing the death of the author in *The Pleasure of the Text*, Barthes acknowledges the ache that remains for the writer's presence: "but in the text, in a certain way, I *desire* the author. I need his figure . . . as he needs mine" (Barthes 27). This codependency is staged in Brooke-Rose's "posthumous" fiction. Walter Benjamin reminds us in "The Storyteller" that the form of the story, unlike the form of the novel, is historically associated with oral rather than written production. Thus, Brooke-Rose's use of an "I" narrator who tells his story (an element she will eschew in almost all of her novels), exposes the nostalgia behind the "longing" for origin in the body of the author. In exposing this process of estrangement, Brooke-Rose does not minimize the aspect of mourning.

Like all of Brooke-Rose's writings, this story of palpable absence dramatizes a cultural narrative, an elegy that is historical. By this I mean more than to acknowledge the fact that the fiction "theorizes" a poststructuralist insight. For Brooke-Rose's fiction is historical in the way it records in "new terms" what she calls the "unreal" reality of the post-traumatic second half of the twentieth century. In *A Rhetoric of the Unreal* (1981), published approximately a decade after *Go When You See the Green Man Walking*, Brooke-Rose tries to account for the "return of the fantastic in all its forms" in twentieth-century literature, theory, and philosophy (*Rhetoric of the Unreal* 7). She sees this important return as a symptom of a 'reality crisis" in the twentieth century according to which there is a pervasive sense of unreality (*Rhetoric of the Unreal* 3–4). In her novels, reality is already an *effect*, issuing from some unspecified cause of separation, an abjection associated with the displacements of the twentieth century: e.g., World War II in *Between*, an unspecified, probably nuclear, apocalypse in *Out*, scientific "post-humanism" in *Such*; technology that threatens to render humanism obsolete in *Amalgamemnon*. In choosing the phantom limb as her narrator in "The Foot," Brooke-Rose puns on the idea of *extremity*. The foot is the extremity that used to link the body with terra firma, the pedestrian, the "real." Without this link to the earth, reality becomes unreal, fantasmatic. Yet the word "extremity" also conveys the sense that crisis is a part of our everyday lives:

> And yet it is obvious that to be effective pain must attack the most active therefore vulnerable part of the central memory-image, the extremities once in touch with earth air fire and water, the soles that bear the whole weight of existence as man transmutes his structural archetypes from curled to lying to upright position and learns the shapes of time food light dark play by fingering breasts limbs balls cuddly animals. ("The Foot" 45)

Curiously, this passage from "The Foot" prefigures Brooke-Rose's last novel, *Subscript*, in which she traces the increasing sophistication and sentience of man as he evolves from the prokaryote cell. Throughout her work, Brooke-Rose's testifies to a "corpus crysis" (*Thru*, 736) in language and history. The crisis is revealed along the pulses of the body; it is a "corpus" crisis, beginning with the legs whose malfunction calls into question what man's evolution has wrought. Man must adapt to his environment or face the possibility of his own extinction. In *A Rhetoric of the Unreal* she speaks of "a radical change" occurring "which man must undergo or perish" (6). "Never before," she says, "has man been so squarely faced with the possible annihilation of mankind and all his works, his planet and perhaps more. . . . These essential differences [between our century and others] . . . are deeply linked to the sense we have that the real has become unreal" (*Rhetoric of the Unreal* 8). In her powerful essay, "The Dissolution of Character in the Novel," Brooke-Rose discusses the prevailing sense of characters as verbal structures "more and more swollen with words, like stray phalluses, cut off from the real" ("The Dissolution of Character" 186). The narrative construction of a "foot fetish" in "The Foot" enacts this sense of loss and unreality that marks the twentieth-century in particular. Specters populate Brook-Rose's fiction, clinging to their power to haunt sensuously, palpably. Painfully and in pain, they acknowledge their obsolescence and cling to their material existence in an attempt to be a body that *matters*. Brooke-Rose's fictions "speculate" by materializing their theories of narrative in the equivocal figure of the specter. But the pain awaiting conversion, through discipline, into fictional power (to paraphrase Dickinson) is not purely personal. It is public and historic.

Like the phantom limb of "The Foot," the specter is a revenant, an unwelcome guest whose appearance cannot be controlled. In *Specters of Marx: The State of the Debt, the Work of Mourning, and the International*, Derrida speaks of the figure of the specter in relation to the question of repetition. It is a figure of iterability that cannot be put in its place or time. He calls this haunting by specters "historical, to be sure, but it is not *dated*, it is never docily given a date in the chain of presents, day after day, according to the instituted order of a calendar" (4). In his own analysis of the rhetoric of the unreal that the twentieth century has inherited, Derrida invokes Shakespeare, specifically, the specter of King Hamlet at the beginning of *Hamlet*, who begins the play with the injunction, "Remember me." Derrida describes "this pre-originary and properly spectral anteriority of the crime—the crime of the other, a misdeed whose event and reality, whose truth can never *present themselves* in flesh and blood, but can only allow themselves to be presumed, reconstructed, fantasized" (21; emphasis in original. Emphases in quoted material are original to the text unless otherwise noted.). But for Derrida, this spectrality is not confined to our sense of being haunted by the past. It refers to a haunting, a nonpresence, at work in the present and anticipating the future. He describes this nonpresence of the present as the "non-contemporaneity with itself of the living present" (*Specters* xix). According to Derrida, reality is shot through with its spectral twin. As in Brooke-Rose's fiction, this "non-contemporaneity" is exacerbated by a number of features of contemporary life imported with the speed of the technological revolution. Describing the "spectral effects" at work in the twentieth century, he cites "the new speed of *apparition* (we understand this word in its ghostly sense) of the simulacrum, the synthetic or prosthetic image, and the virtual event, cyberpace and surveillance, the control, appropriations, and speculations that today deploy unheard-of powers" (*Specters* 54). It also derives from the sense of the already dead and the non-yet-living, the specters with whom we commune in the present. This spectral invasion is also a question of ethics, of attending to the invisible others who cannot claim attention for themselves.

Brooke-Rose, too, is concerned with those "who *are not there*, of those who are no longer or who are not yet *present and living*" (*Specters* xix). These are the specters haunting her texts spanning past and future: *Subscript*, THE story of survival and extinction; *Amalgamemnon*, a novel in future and conditional tenses which predicts the end of humanism and, in "unrealized tenses," imagines the alternatives; *Xorandor*, a computer fiction in which she imagines us on the eve of the destruction of the human archive.

I propose Brooke-Rose as a candidate for the new writer/scholar that Derrida conjures in *Specters of Marx:* "There has never been a scholar who, as such, does not believe in the sharp distinction between the real and the unreal, the actual and the inactual, the living and the non-living, being and non-being ('to be or not to be,' in the conventional reading), in the opposition between what is present and what is not, for example in the form of objectivity. Beyond this opposition, there is, for the scholar, only the hypothesis of a school of thought, theatrical fiction, literature, and speculation" (*Specters* 11). Derrida posits the existence of another scholar, one who could think "the possibility of the specter, the specter as possibility. Better (or worse) he would know how to address himself to spirits. He would know that such an address is not only already possible, but that it will have at all times conditioned, as such, address in general" (*Specters* 12). Brooke-Rose's fiction and theory take up the theoretical wager, this hypothesis, the specter as possibility. Her work explores the palpability of absence, the sensuous reminder, remainder, anticipation, of event.

It should be clear from my description that Brooke-Rose's form of postmodernism provides a vision of inevitable human constraint and loss. It does not conform to the kind of ludic postmodernism privileged by Linda Hutcheon in *A Poetics of Postmodernism: History, Theory, Fiction* (1988). Hutcheon sees in postmodern literature a break and liberation from modernist anxieties, an open-ended plurality that leaves behind the anxious formalisms of the modernists in favor of a more insouciant attitude. She offers a rather glib inventory of what is jettisoned with postmodern experimentations, "such principles as value, order, meaning, control, and identity . . . that have been the basic premise of bourgeois liberalism" (Hutcheon 13). Although "control" and "identity" are concepts that come in for some skewering in Brooke-Rose's fiction, value, order, and meaning stubbornly reassert themselves in new forms that bind the fiction to the theory it materializes. Technique materializes theory through what Brooke-Rose calls "constraint" (I will return to this concept in a moment). Rigor, formulation, and form constrain Brooke-Rose's essays and fiction; they constrain as spurs to invention. They are not abandoned in jouissance.

With the assistance of an unusual essay by Vivian Sobchack I can further distinguish Brooke-Rose's work from Hutcheon's version of postmodernism. In an essay entitled "Beating the Meat/Surviving the Text, or How to Get Out of this Century Alive," Sobchack attacks Baudrillard's interpretation of the cuts, slashes and amputations in J. G. Ballard's *Crash,* an interpretation that celebrates the dematerialization of the text. Sobchack critiques the way that Baudrillard, in particular, and millennial discourses about cyberspace and technology, in general, "decontextualize our flesh into insensate sign or digitize it into cyberspace where, as one devotee put it, 'it's like having had your everything amputated.' In the (inter)face of the new technological revolution and its tranformation of every aspect of our culture (including our bodies), we have to recognize and make explicit the deep and dangerous ambivalence that informs the reversible relations we, as lived-bodies, have with our tools and their function of allowing us to transcend the limitations of our bodies" (Sobchack 209).

Now Sobchack, it should be noted, is writing from a particular and highly unusual position, a position she makes explicit to establish her authority: the position of an amputee who has lost her leg to cancer and who tries to come to grips with her prosthesis, her new "cyborg" existence. Her essay is a biting attack on the too confident transcendentalism and happy metaphor hunting in which contemporary theory sometimes engages. Indeed her critique of the decontextualization of the body provides an important corrective not only to Linda Hutcheon and Baudrillard but also to discourses of the posthuman in cybernetics. In this, context, too, "The Foot" is an important text to consider. Although I have read "The Foot" in part as an allegory about narrative, it also clairvoyantly introduces the information age, the noncontemporaneity of the present for the "posthuman subject." N. Katherine Hayles defines this subject as "an amalgam, a collection of heterogeneous components, a material-informational entity whose boundaries undergo continuous construction and reconstruction" (Hayles 3). As Hayles puts it in her analysis, which also critiques the dematerialization that is the object of Sobchack's criticism, "information loses its body" (Hayles xiii). "The

Foot" inaugurates the theme of information and its embodiments and disembodiments that will recur more explicitly in Brooke-Rose's later novels. Both the false messages relayed by the phantom limb to the victim and the attention to the boundaries and limits of the body are themes that will recur.

Considered in the light of information theory, the sensuous haunting by the phantom limb creates a reverberating loop between body and mind, a circuit of information. Brooke-Rose's notes for the chapter reveal not only her determination for scientific accuracy but also her focus on how messages deceive the amputee into an illusory image of the body. The falsely "reverberating loop" is explained in Hayles's history of cybernetics, which explicitly describes the phenomenon of the phantom limb in terms of signs and signals at work: "[McCulloch] proposed that neural nets can set up reverberating loops that, once started, continue firing even though no new signals are incoming. To distinguish between firings signifiying an external event and those caused by past history, he called the former 'signals' and the latter 'signs.' A signal 'always implies its occasion,' but a sign is an 'enduring affair which has lost its essential temporal reference" (Hayles 59). In "The Foot," Brooke-Rose's drama of narrative as fetish, the sign is caught in reverberating loops of self-haunting. Brooke-Rose conveys both the pathos and the pain that Sobchack resolutely seeks to retain for postmodern discourse. Yet in the end, I would contend that despite its power, Sobchack's essay loses some effectiveness in its unquestioning recourse to the authenticity experienced by the lived body, that is, the author's experience. It contrasts with the impossibility of retracing the link to the lived body in "The Foot" and Brooke-Rose's emphasis on the phantom limb as sensate sign. In Brooke-Rose's fiction, pain is "stranded" through the discipline of language. She refuses to essentialize the body's experience.

THE SIGN AS SPECTER: *THE TURN OF THE SCREW*

Brooke-Rose's brilliant tripartite analysis of James's *The Turn of the Screw*, republished in her book, *A Rhetoric of the Unreal*, reprises, in the form of literary criticism and theory, the theme of the spectral sign. In 101 pages, it takes James's tale as its model of the return of the fantastic in fiction. Indeed, following Todorov, Brooke-Rose considers James's text as the example, par excellence, of the "pure fantastic" (128). According to Todorov, the pure fantastic is a category of reading in which two plots (fabulas), one supernatural and one natural, coexist perfectly such that the reader cannot resolve which one is to be preferred. Brooke-

Rose is mindful, of course, that this seminal turn-of-the-century tale has inspired a history of readings which indeed choose between a ghost story (the supernatural) or a psychic tale of hallucination (the "natural"), but Brooke-Rose's point, and Todorov's, is that a scrupulous and "objective" reading of the text demonstrates that the clues support either reading without tipping the balance toward one or the other (the unreal or the real). Her exhaustive essay reads *The Turn of the Screw* as "an endless spiral" (*Rhetoric of the Unreal* 173), in which either reading can be supported structurally by the series of contrasts and oppositions mirrored on multiple levels without recourse to a single originating event.

Indeed, the absence of a single precipitating event for the trauma of the ghosts' appearance (whether as emanations of evil or emanations of the governess's psychic state) leads Brooke-Rose to dwell on the psychoanalytic concept of trauma as a metonymic relation between two events that share certain features, "a displacement through which the elements shared by both cause the second to symbolize the first and reactivate it" (159). As opposed to a simplistic psychoanalysis of the governess (a project that Brooke-Rose abhors), her own analysis of the "natural" reading (i.e., the nonsupernatural interpretation) posits that the *text* itself is symptomatic, i.e., a complex transmission of signs fundamentally dependent upon displacement and substitution. In a reading that combines the tools of structuralist analysis, complete with tree diagrams and tables of repetitions and variations that occur in the text, with the methods of psychoanalysis that focus on what is not said or said obliquely (with discussion of Lacan, Freud and Breuer, and Shoshana Felman), Brooke-Rose considers the ghostly effects of letters *in* the text and the language *of* the text. Her original essay on James's text, "The Squirm of the True II: The Long Glasses—a Structural Analysis," revised and reprinted in *A Rhetoric of the Unreal*, anticipates by one year Shoshana Felman's psychoanalytic essay, "Turning the Screw of Interpretation," published in 1977.[4] In her revised essay, which takes Felman's work into account, Brooke-Rose focuses on the metonymic displacements and inversions that structure the text and prevent us from mastering its content (i.e., solving its puzzle). She paraphrases Felman's reading of the "signifying chain of letters" in James's text that functions as "a chain of ghosts, the erased letter being like the return of the dead, and both like the story of the unconscious, the return of the repressed through the insistence of the signifier" (*Rhetoric of the Unreal*). In cataloguing the quadripartite structure of the text (based on a series of four-sided frames), Brooke-Rose notes that the four storytellers, Griffith, Douglas, the "I-narrator," and the governess, all are transmitters of the tale for which we are given no "original." She comments that this transmission process "further emphasizes the loss of origin, the curiously Derridean *trace* of lost origin and the curiously Lacanian 'rehandling of the signifier' in a complex chain of transmission, each transmittor or addressor having first been a receiver or addressee, a reader who turns narrator" (*Rhetoric of the Unreal* 173). In this frankly Derridean reading, the missing letters set off a complex transmission of information with neither identifiable source nor destination.

But unlike Felman, Brooke-Rose seeks to anchor her discussion of the ghostly effects of James's text narratologically, in the precise and careful *structuring* of its mirroring processes, including, but not limited to, the thematic of the letters and story telling in the text. A fulcrum between structuralism and poststructuralism, Brooke-Rose's essay tries to show how a poststructuralist reading depends upon a precise formulation of the structures of a text, that "indeterminacy" and "ambiguity" are not antithetical to method and methodology.[5] It also demonstrates that in the work of a "master" such as James, fiction, in its traumatic knowledge, anticipates theory. Although Brooke-Rose mentions that according to previous critics, James could have been acquainted with Freud's and Breuer's 1895 *Studies on Hysteria* (*Rhetoric of the Unreal* 159), she maintains that a psychoanalytic reading of his text need not depend upon such influence. "James, however, must have been perfectly aware that mirrors and their adjuncts (windows, spectacles, telescopes, etc.) are a constant motif in the supernatural, notably in E.T.A. Hoffmann. Nor is it so by chance. In this text, this odd detail about the governess's upbringing, and the castration shock it ought in theory to provoke, is a fine example of the writer's intuition having little need of specific reading in contemporary or (of course) later scientific discoveries" (*Rhetoric of the Unreal* 398, fn 7). What fiction "knows" is an issue that Brooke-Rose engages in multiple forms and valences, as critic, theorist, and fiction writer. The pleasures, methods, freedoms, and constraints operate variously in texts in which she represents both the systems and intuitions of contemporary discourses. Throughout this oeuvre, however, we witness a fascination with the pressure of what's missing and an exploration of the ties that bind precisely because they are already severed.

THE FASCINATION OF WHAT'S MISSING

For Brooke-Rose, the fascination of what's missing is a fundamental matter of technique as well as philosophy and theme. The two are indissoluble. Invisibility, nonpresence, severed ties that bind through haunting—these themes, engaged in her fiction and criticism, correlate with the most distinctive feature of her experimental writing: her use of lipograms. Lipograms are techniques of omission, self-imposed by the author, in which a grammatical or alphabetical feature is deliberately left out. Strictly speaking, the word "lipogram" means "lacking a letter," although I join Brooke-Rose in using the term more inclusively to refer to a number of technical "constraints." *Invisible Author: Last Essays* is devoted to her explanation of her constraints as well as an attempt to tease out the link between these technical omissions and her own invisibility as a writer. Brooke-Rose's constraints include: the omission of the verb "to be" in *Between;* "to have" in *Next;* personal pronouns and possessive adjectives in her autobiography *Remake* and in sections of *Subscript* (depending on the "consciousness" of the organism she is representing); and constative sentences in *Amalgamemnon*. The most significant and consistent lipogram Brooke-Rose invents in her fiction is a narratorless narrative that eschews the past tense and first-person. With no retrospection (hence, no one vantage point for looking back) and no origin or voice speaking the text, she constantly raises the question "Who speaks?" In chapter 7 of *Invisible Author*, called "The Author is Dead: Long Live the Author," and in a reprisal in *Life, End Of,* Brooke-Rose describes her technique, adapted for her own purposes from Robbe-Grillet's nouveau roman, as a "speakerless present . . . [an] impersonal, speakerless (narratorless) narrative" (Brooke-Rose, *Invisible Author* 152).

These "constraints" fund invention. They turn deprivation into power and jolt the novel into experimental form using limitation as a window to creative freedom.[6] Brooke-Rose's invention of a new, characteristic style asserts a vital alternative. In her focus on lipograms and other constraints in her experimental novels, as well as her emphasis on writing as craft and practice, Brooke-Rose resembles the group of French writers known as Oulipo, a group of writers who founded an association in 1960 which began as a colloquium devoted to the work of Raymond Queneau. The name stands for *Ouvroir de Littérature Potentielle*. Queneau described the objective of Oulipo: "To propose new 'structures' to writers, mathematical in nature, or to invent new artificial or mechanical procedures that will contribute to literary activity: props for inspiration as it were, or rather, in a way, aids for creativity."[7] The idea of "the artisinal nature of literary work . . . central to Oulipian poetics" (Motte "Introduction" 10) characterizes Brooke-Rose's treatment of technique as well. Writing with constraints emphasizes the discipline and craft of writing as well as its difficulty as labor. In his edited collection of some of Oulipo's most important writings, Motte points out that "the

French word *ouvroir* has three principal meanings: it denotes the room in a convent where the nuns assemble to work, a charitable institution where indigent women engage in needlework, and a 'sewing circle' where well-to-do ladies make clothes for the poor and vestments for the Church" (Motte, "Introduction" 9). Motte does not emphasize the paradox that although all the forms of labor listed pertain to women's work, most of the Oulipean writers were male.[8]

Yet, unlike the Oulipeans who advertised their lipograms both within their fiction and in manifestos, Brooke-Rose challenged her readers to discover them. Where the Oulipeans publicized the use of their constraints, sometimes affixing a "user's manual," Brooke-Rose tended to embed them. In doing so, she has run the risk that her technical "absences" would go undetected. In essays and interviews, Brooke-Rose sometimes laments the fact that her lipograms often went unnoticed by her readers. *Invisible Author* attempts to redress the peculiar "overlooking" of Brooke-Rose's main grammatical lipogram: the refusal of the third-person, past tense narrative. The book begins with the question, "Have you ever tried to do something very difficult as well as you can, over a long period, and found that nobody notices? That's what I've been doing for over thirty years (Brooke-Rose, *Invisible Author* 1). In *Invisible Author* she explores the "problem of 'visibility/invisibility' raised by the lipogram" (3). For, despite able criticism and positive reviews, critics and reviewers failed to comment sufficiently (in Brooke-Rose's eyes) on the importance of this absence. She contrasts the lack of attention paid to her use of the lipogram with the attention that Georges Perec attracted in writing *La Disparition* (1969), in which he omitted the letter "e." Brooke-Rose published *Between* in 1968, a few months before *La Disparition* (translated by Gilbert Adair as *A Void* in 1994). She clearly resents the fact that the critics were intrigued when Perec announced that he had used a lipogram in *La Disparition*; yet when she revealed her own self-imposed omission to a friend and reviewer, Hélène Cixous, no one, including Cixous, seemed to care.

As much as the joint interest in lipogram, the contrast between Brooke-Rose's use of constraints and those of the Oulipeans is instructive. Never a joiner of groups, Brooke-Rose worked alone all her life, despite her friendship with other writers in England and France. Indeed, the only reference to Oulipo in her essays on her craft in *Invisible Author*, comes in one footnote reference to Georges Perec: "Perec belonged to the club Oulipo (Ouvroir de Littérature Potentielle), headed by Raymond Queneau at the time, whom I greatly admired, and which relished formal tours de force of this kind. I was once invited (by a lesser member) to join, which was a huge honor, but I refused, for fear, perhaps, of being drawn into such attractive games" (*Invisible Author* 183, n.5).[9]

Perec and his translator, for example, offered more markers of absence than Brooke-Rose in *Between*. In chapter one of *A Void*, the reader is introduced to the main character, Anton Vowl, whose surname itself marks the absence of the letter "e" in the word "vowel." In addition, Anton, the character's Christian name, is an anagram for "not an," adding to the clues of the absence of the letter "e." Every time we see his name, then, we are reminded of the absence of the most common letter in the French language. Indeed, later on, the character himself disappears. Although the English title, *A Void*, names an absence, the French title *La Disparition*, meaning disappearance and passing, more keenly suggests an element of ghostly trace. It is worth noting that in 1972, Perec wrote *Les revenentes*, literally, "ghosts," in which "e" is the only vowel employed. A headnote to *A Void*, published in 1994, after Perec's death, informs the reader: "After writing *La Disparition* (*A Void*), he took all his unused e's and devoted them to a short text, *Les revenentes*, in which e is the only vowel employed." (Perec np)[10] Talk about a return of the repressed!

How absence signifies, technically, ontologically, emotionally is a question Brooke-Rose will raise throughout her oeuvre in different genres and with different techniques of omission.[11] Although there is often something elegiac in these hauntings, they are also intimations of obsolescence. Like the phantom limb, desperate to continue to signify in the young woman's life, Brooke-Rose's characters feel themselves becoming increasingly obsolete, losing their significance. Writing of what he calls "obsolete objects in the literary imagination," Francesco Orlando sees in literature a range of affective reactions to the obsolescence hastened by the speed, mechanicity, and remakes of modern life. His categorization of different types of images of "nonfunctional corporality," might usefully help classify the "lightness of being" Brooke-Rose explores: (1) living human (2) nonliving human, (3) living nonhuman, and (4) nonliving nonhuman.[12] Orlando is most interested in the fourth category, the "nonliving nonhuman" and least interested in the first category, which includes what happens to the human body in its weakness, decrepitude, and infirmity. Brooke-Rose's novels, however, take up the full range of this problematic.

As the title suggests, *Out*, her first consciously experimental lipogramatic novel, represents abjection, its central consciousness a sick, lethargic, and out of work humanist. *Next* (with its lipogram of "to have") explicitly represents the abjected as a social class, the homeless.

In most of her novels, humanism is a dead letter, and with it those writers, characters, and professors whose expertise is no longer valued, as with the multifaceted Cassandra-like consciousness of her novel *Amalgamemnon*, crafted in future or "unrealized" tenses only. But it is in *Remake* and, more painfully, in *Life, End Of*, that the central consciousness finds itself in a Yeatsian predicament, fastened to a dying animal. It is here, in her memoir, that "nonfunctional corporeality" renders the writer's cruelly ironic predicament most acutely. Losing the use of her legs and her eyesight, the worker in difficult prose is no longer able to climb the stairs to her library, to read, and, finally, to write, her pleasure in the artisinal nature of her work now denied.

Brooke-Rose's books catalogue as well the "nonliving human"—the specters that haunt the living like the phantom limb; the ghosts she analyzes in James's *The Turn of the Screw*; Larry, the psychiatrist, who has returned from the dead and is the central consciousness of her novel *Such*; the literary characters who wander the pages of *Textermination*, nervously resisting their own extinction in the cultural memory; and, in the broadest archeological sweep, the extinct species of her Darwinian novel, *Subscript*. In *Subscript*, she also takes up the record of the "living nonhuman" (or prehuman), from the earliest cells to the invertebrates and vertebrates that comprise the species before the appearance of homo sapiens. And in *Xorandor*, she examines the "non living nonhuman"—the computer, Xorandor, whose progeny do nothing less than threaten the human archive.[13]

As Brooke-Rose destabilizes the ontological foundations of her "beings," it is language that concerns her. She invents new terms for her literature of speculation. In novels and in essays, she creates "techniques for living," a phrase she uses in her novel *Out*. Again and again, language is the site of both the threatened textermination and of survival. Indeed, originally entitled "Textermination," Brooke-Rose's most metatextual novel *Thru* offers constant reminders of the way that "persons" emerge grammatically and ontologically on the page ("out of the Zero where the author is situated, both excluded and included, the third person is generated, pure signifier of the subject's experience" (*Thru* 647). *Thru* traces the path of "the sign that watches, helpless and in great pain, the engendering of its own projected trajectory struggling along" (Brooke-Rose, *Thru* 737). In "splitting" herself as theorist and novelist in *Thru* and elsewhere, Brooke-Rose stages the drama of the sign watching the engendering of its own trajectory in the theater of theory. Here, and throughout her work, technique is inseparable from techniques for living.

CHAPTER 2

Dead White Males

OUT AND SUCH

OUT (1964)

If Brooke-Rose's short story "The Foot" presents an abjected narrative "I," her novel *Out*, written almost simultaneously, represents an entire abjected society. The novel is a neocosm, in Cristopher Nash's terms, an "alternative-worlds fiction" (Nash 60). *Out* is a post-apocalyptic fantasy in which the "color bar" is reversed after a cataclysmic event (presumably some kind of nuclear episode). Unlike the "Melanian" races, the "colourless" have been susceptible to radiation, producing major mutations in their bodies and psyches. Whites have become sickly and powerless and blacks are healthy and in control. Nation states have regrouped in major new political configurations (e.g., Afro-Eurasia, Sino-America) and geographic displacements and internments have occurred. The binary opposition of race still determines social hierarchy, now, however, with a revolutionary reversal.

The narrative microscopically depicts the environs of a sick and unemployed white male who spends most of his time tended by his wife in their small shack. This former humanist makes occasional forays to the "Labor Exchange" to look for work, but is basically relegated to picking up menial "odd jobs" around the estate of his wife's employer, Mrs. Mgulu. The unnamed man is a perceiver and object of attention but not an I- narrator or lyric center: "A fly straddles another fly on the faded denim stretched over the knee. Sooner or later, the knee will have to make a move, but now it is immobilised by the two flies, the lower of which is so still that it seems dead."[1] Rather than actively perceiving his proximate surroundings, the man passively registers objects in the environment, objects including his own body. *Out* is the first novel in which Brooke-Rose forged what would become her signature constraint, the narratorless narrative sentence. Describing this technique in *Invisible Author*, she says: "there is no seer, only the seen, no "énonciation . . . only énoncé" (*Invisible Author* 138). Like Beckett's "unchosen beings" (Brooke-Rose's phrase),[2] the man exists OUTside the power structures of society, with neither the opportunity nor the will to be an agent in his own drama.

The narration is awash in passivity—"sooner" and "later" merge in lethargy, symptomatic of the enervation experienced by society's whites. The narration is strictly present tense; no authoritative act of narrative retrospection is possible. The passive constructions in the narrative mimic a loss of both energy and action: "Sooner or later some interruption will be necessary, a bowl of gruel to be eaten, for instance, or a conversation to undergo. Sooner or later a bowl of gruel will be brought, unless perhaps it has already been brought, and the time has come to go and get rid of it" (*Out* 11–12). Protagonist, plot, exposition, event, and suspense—these elements of traditional narrative are largely absent. The novel begins with a man so abjected that he cedes his minimal desire to two copulating and near dead flies whose "drama" keeps him immobilized. Rather than positing meaningful alternatives, the conjunction "or" in the phrase "sooner or later" signifies the man's, and the narrative's indifference.[3]

Something has happened, but when or how is never recounted. "Did you ever find your trauma?" (*Out* 120), the man asks Mrs. Ned, a white woman, but the origin of the present predicament is irretrievable. We learn that there has been a general "displacement from cause to effect" (*Out* 120). "Somewhere in the archives there will be evidence that this occurred, if it is kept, and for those who risk to look it up. Other episodes, however, cannot be proved in this way" (*Out* 79). The historical sense enabled in traditional past-tense narration is itself displaced onto some imagined, but uncertain, archive. Thus, narrative, along with society, suffers symptoms of a disease. A doctor tells the man "diagnosis only prognosticates aetiology" (*Out* 140), meaning, we learn later, that "no ultimate cause or ultimate cure" is possible, only an accommodation to the present reality (*Out* 151). A rupture has occurred as a result of some prior injustice or circumstance, but despite the many attempts to determine "what did you do avant la guerre," there are no causes—only symptoms needing treatment. The lack of movement, the inertia, doubles the meaning of "patient," as sick characters and ailing narrative wait for something to happen. Society, and, mimetically, the narrative, are riven with what would now be termed posttraumatic stress syndrome, a condition summed up in the line, "The weeds are scattered all over the scorched earth" (*Out* 197). The reader arrives somehow belatedly, unable to get her bearings.

The present-tense narrative sentence Brooke-Rose developed in *Out* is, in her own view, her most significant technical innovation, one that permeates her fiction. Lipogrammatic, the narrative sentence refuses traditional past tense narration. In a chapter entitled "The Author is Dead: Long Live the Author" in *Invisible Author*, she places her development of this narrative sentence, beginning with its use in *Out*, in the context of the French "nouveau roman," as initiated by Robbe-Grillet, most prominently, along with Nathalie Sarraute and other French experimental writers. This technique deliberately eschews the third-person past tense narration of the traditional novel, that "reassuring guarantor of real events" (*Invisible Author* 132) and relies, instead, on the present tense. Indeed, Brooke-Rose sees Robbe-Grillet's eschewal of the past tense as the technique that inspired Barthes to declare the "death of the author."

Brooke-Rose read Robbe-Grillet's *In the Labyrinth* when it was published in French in 1959 and translated it in 1967, three years after *Out* was published. (Her translation won the 1969 Arts Council Translation Prize.) She regards *In the Labyrinth* as the purest example of Robbe-Grillet's narrative innovation, a "speakerless, narratorless narrative" (*Invisible Author* 151). It is not the present tense, per se, that she finds so fruitful in Robbe-Grillet, but its *paradoxical uses*. First, Robbe-Grillet used the present tense and its deictics, traditionally a speech form, in combination with an impersonality associated with the past-tense narrative sentence of the traditional novel. This, she calls the "'scientific' present tense (as in a scientific law)" (*Invisible Author* 138). Second, Robbe-Grillet's creation of a "scientific" present was limited to a zone of consciousness instead of the omniscient perspective of science. The third and probably most important paradox is that Robbe-Grillet "never evokes an act of seeing or a consciousness, that is, there is no seer, only the seen" (*Invisible Author* 138). These paradoxes add up to the distinctive narrative sentence of the "speakerless, narratorless narrative" (*Invisible Author* 151) Brooke-Rose describes Robbe-Grillet's "astonishing use of the NS [narrative sentence], in which 'no one speaks'" (*Invisible Author* 139). Yet, the narrative sentence is "in the present tense, in which someone necessarily speaks, yet we don't know who, since he never says 'I,' or anything about himself; he is the very 'no one speaks' of the NS" (*Invisible Author* 139). In characterizing Robbe-Grillet's technical innovation, Brooke-Rose points to a zone of consciousness, rather than a perceiver or speaker. In her translation of *In the Labyrinth,* Brooke-Rose is careful to maintain these paradoxical features and the strange kind of myopic description that results: "Here the sun does not enter, nor does the wind, nor the rain, nor the dust. The fine dust that dulls the shine of the horizontal planes, the varnished tabletop, the polished parquet, the marble of the mantelpiece and that of the chest of drawers, the cracked marble of the chest of drawers, the only dust here comes from the room itself: from the gaps in the parquet possibly, or from the bed, or the curtains, or the ashes in the fireplace" (Robbe-Grillet, *In the Labyrinth* 7–8).

In his 1963 manifesto, *Pour un Nouveau Roman,* Robbe-Grillet describes his technique as counteracting the anthropomorphism of traditional humanism. He desires to be on record as launching a sweeping critique of the use of metaphor to connect man and nature: "To reject our so-called 'nature' and the vocabulary which perpetuates its myth, to propose objects as purely external and superficial, is not—as has been claimed—to deny man; but it is to reject the "pananthropic" notion contained in traditional humanism, and probably in all humanism" (*Towards a New Novel* 57). Yet Robbe-Grillet's emphasis on the scientific and antihumanistic implicitly contradicts his reliance on the psychologizing effect of avoidance and obsession in *La Jalousie* or the state of delirium in *In the Labyrinth.* Indeed, in analyzing Robbe-Grillet's technique in *In the Labyrinth,* Brooke-Rose calls the sudden and confusing changes in perspective in the nouveau roman "baroque," and attributes them to the delirious experience of the dying soldier, its protagonist. The novel, she says, is

> presented instantaneously, yet out of time, experienced and re-experienced through the dying soldier's delirium, when all the data of the preceding days have acquired a dream-like intensity that nevertheless confuses time, accuracy and even subjective identity, so that the soldier could be seeing himself from outside himself as well as reliving inci-

dents and collocations of data with omissions, shifts, or added detail, as if through the expanding and contracting lens of memory and imagination; but instantaneously, merging with direct experience." ("The Baroque Imagination of Robbe-Grillet" 418)

Although the metaphor of the lens suggests the technological apparatus of science, it is linked inextricably here to the psychological state of the soldier.

By her own admission, Brooke-Rose was "influenced" more by Robbe-Grillet than Nathalie Sarraute, another writer of the *nouveau roman*; yet it is Brooke-Rose's description of Sarraute's narrative "tropism" that most aptly characterizes the quality of her own cold narration in *Out*. Sarraute's novels, she says, explore "the imperceptible movements at the threshold of consciousness as if they were biological tropisms." In this summary, she contrasts Sarraute with Robbe-Grillet, who "externalizes and objectifies" (Brooke-Rose, "Imitations Are Proof of New Writing's Power" vii). Yet this description of biological tropisms captures the way Brooke-Rose treats the human beings in her fiction as equivalent to other sentient matter undergoing chemical and physical reactions, in a kind of reversal of the pathetic fallacy. Like plants with the basic responses of turning toward and away from the light, her sickly white man's emotional spectrum has been reduced to the most basic reactions of approach and avoidance. The avoidance of risk is his most noticeable characteristic, his signature tactic for survival. Danger lurks everywhere amongst ordinary actions:

> The feeling is one of heterotrophism. The left foot treads the length of a cemented line. Between the tiles, the right foot carefully selects another line of cement parallel with the edge of the path. The amount of free energy that becomes available for the performance of useful work does not correspond to the total heat change but is equivalent to about ten thousand calories per gram. molecule, the remaining two thousand being involved in the intra-molecular changes of the reaction. It is possible to walk on such parallel lines only, almost without touching the diagonals. (*Out* 39)[4]

In Brooke-Rose's version of the narrative sentence as "scientific law" a deep estrangement takes place in the writing, a wrenching of narrative from the human perspective. This is a process of estrangement that transcends the more subjective rationale of alienation at work in Robbe-Grillet's fiction. In this greater narrative defamiliarization Brooke-Rose can be compared to the writer whom she considers the *greatest* of innovators: the author of what she calls the new "Anti-novel" novel. As early as the fifties, Brooke-Rose wrote essays on and reviews of Beckett for the English-reading public, such as her 1958 essay, "Samuel Beckett and the Anti-Novel," published in John Lehmann's *The London Magazine*. It is here that Brooke-Rose acknowledges Beckett's role behind the development of the nouveau roman, specifically, his experiments with a narrative amnesia that had a profoundly defamiliarizing effect, transforming both the characters and the novel into a species of mutants. In this essay, Brooke-Rose comments on the "out of time" quality of Beckett's narratives, which she describes as "out of focus and as if observed, not so much by a foreign visitor as by someone outside the human race, outside the world and outside time" ("Samuel Beckett and the Anti-Novel" 40). Beckett shifts the focus of the narrative lens, estranging man as the narrative almost graphs his position: "Hence the weird almost mathematical style in Watt, a style with a slight legal flavour, allowing for all contingencies, a style based on permutations of possibilities. For not only does any one action have numerous explanations, but metaphysically speaking there are also numerous other possible actions which, though not actualized by us in any one instance, exist nevertheless in a timeless mind" ("Samuel Beckett and the Anti-Novel" 41).

It is in *Out* that Brooke-Rose mixes Robbe-Grillet's myopic, cold descriptive sentence with Beckett's agnostic list of possibilities played out in the narrative. As in Beckett, but not Robbe-Grillet, *mutation and permutation come together*. Scientific and narrative experimentation merge visibly in the text. In *Out*, the obsessive play of variables, the almost compulsive enumeration of possibilities is not confined to the psyche of the central consciousness but becomes a property of narrative experimentation, possibilities entertained and discarded:

> Mr. Swaminathan's eyes strike an atonal chord, confusing the neural cells which complain by discharging a high mad microvoltage. It is not, however, his eyes which do this but the memory of his eyes having possibly done so, or the psychic presence, now hammered into by the high-pitched ring of metal hammer on metal chisel. A recording engineer might perhaps separate the components of the mixture. If the hammering were extracted, the lost sentences that came and went and returned in reconstructed form might be recovered and heard. (*Out* 98–99)

The "expanding and contracting lens of memory and imagination" that Brooke-Rose speaks about in Robbe-Grillet is literalized in a text that proposes various instruments for recording experience. In an ironic twist on the French novel's "scientific" present tense, scientific instruments, "scopes" of all kinds, are advanced in the narrative as possible modern technologies for returning the narrative to old certainties. The narrative suggests that these instruments might be useful in charting physical, emotional, and narrative movements, but the narrative does not "commit" to using them:

> A microscope might perhaps reveal animal ecstasy among the innumerable white globules in the circle of gruel, but only to the human mind behind the microscope. And besides, the fetching and the rigging up of a microscope, if one were available, would interrupt the globules. If, indeed, the gruel hadn't been eaten by then, in which case a gastroscope would be more to the point. And a gastroscope at that juncture of the gruel's journey would provoke nausea. (*Out* 15)

Here, the contents of bowels, stomachs, and minds receive equivalent treatment in the deadpan narrative. Although the "human mind" is granted as the only consciousness capable of projecting "ecstasy," each potential act of measurement, whether by instrument (gastroscope) or human intervention, runs the risk of nullifying the activity itself. And, assuming the bowl of gruel/Petri dish contents had been consumed already, the instrument would provoke nausea and disgust rather than an imagined orgy of ecstatic globules.

There is indeed something "baroque" about this style, which yokes together by violence disparate things, to paraphrase Dr. Johnson on the Metaphysical poets. This is a kind of "analogical thinking" that Brooke-Rose recognizes in Robbe-Grillet, despite his overt claim to eschew all forms of metaphor. Indeed, Brooke-Rose protests that Robbe-Grillet means only certain kinds of metaphors associated with "humanizing" nature. She explicitly counters his sweeping refusal of metaphor by pointing to the "analogical thinking" present in the nouveau roman and points to the Baroque poets as precursors of the genre. In the "best baroque poetry," she says, metaphor is

> neither just decorative nor anthropomorphic but functional, one of the many means developed by those poets for the purpose of resolving the contradictory aspects of emotional experience in relation to the changing validities of time and the physical world. When Donne turns a flea into 'our mariage bed, and mariage temple" or says to the sun "This bed thy center is, these walls, thy spheare," or of his lady-love

"She' is all States, and all princes, I," he is shifting the perspective quite as suddenly as Robbe-Grillet does with a swift verbal close-up or a camera swerve away from, say, the eyes of A, the 'narrator's' wife in *Jalousie*, to the parapet of the terrace and then to the banana-segment in the distance. In Donne the shift is part of a complex argument, but the argument itself is a way out of an emotionally untenable position stated as an intellectual dilemma. Today, the process is necessarily much less overt, reflecting unconscious or semi-conscious fears, and Robbe-Grillet's unpronounced [sic] narrator averts his eyes from a visual image because it may, and eventually does, lead to other visual images which are too painful." (Brooke-Rose, "The Baroque Imagination" 408–9)

Brooke-Rose the critic and Brooke-Rose the experimental novelist merge in these perceptions, as she tries to capture the function of Robbe-Grillet's deliberate juxtaposition, with its disjunctive formal and emotional effects. In updating this "yoking" with Robbe-Grillet's example, Brooke-Rose both localizes the sudden shifts of perspective in the pain and desire of the protagonist and acknowledges the avoidance as a narrative property, a textual reaction to the altered properties of a radical new world order.[5]

Even as she pays tribute to Robbe-Grillet's influence, Brooke-Rose ups the ante of the narrative stakes. Her own "paradoxical" narrative sentence is more radically severed than Robbe-Grillet's from the subjective, anthropomorphic rationale that he intends to leave behind. In *Out*, Brooke-Rose's narrative technique is neither as phenomenologically based as Robbe-Grillet's nor as existential as Beckett's. In her version of the French new novel, Brooke-Rose makes the breakdown of narrative symptomatic of a *social* breakdown. For *Out* is a dystopia, a type of science fiction in which we find "new configurations of inner and outer space."[6] Brooke-Rose imagines a scenario of revolutionary reversal which is like a photographic negative, with black and white power relations reversed, sometimes explicitly, in the technology of representation: "In the white wall the glossy black door opens suddenly. The woman stands framed by the whiteness, pert and petite and pretty in a white linen dress the neckline of which embraces the glowing basalt of her throat as a crescent moon the night sky. It is more difficult as a negative. The background is of pale flowers and cypress hedge receding. . . . The negative creates a silence" (*Out* 175–76).

Language, geography, and physiology bear the effects of this radical reversal of black on white, "negative" on positive. Whites, formally the norm and therefore unmarked in language, are now described as "colourless," their lack of color marked linguistically (*Out* 146). Their "waxiness" (*Out* 175) is a symptom of deficiencies in liver and spleen. In *Out*, Brooke-Rose ironically rewrites "the white man's burden" (*Out* 140) in a fantasy of a new (and white) "invisible man." What is unusual about Brooke-Rose's dystopic fiction, however, is that it links social critique to narrative experiment. As opposed to much science fiction, which leaves a more or less "transparent" prose intact in order to create a coherent "neocosm" or alternative world, in Brooke-Rose's fiction, discourse becomes symptomatic.

Here again, Brooke-Rose literary critic and Brooke-Rose experimental novelist intervene in literary history. Although a student of science fiction, Brooke-Rose herself finds it formally unadventurous: "One of the most striking features of much science fiction until fairly recently has been its lack of imagination with regard to narrative technique, as opposed to its imagination with regard to ideas. It took over wholesale the techniques of the realistic novel" (*Rhetoric of the Unreal* 82). Working against this tradition, Brooke-Rose creates a mutant narrative about mutation. Her strict omission of past tense narration and its corollaries—narrative memory, event, authority, and, even, desire—mimes the social deprivations of the colourless characters. The disappearance of retrospective past tense narration (the "guarantor" of the real), signals an ironic punishment for the former subjugators; it brings a loss of narrative memory that severs them from their power to call the shots. The unrelenting narrative present in *Out* is a "sentence" meted out to the once powerful white society: "—It's because of there being no past, and no future, ma'am, it's so difficult, living in the present" (*Out* 124), the white man tells Mrs. Mgulu, his wife's employer, who takes pity on him and gives him work. "—You fed on our past," he tells her, "and drained us, now you deny the past but need to remind us, it's an empty ritual for you, a weakness. But it hurts" (*Out* 124). Trapped in repetition, uncertain of the difference between projection and event, imagination and occurrence, the dying white man suffers.

The sickly white imagination swells uncomfortably and uncontrollably, a symptom without a demonstrable cause. History in *Out* is recoverable only as a series of possible textualizations of the past, "an absent cause", as defined by Fredric Jameson in *The Political Unconscious* (35). Nonetheless, history leaves its indelible wound on the bodies of the characters and the body of the narrative. Brooke-Rose's novel is postcolonial as well as postapocalyptic: the empire strikes back against the vampiric colonizer, giving new meaning to the phrase "the white man's burden." If colonialism is the obvious satiric target (and the source of the original "moral" imperative behind the phrase and its conception), any redress provided by liberalism, with its dream of equality is exposed as illusory. The "displacement from cause to effect" (*Out* 120) signals the lost cause of liberalism and the specious idealism of the liberal "interest" in all races and peoples. A poster hanging above the entrance to the Labour Exchange proclaims, "We had a dream. It's a disgrace" (*Out* 82).

Despite the ironic justice underlying the reversals of power, sloganeering and subjugation continue in their new lodgings. Although the past is "denied" by the newly powerful, the empty mantra of the new bureaucrats actually commemorates the failed dream: "Exalting all colours to the detriment of none, don't you know your slogans?" (*Out* 125) says Mrs. Mgulu to the man. The "revolution" produces no miracles, only more bureaucracy, more bourgeois policings of the norm, albeit with a different-looking norm produced. "—And if the past proves nothing why do they keep asking about my previous occupation?" the white man says to Mrs. Ned, and she replies: "—They're bureaucrats. They're behind the times" (*Out* 118).

Thus novelistic "transgression" and societal subversion are linked mimetically in Brooke-Rose's first use of her characteristic narratorless narrative. The categories of identity, history, and community have been radically altered in the postapocalyptic reordering of society; transgressions of time, mode, and voice reveal a corresponding lack of faith in the categories of narrative. In an essay on similar "transgressions" in the nouveau roman, Brooke-Rose uses Genette's structuralist system to analyze the creation of a disorienting, perpetual present. Robbe-Grillet and other French writers of the new novel, she says, exploit a fusion of time to create a "slow down" of narrative time. By using the present, whatever the order of events, Brooke-Rose says that these practitioners of the novel leave the reader disoriented: "we never quite know when (and whether) something is occurring, or re-occurring (or being recalled), the only time markers being contingent ones, such as slight differences in the retelling, in the position of objects, or in the climate" (*Rhetoric of the Unreal* 314). These fictions participate in a kind of narrative "slowdown" which renders the element of "story" wholly problematic, as the categories of foreground and background become indissoluble. In these novels, Genette's category of "order," too "becomes irrelevant, since the very notion of 'event' is transgressed" (*Rhetoric of the Unreal* 315).

Thus, although *Out* retains the lineaments of a plot, as most analysts have observed, events are difficult to chart, both because (1) it is impossible to know whether a particular event is told many times but happens once (repetitive telling) or told many times and happens many times (singulative telling) ("Transgressions," *Rhetoric of the Unreal* 317), and (2) it is impossible to distinguish between scenes that are in the mind or in the world. This transgression is commented on continually and metanarratively in the text: "Unless perhaps a certain period has already elapsed since that episode, if indeed it occurred." Not only are there new configurations of outer and inner space, but the demarcation between the two is deliberately obfuscated. In this forensic nightmare, we, and the man, are deprived of "proof" of existence and event ("It would help me so much, it would help to confirm my existence," the man tells Mr. Swaminathan).

These technical "transgressions" create a sense of narrative inertia, as the time of narration greatly exceeds the time of the story. This technical inertia is a "technique for living," of sorts, for the phrase, "[e]verything that moves increases risk" (*Out* 57), echoes repeatedly in the text. It is a mantra that pertains to both the man and the narrative; the narrative makes a tropic swerve from certain topics and a phobic refusal to commit to story: "Sometimes it is sufficient merely to imagine an episode for the episode to occur, though not necessarily in that precise form" (*Out* 68). In this desultory mix of supposition, conjecture, erasure, and iteration, narrative authority vanishes and narrative desire appears moribund.

Postapocalyptic and postcolonial, *Out* also locates us in a "postpsychoanalytic age" in which transference, the belief, established over time, in the authority of the doctor/analyst, is no longer possible.[7] In the absence of traditional trusted "authorities," licensed to report both psychological and epistemological realities, substitute techniques and specious authority figures proliferate. The "psychoscope" takes over the function of the trusted retrospective narrator; supposedly it "telescope[s] a whole life-time after all, and quite, quite objectively" (*Out* 150). The swami-like figure of Mr. Swaminathan, Mrs. Mgulu's "managing agent," presents himself, one of many bureaucrats and functionaries who intrude on the white man's consciousness. Surveillance performed by the omniscient narrator is replaced by a series of stand-ins policing his thoughts. No one can set the story straight; no one can provide knowledgeable exposition. Mr. Swaminathan polices the white man's desires and withholds his approval like a stern father. Yet, although these substitutes appear in the text as separate characters with speaking parts and agency, it is also suggested that they function as figments of the white man's imagination, as introjected authorities:

—Mr. Swaminathan, you said in the street that memory is a primitive weapon.
—My dear chap, memory is not a place but a racing function of neural cells giving off dismal rhythms at less than ten microvolts, which are driven into by the high-pitched ring of hammer on chisel into marble. What did you say your occupation was before the er—?
—I was a humanist.
—I didn't mean your politics . . . You're a square peg in a round hole aren't you?

The conversation cannot take the form of the hammering because during the hammering there is no conversation, and during the conversation, if it occurred, there was no hammering. Without a recording engineer no chemistry of identity can put those two elements together in time. . . . Either the conversation has partially occurred, the beginning, for instance, the remainder being suppressed, selected, manipulated, transformed, schematised, because inunderstood. Or the conversation has wholly occurred, and been wholly manipulated, transformed, schematised, because inunderstood . . . A corollary is that the conversation has wholly occurred and that Mr. Swaminathan is mad. . . . A second corollary is that the conversation has wholly occurred and is wholly sane but beyond the grasp of sick white reasoning." (*Out* 108–9)

In a scene in which the man receives "psychoscopy," Mr. Swaminathan merges with other authority figures, doctors, priests, fathers, and God. "Will you lay down the white man's burden?" the doctor adds, and the next line of dialogue, presumably thought by the white man himself is "—He is dying. Absolve him . . . That are heavy laden. Take it up, take it up for me . . . Oh, father, doctor, touch me, cure me, oh Mr. Swaminathan, I love you" (*Out* 140). Yet the past cannot be absolved or forgiven, the guilt of the "white man's burden" is not expunged. Some quick fixes are proposed, spurious "technique[s] for living" (*Out* 132), like the one Mrs. Mgulu proposes, can be provided by a Doctor Fu Teng. The new elite babble on about "rehabilitation" and reclamation (*Out* 146), but the effects of trauma persist. Despite Mrs. Joan Dkimba's assertions that "it's quite incredible but people do forget, oh yes, new generations, despite history and everything" (*Out* 150), and no matter how many instruments attempt to sanitize the past, a residue remains. Indeed, like the phantom limb in "The Foot," absence *physically* aches: "The absolute knowledge that Mrs. Mgulu writes no notes and walks along no highway and does not nod and aches there by her absence, the absolute knowledge enters the body through the marrow bone, and up into the medullary centers, down the glosso-pharyngeal nerve no doubt or the pneumogastric, at any rate forward and down into the throat which tightens as the knowledge spreads into the chest and hurts" (*Out* 163).

The fixers, including a peremptory narrative voice that exhorts the man to "comment and percolate" suggest that ridding the mind of painful thoughts is like emptying the bladder: "We can make our errors in a thought and reject them in another thought, leaving no trace of error in us. Comment and percolate. Sooner or later the bladder must be emptied, leaving no trace of urine in us. Explicate and connect. The grey base of the olive-tree darkens and steams a little" (*Out* 53).

These easy prescriptions, these spurious "techniques," cannot heal the trauma. Yet, amidst these false cures, hints of possible connections and possible meanings appear. The new instruments of narrative just might detect a meaningful moment before it is quickly erased: "A periscope, held backwards, might perhaps reveal whether the turning away of the red network of veins and the moving off, beyond the red poinsettias, of the broad-brimmed hat over the deeply lined red neck has been totally accomplished, or whether there has been another turn, and a pause, and a watching there still" (*Out* 39). A look, a phrase of dialogue—something possible but not verifiable "happens" in the novel, before suffering the typical fate of erasure. One is left with a fleeting sense of emotional connection, a pale shadow of what real human interaction might look like. Narrative conjectures, narrative investments in possibilities, however quickly "erased," begin to take on a resonance.

Thus, out of the strict lipogrammatic denials of the prose—a prose without history, author, narrator, or story—some emotional valence survives. Here, a comment Brooke-Rose makes about Robbe-Grillet's experimental program is helpful. In her review of Robbe-Grillet's *Jealousy*, Brooke-Rose praises his experimental technique but goes on to say: "To me, however, the most fascinating aspect of Robbe-Grillet is the extent to which his novels come off best where he fails these theories, investing objects, willy-nilly, with emotional and moral significance . . . " ("Review of *Jealousy*" 74–76). Within the Petri dish, the human organism strangely adapts. Within the cold, withholding narrative Brooke-Rose deliberately constructs in her novel, objects and perceptions are invested with emotional significance. Constraints produce adaptations. Even lost words can become valuable: "The dialogue runs smoothly along the kindness in the soft black eyes, orchestrated by a depth of racial memory. . . . The dialogue flatters as the smooth face turns its curved oblongs of reflected sunlight off towards the olive grove and a monologue moves away on the other side of the dark neck and the crinkly black ball . . . " (*Out* 181). What emerges in the narrative of *Out* is a certain poignancy, for despite the politics of amnesia on the part of the strong and the strategy of emotional avoidance on the part of the weak, iteration, conjecture, enumeration of possibilities, begin to look like desire.

In *Out*, Brooke-Rose breaks the rules of the French rule-breakers. In her essay on narrative transgression in the nouveau roman, she points out the near absence of both "heterodiegetic analepsis (reference to a prior event told by an external narrator outside the characters) and "marked prolepsis, which gives story information in advance (the canonic 'we shall see later that' or 'I never saw/was never to see him again')" ("Transgressions" in *Rhetoric of the Unreal* 314). In her own novel, however, a strange form of marked prolepse *does* make repeated appearances in the following refrain: "Sooner or later some interruption will be necessary" (*Out* 11); "Sooner or later movement, which is necessary but not inevitable, will lead to attainment" (*Out* 16). This is hardly a case of imparting "story information in advance." Indeed, the distinction between sooner and later doesn't really matter in this prison of iteration. Yet, the repetition of the phrase begins to seem like a mantra, an insistence that sooner or later, some events WILL occur. The phrase "Sooner or later some interruption will be necessary" reintroduces the desire for a plot. Both the protagonist and the narrative need motivation and the exigencies of storytelling (even experimental storytelling that jettisons "story" and "history") demand it. The boredom in the phrase gives birth to the possibility of prediction. Instead of the sentimental occurrences of plot in a conventional novel, propositions gather emotional effects as they begin to resemble desire.

The novel closes, however, not with hope, but with a dream of annihilation. Ultimately, in *Out*, Brook-Rose refuses to sentimentalize these moments or to have them function as more than a trace. At the end of the novel, the white man dreams of a funeral pyre, the site of the extinction of "the human element," which "disintegrates and radiates into the huge consciousness of light, under the eyelids a gold triangle, a yellow shower" (*Out* 198). Inner and outer space converge in catastrophe. Another apocalypse is staged, albeit in dream mode: "A moment of agony, of burning flesh, an aspect of the human element disintegrating to ash, and you are dead. But that's another story" (*Out* 198). The death of the dreamer leads to the birth of a new novel, a further chapter in the narrative of the dead white male. This Christ-like new "story" is the story told in *Such*, a novel that records the near-death experience of another white male, who returns, like Christ and Lazarus, from the dead and is "reborn."

In *Out*, the elements of traditional narration are obsolete; humanity itself is a dead letter. Some historical event has altered the trajectory of history, some event strong enough to destabilize the tenacious racial structure of power and domination. This new world, this "nouvum" requires a whole new calculus of emotions, of ethics, of politics. In a world where man can only project ecstasy onto flies and where "recumbent humanity" is scrutinized by instruments of science as coldly and efficiently as amoeba under a microscope, sentimentality is obsolete. Yet out of the constraints, out of the deliberate deprivations of traditional techniques, something new, something painful, and something powerful is created. The novel ends. We move OUT. We are evicted.

"We had a dream. It's a disgrace." If one were to search for an analogous piece of fiction as cold and deliberately unlovable and unloving as *Out*, one might propose J. M. Coetzee's *Disgrace*, one of the most demanding novels emerging out of the earth-shaking reversals that have occurred in South Africa with the end of apartheid. "A risk to own anything: a car, a pair of shoes, a packet of cigarettes. Not enough to go around, not enough cars, shoes, cigarettes. Too many people, too few things . . . " (98). Coetzee's novel is in the present tense, like Brooke-Rose's. Like *Out*, it deliberately eschews the comforts of most fiction, like narrative retrospection and identification with a sympathetic consciousness—the Enlightenment calculus of emotions and knowledge that has underwritten the tradition of the novel.[8] Like the white man in *Out*, Coetzee's protagonist, Lurie, is a former humanist, a humanities teacher who loses his job after an affair with a student. Abjected from society, he is neither abject nor apologetic. During the course of the novel, he tries to come to grips with the rape of his only daughter as well as an "offer" of protection and a kind of marriage from the taciturn and angry Petrus, the gardener on his daughter's farm. Both class and color reversals of power occur in postapartheid South Africa. Like the man in Brooke-Rose's novel, Lurie is a white man so off-center and off-putting that he tests the reader's patience and powers of identification. Like *Out*, *Disgrace* refuses to represent either art or truth and reconciliation as panaceas that will undo the pain of a history of racism and oppression. Like Brooke-Rose, Coetzee links technique with survival, new "techniques for living." The tone and tense of prose narrative respond to the growing uncertainties, the new configurations of desire, the demand to address the past without pretending to erase it. "A tape-recorder might perhaps reveal certain phrases that came and went, leaving no trace of error in us," we read in *Out* (*Out* 57), but for both Coetzee and Brooke-Rose, the trace remains. In both novels, the present is, indeed, a sentence, an effect that bears the painful traces of the past but does not neatly assign it a place in retrospective knowledge. Both authors trust the genre of the novel to represent the painful residue of this suffering, but it is a novel radically reformed. For both, technique fuses form and content in presenting a disgraced and scorched environment. A new kind of fiction is needed, one that casts a cold eye on life, on death.

SUCH:
THE DEATH AND AMAZING RECOVERY OF THE WHITE MALE (1966)

"A moment of agony, of burning flesh, an aspect of the human element disintegrating to ash, and you are dead. But that's another story" (*Out* 198). *Such* is that other story, a story, if one can call it that, of a dead psychiatrist named Laurence, whose heart, we learn only later, has stopped on the operating table.[9] Clinically dead, Larry has been placed in a coffin and buried before the first page of the novel. The novel begins without attributing a name or form to the consciousness recorded in the first paragraphs: "Silence says the notice on the stairs and the stairs creak. Or something creaks in the absolute dark, the notice having come and gone like things. Someone creaks, leveling out nails perhaps with the pronged side of a hammer . . . Voices hang on a glimpse of five moons, five planets possibly. The layers of my atmosphere, however, distort the light waves traveling through it and upset the definition" (203). The juxtaposition of the possessive pronoun and the cosmic distance unsettles the reader's perspective. It is impossible to know where we are.

Brooke-Rose has called the novel her "least 'mimetic,'" and points out that it began only with a sentence that she thought of as she heard the noise of creaking stairs in a hotel somewhere in Portugal. The sentence grew "out of what was neither a technical nor a philosophical idea" (*Stories, Theories and Things* 14); nevertheless, thematically, *Such* takes the premise of *Out* one step further and stages the death, rather than the dying, of the protagonist. How does a writer tell a story of a dead white male, a writer who is interested in experimenting with fiction and departing from canons and clichés? A woman writer who wishes to depart from and at the same time is drawn, almost compulsively, to the "banality of the same untender story" of flawed relationships between men and women? In *Out*, Brooke-Rose represents the dying gasp of this subject in a text that focused on the "white" in the complex subject of the "dead white male." As she tells the story in *Stories, Theories and Things*, in the summer of 1964, after writing *Out*, she began a new novel about a simultaneous translator of undetermined sex, but became "totally blocked until, some three years and another novel later, this simultaneous interpreter became a woman" (*Stories, Theories and Things* 6). *Such* is the novel she wrote in the summers of 1964 and 1965, after dropping the as yet untitled novel *Between* "in despair" (*Stories, Theories and Things* 14). In *Such*, the white male is given one more shot in a story in which he dies and is reborn.

Thus the story of the death and rebirth of the white male in *Such* is an allegory of his fate in Brooke-Rose's hands. The dead white male is resurrected as a subject one more time; Laurence, Larry, Lazarus, Someone (all names used in the narrative for the main consciousness) arises after three days and three nights of his death experience, struggling to remember the "journey" he took while lying unconscious. The novel is divided into two parts: Part I begins with his fantastic astronomical voyage, a drama that represents the workings of his unconscious as he experiences the death of the body. It ends with the staged "heat death" of the universe, the point of maximum entropy (and minimum energy for work), a universal death that corresponds to Larry's own death wish. Part II begins with Larry now "reborn," returning to his life and gazing in the mirror, struggling with the "nebulous memory" (*Such* 336 [pun intended]) of his bizarre journey: "[I]nside the mirror the tall thin man stares back, as before death, before recovery, as when life took its normal course through blood vessels, nerve fibres, muscle spindles, bones, flesh *and such*" (*Such* 335; my italics).

According to the *OED*, "such" is "a demonstrative word used to indicate the quality or quantity of a thing by reference to that of another or with respect to the effect that it produces or is capable of producing." Brooke-Rose points out that "such" is the only "adjectival title" among the prepositional titles in her Omnibus collection (*Invisible Author* 54). The word points to what comes before or after, either continuing or summarizing what has been said or proposing a new comparison. In the sentence quoted above from Part 2 of the novel that describes the life of the body, with its nerves, muscles, organs, blood, bones, "flesh *and such*," the phrase alludes to what has come before. It functions like "etcetera," confirming what has been, the ordinary, the habitual, the known. But nothing about this novel takes the ordinary for granted. Larry's near-death experience jolts "ordinary" human existence off its axis. During his near-death experience, the former physicist turned psychiatrist has his certainties blasted, including the explanations of life provided by both physics and psychoanalysis. Although his "death and amazing recovery" (223; 247) is the story journalists and scientists alike want to hear, Larry finds this story impossible to tell.

Indeed, the bizarre psychic journey Larry takes in Part 1 of *Such* can only be told in metaphoric terms: it is not life "and such," but life "such as" only astrophysics can describe it. The narrative in Part 1 turns life inside out, the psychic journey told as star trek. As Sarah Birch, Michela Canepari-Labib, and Christine Brooke-Rose herself have pointed out, the novel relies on a fundamental analogy between inner and outer space and draws its technique from the language of astrophysics.[10] Astrophysics, or the application of the theories and methods of physics to the study of stellar structure, evolution, and origin, is applied to both Larry's psyche in Part 1 and his "posthumous" views of his relationships with other people once he comes back to life. In *Such*, Brooke-Rose takes the study of the waves emitted and absorbed by celestial bodies and uses it as a metaphor for the distances between people. "I had discovered," she says in *Stories, Theories and Things* "that scientific language, when taken 'literally' (non-scientifically) becomes metaphoric" (14). In *Invisible Author*, she describes Larry as "a man who has died briefly and sees distances between people as a radio telescope sees the stars" (58). Larry registers loneliness, relationship, anger, jealousy in terms of the movement of radio waves and subatomic particles. A woman "bombards the square room with the particles of a vague discontent" (*Such* 282). The rival who seduces Larry's wife while he is technically dead is described as riding her "in the nearby remoteness of his ulterior motive which I read like the distant stars" (*Such* 228). Terms that we normally use to describe the defenses and vulnerabilities of human communication, such as emotional "opacity" or "resistance" are restored to their physical origins, sometimes passing from dead to live metaphor in a single instance. "Something," the woman cicerone who accompanies him on his journey like Dante's Virgil, tells him, "And so I find it hard to get through to you. The layers of atmosphere distort the light waves traveling through it and upset the definition" (*Such* 236). Just as the parabolic dish focuses radio waves into a concentrated signal that is filtered and amplified, we read of "parabolic gestures that create situations," and "angular attitudes that send things off into elliptical orbits until the crowd yells, hisses, stamps its feet" (*Such* 362).

The psychiatrist who has spent his life "collecting silences," attempting to separate himself from the chaos, need, and burdens of human responsibility, experiences the breakdown of the barriers he has erected. He begins to hear things he never heard before, an emotional music of the spheres:

> the vibrant hum of waves merging, doubling, trebling each other and overlapping, expanding, bursting the walls, the street, the entire sky in ultra-violet light when before dawn the degree of ionization in the lower atmosphere has fallen off and the higher layer then reflects, something at least. (*Such* 363)

"Something" is not only his female guide during his fantastic journey, but also a part of his own psyche, like all his guides on this fantastic journey. Something seems to function as the voice of Eros or the life instincts within him, combating Thanatos, the death drive. She is the force toward connection, toward creating greater unities; she represents the instincts of self-preservation and union. (I will return to this Freudian landscape in a moment.)

Creating what one might call a series of subjective correlatives, Brooke-Rose maps outer space onto the deeper psychic level of instincts and drives. Thus, the vehicle in which Something and Someone travel is a "means of communication" with his own psyche first and foremost. It is a "programming of . . . basic urges with Erase, Shift Count, Inhibit" (292). Their vehicle

> drives heavily from bump to bump, holding the road well with its thousand hundredweight. The driving depends on perfect co-ordination between Something and me. I watch the fuel, manipulate the gears, she keeps the speed steady and handles the steering wheel. The little orange lights flicker like stars on the grey control panel, each over well-lit letters that say Erase, Uninhibit, Shift Count, Pot Drawer, One-shot trigger and things like that. We thus have no need for a back-seat driver and our two sons can sleep behind the tarpaulin. (260)

The mechanisms of "drives" are comically literalized in the various vehicles that transport Someone and Something over land, sea, and space. In creating a landscape that doubles inner and outer space, Brooke-Rose plays on the overly literal acceptance of Freudian topologies of the unconscious and transforms it into a poetic scenario. In her essay, "Id is, is id?," first published in *Discourse in Psychoanalysis and*

Literature, reprinted in *Stories, Theories and Things,* she criticizes the "certain literalness" of some Freudian disciples in their faithful acceptance of a "new theology" ("Id is, is id?" 37) of the unconscious. She acknowledges, however, Freud's own poetic use of topology in his "incredible search for a mechanical analogy" to psychic processes, like memory and the unconscious (35). "Freud himself was a poet in this respect, and as poet and doctor he gave an explanation of the functioning of the unconscious on an (as yet then unelaborated) model of human languages, an explanation which was both neurologically and linguistically more satisfying than he perhaps fully understood at the time" (37).

Critiquing the rigidity of Freudian typology, Brooke-Rose bends Freud's dynamic and linguistic models of the psyche to her own purposes in *Such.* According to Freud, instincts, or drives, bridge the gap between "the somatic and the mental" (Laplanche and Pontalis 364). His dynamic model represents "psychical phenomena as the outcome of the conflict and of a combination of forces—ultimately instinctual in origin—which exert a certain pressure" (Laplanche and Pontalis 126). In Freud's model, the word "'dynamic' is employed in particular to characterize the unconscious, in so far as a permanent pressure is maintained there which necessitates a contrary force—operating on an equally permanent basis—to stop it from reaching consciousness" (Laplanche and Pontalis 126). The analogy between the physical and psychical journey in *Such,* with its concentration on energies and forces, borrows from the language of astrophysics in order to describe relationships and psychic processes. But it is related as well to the dynamic landscape of the Freudian psyche, itself based on an economic view of quantities of energies that flow and conflict with one another. Indeed, as Laplanche and Pontalis point out, the original context of Freud's ideas of "free" and "bound" psychical energies was the *second* principle of thermodynamics (gradual loss of energy) (172).

The relation between the physical and mental is also established in the dual career of Larry, the physicist turned psychiatrist who works in a department of astrophysics in a university. A "scientist" with two vocabularies for mapping the universe, ironically he has so repressed his own desires that it is only through the experience of his death that he breaks through the resistances he has built up over a lifetime of denial. Professor Head, a colleague in the department and the wise spokesperson for an advanced scientific theory that still admits the mystery of the universe, tells Larry that physicists attempt to obtain answers from the particles of the universe while psychiatrists attempt to map the "geometries of the soul." Speaking to Larry during his recovery, Professor

Head upholds the physicist's approach: "We do our best. We tap the silent telephones of outer space, we bounce our questions on the galaxies which answer out of aeons. But they give no names, no explanations, only infinities of calculations. You on the other hand give names to the complex geometries of the soul, you explain perhaps, but do you heal, within space-time I mean. These maps represent something, certainly, but not the ultimate mystery of the first creation that has gone for ever with its scar inside one huge unstable atom" (271).

Before his death, Larry has deluded himself into thinking that labeling is the same as therapy, the removal of a scar. His method of analysis represents the most leaden application of Freud. But Larry's experience of death helps him discover the limitations of this notion of therapeutic cure. After returning from his "journey," Larry announces his resignation from the hospital staff. He says, "For a long time I've had no future as a spy. The great failure of our century. We give names to sicknesses, but we don't heal, merely create new dependencies" (341). This realization takes place in the context of the more or less "realistic" dialogue that dominates Part II of the text after his "rebirth" (still punctuated by long sections of the "nebulous" memory of his experience). Something makes the same accusation in the fantasy world of the dream journey in Part 1. She accuses him of hiding behind his psychiatric labels, what she calls his "five geometries" (215). Something chastises Someone for the resistances he creates, the defenses that present him from truly "hearing" what others are saying and understanding his own inner voices as well. His "atmospheric density" gets in the way (217). In a sense, his heart has been dead before it literally stops on the operating table. When he returns to life in Part II, his wife, Brenda, tells him that the doctors could find nothing organically wrong with him, "just nerves" (305).

In an explicit reference to Dante, Larry makes his journey "midway through life in the dark wood" (303). His "mid-life crisis" fuses the more typical meaning in ordinary parlance with a more radical turn from mid-life to brief death. His journey into death is a stripping away of the defenses that enable him to shut out both his own inner voices and the needs of others. It is Something who counsels him in this process, literally giving birth to the layers of Someone's psychic development and helping him to recognize them. At the beginning of the novel, the as yet unnamed dead man climbs out of his coffin to find himself in a landscape that is both an interior of a building—an amphitheatre (part operating theatre and part theater of the absurd, with actors going up and down the stairs)—and an interstellar space, replete with five moons or planets: "Between each desk of the amphitheatre the floor sinks like a blanket of interstellar cloud. The silence has a creaking quality" (204). On the "outer orbit," an unnamed woman appears, who describes herself as a "girl-spy." A dialogue follows, as the man tries to orient himself:

> ——Don't you have a name?
> ——Do you need to tell me apart?
> ——No, but I'd like to call you something.
> ——All right then, call me Something.
> ——Wouldn't you like to call me something too?
> ——Oh, no, we'd only get confused.
> . . . .
> ——But I don't know my name.
> ——You will. In the meantime, if you insist, I'll call you Someone. (205)

"Something" carries a row of quintuplets, born, as in Greek myth, from part of her anatomy, in this case from her knee. They are described as planets, moons, or cylinders. Someone wants the children to be baptized and in an elaborate "naming" process, Jonas the trumpeter plays the five children into existence. These astral blues brothers and sisters take their names from jazz classics: Gut Bucket Blues, Potato Head Blues, Tin Roof Blues, Dippermouth Blues, and Really the Blues. Each planetary "child" moves off into orbit. The planetary "children" are "slices" of himself, impulses or "cylinders" which drive him but that he banishes from acknowledgment. Someone initially believes that baptism "doesn't just give names, it gets rid of the original cause" (207), but Something protests that naming does the work of repression only temporarily: "—Only for a time, Someone. The original cause comes back. You don't understand much, do you?" (207) and "—Oh, they'll come back. Things do" (206). Each of the "children" will return during Part 1 of the novel. Thus, although Someone wants to jettison his burdens, he finds they return, like boomerangs: "—We all remain," Tin Roof tells him. "You can't get rid of us merely by giving us names and sending us into oblivion. Oblivion has its orbits, like everything, you know that" (329). Getting in touch with his inner child, as a new age ideology might put it, he hears the voices of earlier selves buried within him.

Larry's journey is thus both a family vacation from hell and an inner descent in which he regresses to encounter the various psychic layers of his own development. The five planetary children come back to sing the blues, the drives and desires that Larry has tried to repress. Not until he "suffers the children to come" (328), as Tin Roof puts it, does the physician heal himself. Larry must recognize the "cylinders" that drive him, including the "ticking of [his] time" (328), his own mortality, and the most basic of human instincts, according to Freud, the death drive.

These planetary children, then, represent different aspects of Larry's psyche. The age of each child doubles the age of the previous one: Three-year-old Dippermouth (who has a clock face, tells time and, occasionally, screams in alarm), expresses, according to Brooke-Rose, "a small child's need of constant attention, the times expressing only smile and opposite" (Brooke-Rose, e-mail, 10/20/03). Dippermouth is the first basic indicator of Larry's flawed "means of communication" ("You can't photograph means of communication that work by magnetic impulses, except as they appear on dials," Telford, an old friend, later tells Larry, "and the viewer soon gets bored with dials and wavy lines and mathematical formulae" [367]). The three-year-old Dippermouth is followed by Gut Bucket, with the deeper and more contained emotional life of the six-year-old, and then Potato Head, the more opaque twelve-year-old girl (Brooke-Rose has called her "the opposite sex aspect of any psyche at that age, very affectionate but dumb, i.e., not really recognized" [Brooke-Rose e-mail, 10/20/03]). Tin Roof, the outspoken and "unscreened" twenty-four-year-old, is next, and, finally, the adult reality (Really) of the psychiatrist at forty-eight (328) (According to Brooke-Rose, Really represents "the illusion we have at any adult age that our then reality is THE reality" (Brooke-Rose, e-mail, 10/20/03). In his journey into death and the unconscious, full of violence, danger, and romance, forgotten parts of Larry's existence are "reborn," returning with all the ferociousness of intergalactic gasses. He finds "a forgotten area of particles that come whirling back to form filaments of gas in violent motion or extragalactic nebulae colliding perhaps on the outer rim" (390). The flesh and blood man dies and is reborn to middle-aged reality, the "sort of presence to hold on to" (305). But he comes back to life only after he has experienced the nadir, his own death, and the decay and degeneration that "lies inherent in all living existence" (303). Like Marlow in Conrad's novel, he is indelibly marked by his trip to the heart of darkness. But through his bitter knowledge, Larry returns to life equipped with a deeper recognition of his own relation to others: "I feel that during my death I became everyone I know, even my patients perhaps, whose names and the names of whose neuroses I can't remember, whose aggressions, inabilities and blindnesses I have absorbed over the years, unless mine perhaps" (304), Larry confesses to Professor Head.

This oceanic feeling is a prelude to a greater ability to "read" other people's distances and desires.

His death journey leads Larry toward understanding that he must relinquish the fantasy of the precision of language and the map of identity, both as former physicist and as psychiatrist. The scientist "works wonders with the precision of his language" and "arabesques his way through the equations of energy contained until the chemistry of anger and hurt pride lies quietly balanced in the test-tube, on a dial, on a page that turns a new leaf full of squares and lines intersecting, circles, tangents and cubes, curves too, and the light turns the days into a fifth dimension" (285). Yet, despite the inspiring set of metaphors that astrophysics provides for the novel, science's pretense to precision in mapping the psyche is treated with great skepticism. Larry/Lazarus must content himself with the free energy in language, its errant combinations and uncontrolled detours: "Words drop into the overlapping rings that lasso out to catch faces, voices that swim for dear life through the heavy water, some drown, some float, some gasp in the chilly depth" (377). Larry contents himself, too, with the indeterminacy of identity, the philosophical principle extrapolated from Heisenberg's Uncertainty Principle. As Elizabeth, Stan's wife, says at the end of the novel, "—So we all pretend to come and go as fully ourselves. And all the time millions and millions of particles of us have combined with others or escaped into various orbits to return to us ultimately" (388). Elizabeth tells him "You used to say . . . Someone would come along and find a unified theory that would do away with indeterminate interpretations, you'd say, and revert to causality. I thought perhaps you might" and Larry answers, "But I didn't. In the meantime we do the best we can, some of us preferring to pretend causality exists, and others, others preferring to prefer its absence" (387).

In *Such*, then, "root" causes are exposed as fictions; scientists, like writers, participate in "acts of faith." As Professor Head tells Larry, mathematics at the level of astrophysics is like fiction: both start with a working hypothesis, producing "something" out of nothing, something not to be confused with absolute truth or cause. Professor Head's counsel differs from other male characters in Larry's dream and waking life, who attempt to find the "cause" of his illness—physicians, lawyers, physicists. Their "small and nervous handwriting fills the page at wide impersonal intervals like an equation worked down to the very end and frozen there in resolution as if x could really equal the square root of minus one" (340).

Michela Canepari-Labib reads *Such* as an "attack" on psychoanalysis (Canepari-Labib 45), particularly Freudian psychoanalysis. Yet, I would argue that although Brooke-Rose makes fun of Freudian orthodoxy, she makes use of both the dynamism of Freud's model of the psyche, in which energy flows, is blocked, and transfers from object to object, and his views of language and its relation to the unconscious. Even Brooke-Rose's uncharacteristic reliance on the form of dialogue (found to this extent only in *Xorandor*), enacts a kind of analytic situation. As Benveniste put it in "Remarks on the Function of Language in Freudian Theory":

> All through Freudian analysis it can be seen that the subject makes use of the act of speech and discourse in order to 'represent himself' to himself as he wishes to see himself and as he calls upon the 'other' to observe him. His discourse is appeal and recourse, a sometimes vehement substitution of the other through discourse in which he figures himself desperately . . . through the sole fact of addressing another, the one who is speaking of himself installs the other in himself. . . . Language [*langage*] is thus used here as the act of speech [*parole*], converted into that expression of instantaneous and elusive subjectivity which forms the condition of dialogue. (Benveniste 67)

Like the "other" in analysis, Something is attentive both to the gaps or lapses in Someone's speech and his substitutions. Telford, who seeks to betray Larry into disclosing his secret story, is his "twin" (361), his interlocutor.[11]

The language games in *Such* resemble the mechanisms of displacement and substitution in dreams and jokes, which can offer the "royal road to the unconscious," according to Freud. Particularly in *Jokes and their Relation to the Unconscious*, Freud emphasizes that unconscious wishes and fears censored in waking life find expression through abbreviation (condensation) or substitution by means of displacement, a process in which ordinary things take on great importance (165), or "indirect representation," almost any kind of connection, including a "similarity of sound" (172). Words are 'bent' in the dream and it is the work of analysis to "unbend" them, so to speak, to understand the dreamwork and its relation to the latent content of the dream. As James Strachey says in his editor's preface to *Jokes and their Relation to the Unconscious*, "it was inevitable that as soon as Freud began his close investigation of dreams he would be struck by the frequency with which structures resembling jokes figure in the dreams themselves or their associations" (4). Freud points out that a "favorite definition of joking has long been the ability to find similarity between dissimilar things—that is, hidden similarities" (11). He goes on to say that this idea itself has been expressed in joking form: "Joking is the disguised priest who weds every couple" (11).

Brooke-Rose's "mapping" of psychic processes and human relationships onto the vocabulary and principles of astrophysics "bends" language, like light waves. Something castigates Someone for building up his "resistance," his "density," so that verbal communication with him is distorted. In astrophysical terms, gravitational pull and density bend light waves; likewise, Someone's density creates the bending, even breaking, of laws and of words. Right when he emerges from the coffin, Someone thinks, "The layers of my atmosphere, however, distort the light waves traveling through it and upset the definition" (203), that is, the normal denotation of words. "You chose the way of unconsciousness which bends words to breaking point," Something later tells Someone. "I told you it would take a long time to unbend them and bring them back to life. You'll have to do exercises" (220). Something is the coach for this "unbending" process; Larry's "resistance" and "blindness," are countered by Something's encouragement to analysis. Although he repeatedly says he does not dream, Larry's experience with death functions like dreaming, exposing his unconscious fears and desires in language (and at one point he admits to having a "peculiar dream" [229]). As "girl-spy," Something exerts a kind of analytic pressure, an impulse toward clarification of latent meanings. In particular, she instructs him in a basic principle of both physics and psychoanalysis—that energy passes through matter, a principle that Larry, despite his professional training, has failed to understand. Abstract ideas express themselves in "things" in a process of displacement. "You have to use the word something" [to speak of people's essences]," Professor Head says at one point. "We all communicate through things, superficial things mostly" (284). It is no accident that one of the vehicles the "family" takes on its journey is a "sort of cigar-shaped" conveyance, perhaps a joking reference to Freud's phallic landscape in which a cigar is never just a cigar. Something tries to be the medium through which Larry understands how the tangled web of words operates. This process of unbending the meaning of words is painful, as Someone continually tells Something.

As Freud shows in *Jokes and Their Relation to the Unconscious*, jokes themselves appear frequently in dreams. Larry's death-dream landscape is like a comedy club for stand-up, a place where wisecracks and punchlines abound. The atmosphere moves between a surreal or comic strip animation (Tin Roof takes off the top of his head and eats the contents of his own mind) and slapstick (fat ladies sit on unwilling dead men). We hear repeatedly that Larry the psychiatrist, "dies laughing," a phrase that itself exemplifies the way dead metaphors, like Lazarus, come back to life in Brooke-Rose's novel. Every opportunity to remind us of the "root" meaning (the square root?) of expressions is taken. "Words are a plastic material with which one can do all kinds of things," Freud comments. "There are words which, when used in certain connections, have lost their original full meaning, but which regain it in other connections" (*Jokes*, 34). The ticker tape parade to celebrate Larry's life-saving heroics has the crowd "flush[ing] with pride" which, in this landscape of regression, merges with the flush of a toilet: "the lavatory flushes full, I flush with pride. . . . The whole town flushes with delight" (288). Stance (his wife's lover) tells Larry, "Why don't you take a trip? I can fix it for you in a jiffy" and his wife says, "—How do you know, says my wife on the quick verbal uptake for lack of deeper satisfaction, that he wants to travel in a jiffy./Laugh, I thought I'd died" (227). "Uptake" is both verbal and physical; vehicles of conveyance are carriers of meaning, both within and above the speed of sound. "You might as well ask for the moon" (239) Something tells Someone, and literally, he does, when he searches for Dippermouth.

Double entendres comically literalize verbal expressions: Larry's flesh-and-blood life before death has him consistently "breaking promises" to other people; and in the dream landscape, these "breaks" are restored to their physical properties: "when you break your word, it creates density and upsets the definition" (235), Something tells him. Like the word "uptake," the word "comeback" puns on the central plot situation of Larry's return from death and his penchant for repartee. Upon Larry's "comeback" from death, the first dialogue between Someone and Something (already quoted) is like a stand-up routine, reminiscent of the old classic, "Who's on first?" ("—Do you need to tell me apart?/—No, but I'd like to call you something./—all right then, call me Something./—Wouldn't you like to call me something too?/—Oh, no, we'd only get confused" (205). The story of his inner journey is like an inside joke the journalists seek to tell the waiting public: "—How did it feel exactly repeat feel exactly query what did the joke fat woman unjoke say did you die laughing pardon me you see she said you didn't cry unpardon if I may get in a query edgeways query . . . no comment I feel sick don't puff your cigar-shape at me comment has humour expand human touch your end my reply" (222–23). If the phrase "cigar-shape" signals the phallic landscape of the Freudian dream, here it evokes the territory of Groucho Marx, delivering his one-liners with a flick of cigar ash and rapidly raised eyebrows. "To every man his own afterlife if any" (339), Larry tells his lawyer, in a parody of Marx's famous dictum, but Groucho is a more apt genius than Karl in the novel.[12]

Although Larry would prefer to travel above the speed of words (supersonic) because he "collects silences" (210), Something understands that words themselves are the messy "means of communication" (211). Again, in her role as girl-spy, she demonstrates her understanding of the secret life of words. While Larry tries to use words to fix and distinguish separate entities, Something encourages him to recognize the messy interaction between words and things. At one point, Larry makes explicit the relation between understanding his experience and getting the joke: "—Or have you lost contact with base? Base! Ha! Now I understand. When you say you follow your instructions you mean you follow your base instincts. Well, why didn't you say so? All this talk of laws and meridians within, you had me quite perplexed. Good girl. Come let me rouse your base instincts" (237). At a moment when Someone comes to understand the workings of his own desire, he finds the pleasure of the joke, an experience that Freud describes as a "sudden release of intellectual tension, and then all at once the joke is there—as a rule ready-clothed in words" (*Jokes* 167). The sexual instinct teams with the pleasure of the joke to allow the discharge of energy. Reading *Such* participates in such pleasures as well. This is the pleasure of noticing the recurrent play on words between the "big bang" theory of creation (233) and the "kiss kiss bang bang," the sex and aggression, which characterize the interactions among characters (231, 373). In a jumble of like sounds of the kind Freud describes, Jonas blends with Jonah who has been inside the whale and is a typological figure for Lazarus/Larry. And there is a further play between Freud's "oceanic" feeling described in many near-death experiences (and attributed to religious feeling) and the ocean in which Jonah is swallowed by the whale—"Ah sure done swallow an oceanful of sand crossing Jordan in dat big big fish" (290).

If science replaces religion as the great story of the twentieth century, Freud's schema of warring drives provides a twentieth-century mythology of the soul. "The theory of the instincts is so to say our mythology. Instincts are mythical entities, magnificent in their indefiniteness" (from *New Introductory Lectures on Psycho-Analysis*, quoted in Laplanche and Pontalis [216]).

In "The Dissolution of Character in the Novel," Brooke-Rose refers to Freud as a potential earlier source of the death of character than the French writers of the nouveau roman. She refers to "Freud on dreams and the case histories so much more convincing than any subsequent ghosts of fiction" (Brooke-Rose, "Dissolution of Character" 186). If the classical novel is dead, along with the past tense narration of realist novels, science and psychoanalysis may momentarily revive interest in the dead white male who served as their protagonist. One could say that they offer a "post-dissolution" narrative possibility. In borrowing the poetry of the stars and the supple words of dreams, Brooke-Rose performs the magic rite of restoring the dead—character and novel both. She turns a human body into whirling atoms and human interaction into bombarding particles. At the end of the novel, the narrative sentence, the scientific present, reasserts itself. In the struggle with Elizabeth that seems to lead to Larry's death, he loses his "I." In *Such*, Brooke-Rose takes a telescopic view of human generation: "We love like ancient innocents with a million years of indifference and despair within us that revolve like galaxies on a narrow shaft of light where hangs the terror in her eyes as the life drains away from blood-vessels . . . out of the story of a death and amazing recovery and into the unfinished unfinishable story of Dippermouth, Gut Bucket Blues, my sweet Potato Head, Tin Roof, Really, Something and me" (390). It is an "unfinishable" story because it is astronomical, psychic, and the never-ending story of the blues. In this lyrical evocation of our interstellar apathy, Brooke-Rose returns to the question of being, a problem which has also been referred to as the problem of the "as such" of philosophy, "the great phenomenologico-ontological question of the *as such* . . . the human subject or *Dasein*."[13]

The story of the dead white male is a sensational story of death and "amazing recovery" worthy of the British tabloids. "In narrative," Walter Benjamin contends in his famous essay, "The Storyteller," "death is the sanction of everything that the storyteller can tell" (Benjamin 94). Linking narrative endings with literal scenes of dying in fiction, Garrett Stewart writes in *Death Sentences: Styles of Dying in British Fiction*, "We go to death scenes for the kind of knowledge that is knowledge only insofar as it is pure retrospect, wrenched free from supposed experience into containment and clarity, displaced from inarticulate pain, for instance, to epiphany" (Stewart 45). Yet what are we to make of Brooke-Rose's refusal of "pure retrospect" in her characteristic narrative sentence? What does it mean to write a death sentence without the characteristic "authority" of narrative ending, the view from the deathbed, and to create, instead, a "nebulous memory" constantly confused with the present and represented as cosmic voyage? Far from "containment and clarity," *Such* presents instead a compulsion to repeat the traumatic experience, as if under the pressure of analysis, a reliving rather than a recollection from a distance.

As she stages the death of the white male protagonist, Brooke-Rose simultaneously stages the death of narrative as we know it. Or, more accurately, she stages the life and death of narrative in the fits and starts of the story, which, like Larry, threatens to abort in medias res. The death instincts "strive towards the reduction of tensions to zero-point. In other words, their goal is to bring the living being back to the inorganic state" (Laplanche and Pontalis 97). Before the end of Part I of the novel, Larry confesses that he fears a second life more than he fears death: "I have acquired a painful sensitivity to noise, to radiation and to the taste of love degrading itself away in men and in myself until it levels itself completely and no shocks occur, no movement and no life around my staring eyes and I work out the square root of my time" (291). *Such* stages not only Larry's death, but his death instinct, his movement toward quiescence and the end of desire. At these moments, the narrative itself is threatened with extinction. Indeed, between Part I and Part II of the novel, this extinction is enacted. The novel enacts its own point of maximum entropy, as it represents the heat death of the universe. In a standard definition, "Entropy indicates the degree to which a given quantity of thermal energy is available for doing useful work—the greater the entropy, the less available the energy" (*Columbia Encyclopedia*). Although energy cannot vanish, "it tends to be degraded from useful forms to useless ones. When the universe as a whole reaches maximum entropy, the temperature will be the same everywhere and no energy will be able to be converted into work. This is known as the 'heat death' of the universe."

The male Someone begs to be released from the burden of his centrality, that is, the narrative obligation to give shape to his experience of death, the one man come back to tell the story. Rather than fleeing from the lightness of being, he seeks refuge in it. He wants to relieve the pressure of attachments, figured as throwing the fat lady off his body. He wants, that is, to die. ("I don't want to go back, I don't, I don't" [332], he says at the end of Part I, as the narrative approaches its own extinction mimetically). It is Larry's children who save him, and since they are parts of himself, their rescue signals that in some recess of his outdated being, he desires to live on, to take on more being. Part II of the novel is his temporary stay of execution, a return to "some sort of presence, something to hold on to at least, such as a banister" (335–36), the flesh-and-blood instantiation of the middle-aged man.

In *Reading For the Plot: Design and Intention in Narrative*, Peter Brooks constructs a theory of narrative desire from Freud's theory of the death instincts in *Beyond the Pleasure Principle*. Brooks sees the organism's journey toward death as a model or "masterplot" for narrative desire and its progress toward its own end. According to this model, narrative is a dynamic model in which plot works itself out in narrative time between the two quiescent moments of beginning and end. "Plot," Brooks says, "is a kind of divergence or deviance, a postponement in the discharge which leads back to the inanimate. For plot starts (or must give the illusion of starting) from that moment at which story, or 'life,' is stimulated from quiescence into a state of narratability, into a tension, a kind of irritation, which demands narration" (Brooks 103). In *Such*, the first novel in which Brooke-Rose says she found her voice, the moribund fictional relevance of the white male is revived along with Larry/Lazarus/Someone, in a narrative that flirts with its own extinction along the way. It is as if some of the irritation into narratability remains in the texture of the narrative. On the one hand, the tribulations of the male protagonist are meant to be representative, even allegorical. This allegory instills in the reader an identification with and sympathy for Larry's predicament. On the other hand, the generic male is also gendered male and his representation is mixed with an objectifying aggression. In the metaphors of incision, of clinical probing, invading and querying both his body and his mind, there is a sense of revenge, a surgical impulse to remove the layers of disappointment, blindness, infidelity and deception. Larry's narrative "treatment" is more painful than his sudden death. The "surgeons cut carefully at the bark, removing it in quarter-cylindrical segments" (*Such* 218). Like the phantom limb in "The Foot" and the dying man in *Out*, the physicist turned psychiatrist has narrative "life" at the price of a certain abjection or surgical "cut." Describing the predicament of character in the twentieth-century, Brooke-Rose says that characters are like "stray phalluses," "swollen with words" ("The Dissolution of Character" 186). The image is one of castration—character as verbal fetish disguising the lack beneath. Here, Brooke-Rose refers to both male and female characters in the age of technology and popular culture. Indeed, her female "characters" are as supererogatory as her male—the classicist Mira in *Amalgamemnon*, like the unnamed dying man in *Out*, waits on an unemployment line, and characters, both male and female, in *Textermination* are like ghosts.

Yet when the woman, the object of desire, becomes the subject, something different occurs—an access of energy and tone of insistence, a note of prophetic warning. In *Between*, *Thru*, *Amalgamemnon*, and

Textermination, Brooke-Rose moves from the posthumous male to a female consciousness, a Cassandra-like figure who becomes the central driver of her "disc/horse" (*Thru*). The ache of what's missing is still palpable even in this fresh dramatization of female experience and female-centered narrative, but in *Between, Amalgamemnon*, and *Textermination*, where a female consciousness takes on these narrative burdens, she has the capacity to be in touch with both past and future amidst the sad waste of the present. "Some argue nevertheless that parts of a divided nucleus recede from one another at great speed, the shock processes involving ejection of high energy particles that must ultimately form a human element, a star where the taste of love will increase its luminosity until it cools in quiet rage at all that tenderness that went to waste, accumulating only the degenerate matter of decay" (*Such* 390). The "Orphic discoveries" Stewart speaks of (on the deathbed) are repudiated; in lieu of epiphanies are these fading stars. The white male dies laughing. In 1966, Brooke-Rose returned to the simultaneous interpreter she had envisioned writing about in 1964. Only this time, she realized that the translator was a woman. Brooke-Rose's "metastory" in *Stories, Theories and Things* begins with *Between*. It stages another journey that subverts the classic paradigm of narrative journey, another journey in a sense "between" the beginning and the end, life and death "inside the whale, who knows, three hours, three days of maybe hell. Between doing and not doing the body floats."[14]

CHAPTER 3

Between

A NEW VESSEL OF CONCEPTION

> What would be the narrative of a journey in which it was said that one stays somewhere without having departed—in which it was never said that, having departed, one arrives or fails to arrive? Such a narrative would be a scandal, the extenuation, by hemorrhage, of readerliness. (Barthes, *S/Z* 105)

PUBLISHED IN 1968, Brooke-Rose's novel *Between* is a prime example of the scandalous, "writerly" text hypothesized by Roland Barthes in *S/Z* (first published in 1970). It anticipates Barthes's conjecture about a new kind of narrative based on the trope of the journey. This multilinguistic narrative that thematizes travel and translation presents both a narrative *of* and narrative *as* a journey severed from origin and *telos*. In its travel plot, *Between* thematizes its own experiment with the traditional shape of the journey that underwrites the trajectory of many classic narratives. In the discontinuities and gaps of the narrative, Brooke-Rose does not reject the crucial role of narrative and narrative journey but proposes, with Barthes, a new logic for it. After the "dead-end" of *Out*, and the cycle of death, rebirth, and death in *Such*, she continues experimenting with her new narrative sentence, this time with a female center of consciousness and new logic of narrative journey.[1]

Barthes identifies what he calls the "readerly" text, that is, classic realist narrative, as based on the model of a well-plotted journey, a traditional sequence of events of which he says: "To depart/to travel/to arrive/to stay: the journey is saturated" (S/Z 105). Like a well-guided tour, this type of narrative leads the reader from place to place, establishing an illusion of continuity in the fullness of its presentation: "To end, to fill, to join, to unify—one might say this is the basic requirement of the *readerly,* as though it were prey to some obsessive fear: that of omitting a connection. Fear of forgetting engenders the appearance of a logic of actions; terms and the links between them are posited (invented) in such a way that they unite, duplicate each other, create an illusion of continuity . . . as if the *readerly* abhors a vacuum" (Barthes 105). In contrast, the "writerly" text is a "scandal," a "hemorrhage," language that suggests the violation or wounding from within of the classic text, thus destroying its "logic of actions." This text disseminates meaning rather than fixing it in place. This journey without origin or *telos* thus serves as Barthes's paradigm for a psychological freedom from the compulsion and anxiety betrayed in the figure of the "saturated" journey as sequentially plotted. The journey now funds an optimistic theorizing of a narrative mobility that, unlike conventional narrative, does not circumscribe the movement of desire and free play. According to Barthes, there are pleasures, for writer and reader, in the discontinuities and silences of this "writerly" text.[2]

As Brooke-Rose has noted in essays and interviews, during the sixties she read widely and deeply in both contemporary literature and first structuralist, then poststructuralist theory, often writing about French theory for an English audience. The publication of *Between* in 1968 coincided with Brooke-Rose's move to the University of Paris, Vincennes, at Hélène Cixous's invitation, where she taught courses in literature and theory.[3] With her dual vocation as writer and critic/theorist, her fictional experiments not only "test" theoretical speculation but sometimes precede the theoretical framework that would comprehend them (as she notes of James in her analysis of *The Turn of the Screw*). *Between* was published two years before the French publication of *S/Z* and anticipates Barthes's new kind of narrative journey, with its break from the logic of beginning, middle, and end. In her critical writings and interviews since the publication of *S/Z*, she refers approvingly to Barthes's notion of the writerly as privileged over the readerly. In her own description of realism in *A Rhetoric of the Unreal,* based on the account of the French critic Philippe Harmon, she analyzes it as a kind of saturation. She says that realist texts deploy two strategies that are sometimes contradictory: the circulation of a great deal of information and a readability and clearness that depend on "semiotic compensation," that is, a variety of ways to make meaningful the load of information.

In Brooke Rose's description of her own experimental style in *Between*, the journey figures a freedom from conventional syntax, an errancy or wandering that resembles Barthes's general idea of the writerly: "The syntax of *Between* is free-ranging in that a sentence can start in one place or time, continue correctly, but by the end of the sentence one is elsewhere" (Brooke-Rose, *Stories, Theories and Things* 7). Syntax engages in transgressive travel in an unpredictable trajectory, a metonymic slide from here to there that produces a sense of random movement rather than purposeful direction.[4] In an interview in the *Edinburgh Review*, Brooke-Rose represents the experimentalism of her style in terms of an exploration that is not a quest but a magical and pleasurable crossing of boundaries. As a writer she finds herself "on the frontier of something and I must twist language in some way to pass the frontier, and that's the pleasure" (Turner 31). The pleasure of the text resides in (or, more properly, lambently circulates in) a style that could pass the electronic screening at the airport, a sly smuggling across conventional borders.

In lieu of a "saturated" narrative journey, the entirely present-tense narration in *Between* offers reiterated passages of dialogue and description in several European languages (with English the hegemonic medium). The narrative settles on the European travels of an unnamed female translator of French and German parentage who "travel[s] in simultaneous interpretation" (*Between* 408, 494), translating mostly from French to German. Narrative continuity is replaced by replays and repetitions, with iterated scenes generally not clearly marked as having *taken place*, either temporally or spatially. We hear a dialogue about annulment: the translator's marriage is inferred. One hotel room, one plane ride, one lover blends into another. Informational or semantic gaps occur to disrupt the logic of narrative continuity.

The most persistent scene is the inside of a plane en route to one of many European and, occasionally, Asian cities. The novel begins:

> Between the enormous wings the body of the plane stretches its one hundred and twenty seats or so in threes on either side towards the distant brain way up, behind the dark blue curtain and again beyond no doubt a little door. In some countries the women would segregate still to the left of the aisle, the men less numerous to the right. But all in all and civilisation considered the chromosomes sit quietly mixed among the hundred and twenty seats or so that stretch like ribs as if inside a giant centipede. Or else, inside the whale, who knows, three hours, three days of maybe hell. Between doing and not doing the body floats. (*Between* 395)

The travelers go places but seem to exist in a limbo of movement and disorientation, traveling, but caught—like Eliot's hollow men, like Jonah in the whale—in an interstitial "between" of time and space ("Between the dawn and the non-existent night the body stretches out its hundred and twenty ribs or so towards the distant brain way up beyond the yellow curtain" (*Between* 404). "Welcome aboard this vessel of conception floating upon a pinpoint and kindly sit quietly ensconced in your armchairs, the women to the left of the aisle the men less numerous to the right" (*Between* 442). The plane is a vehicle of transportation, a vehicle of metaphor (the "vessel of conception") that translates us from one place to another: "Beyond the wooden shutters and way down below the layered floors of stunned consciousnesses waking dreams nightmares lost senses of locality the cars hoot faintly poop-pip-poop the trams tinkle way down below in the grand canyon and an engine revs up in what, French German Portuguese" (*Between* 396–97). Brooke-Rose describes her conception of the novel in a Jamesian "metastory": "The I/central consciousness/non-narrating narrative voice/is a simultaneous interpreter who travels constantly from congress to conference and whose mind is a whirl of topics and jargons and foreign languages/whose mind is a whirl of worldviews, interpretations, stories, models, paradigms, theories, languages" (*Stories, Theories and Things* 6–7).

There are references in the novel to the "freedom of the air" and the "inebriating attractions as the body floats in willing suspension of loyalty to anyone" (*Between* 461), that is, to the liberating possibilities of such constant airplane travel, but the "intended effect" of the mobile, hectic style and plot, she goes on to say in the above passage, is "mimetic realism—in brief, perpetual motion in my central consciousness, and loss of identity due to her activity" (*Stories, Theories and Things* 7). Brooke-Rose, who often cautions her readers against searching for authorial "intention," even the one the author hands you on a plate, serves up a metastory that, in its appeal to mimetic realism, partially tames the "scandal" of the writing. The errant style mimics the theme of anomie and rootlessness,[5] a modern condition, which in the "now" of the writing (1968) is replaced by the banality of late capitalism, the global hegemony of mass culture that turns one European place into another. Like the official voice of the pilot and cabin crew, which originates in some "distant brain" and is amplified over the loudspeaker system, the detached, dispassionate narrative voice announces flatly that "air and other such conditioning . . . prevent any true exchange of thoughts" (*Between* 399), as the body floats in "this great pressurized solitude" (*Between* 406).

Translation becomes the central metaphor for the general loss of place in this global village. Despite the disorienting effect of the different languages on the reader and at times on the main character, the rapid language changes in the text suggest an almost frightening fluency of scene, dialogue, character, and relationship. The bilingual interpreter becomes the symptom of this frightening fluency; like the phrases passing through the microphones of simultaneous translation, she herself is a translatable sign. We are meant to hear the double meanings in the phrase "Bright girl, she translates beautifully don't you think? Says the boss" (*Between* 414). The French/German translator crosses national borders, geographical and linguistic, with such facility and frequency that "home" and the destinations of travel cease to be oppositional—there is always something alien about home and something familiar in the foreign locations.[6] In her "metastory," Brooke-Rose insists that this travel is particularly gendered—the female body transported across national boundaries is also the sign of a passive identity which circulates so freely across boundaries that it loses its distinctiveness. In *Stories, Theories, and Things*, Brooke-Rose describes her own false start with the novel, in which the interpreter was conceived as "androgynous."[7] These pages, she tells us, were abandoned when she realized that translation figured a particularly (although not exclusively) "feminine" experience. As she puts it, the novel is entangled "with the notion/imagined experience/theory/ story that simultaneous interpretation is a passive activity, that of translating the ideas of others but giving voice to none of one's own, and therefore a feminine experience" (*Stories, Theories and Things* 7). Successful translation signals a loss of identity; the translator becomes a conduit, like the microphone that is the tool of her trade. Just as the middle-class woman functions, according to Nancy Armstrong, as *the* representative protagonist for the nineteenth-century domestic novel, after the male narrators of "The Foot," *Out*, and *Such*, Brooke-Rose turned to the female translator to figure a particularly twentieth-century consciousness of dislocation , invisibility, and redundancy.[8]

This oxymoronic sense of travel as a routine disorientation contrasts sharply with the exciting potential signified by the airplane in Woolf's writing—in *Mrs. Dalloway*, for example, where it figures, as Gillian Beer says, "'free will' and ecstasy, silent, erotic and absurd" or in *Orlando*, where Shelmerdine's descent in a plane suggests "the free spirit of the modern age" (Beer 145). The sense of translation as weary work contrasts as well with the foreign language as a refreshment of the mother tongue, as it functions for Miriam Henderson as she gazes at a Continental newspaper on her trip to Switzerland in Dorothy Richardson's

Oberland: "The simple text was enthralling. For years she had not so delighted in any reading. . . . Everything she had read stood clear in her mind that yet, insufficiently occupied with the narrative and its strange emanations, caught up single words and phrases and went off independently touring, climbing to fresh arrangements and interpretations of familiar thought" (58). Brooke-Rose presents a more jaundiced, post–World War II view of the possibilities of discovery and escape, a view that echoes Susan Sontag's description of the symptomatic cultural condition of modernity in her influential essay "The Aesthetics of Silence," published in 1967. Sontag's is an essay Brooke-Rose quotes extensively and approvingly in "Eximplosions," her chapter on modernity in *A Rhetoric of the Unreal*. Sontag writes,

> In an overpopulated world being connected by global electronic communication and jet travel at a pace too rapid and violent for an organically sound person to assimilate without shock, people are also as the unlimited "technological reproduction" and near universal diffusion of printed language and speech as well as images and the degeneration of public language within the realms of politics, advertising and entertainment, have produced, especially among the better-educated inhabitants of modern mass society, a devaluation of language.

Art, Sontag suggests, "becomes a kind of counterviolence, seeking to loosen the grip upon consciousness of the habits of lifeless, static verbalization" ("The Aesthetics of Silence" 64–65).

Brooke-Rose describes Sontag's essay on modern art as a "still remarkable, elegant essay, in many ways a proleptic summary of much that has been said since" (*Rhetoric of the Unreal* 343–44) and endorses her assessment that a loss of authenticity is experienced in the modern condition. Much as Dean MacCannell in his now classic study *The Tourist*[9] identifies the tourist as an emblem of modern man in search of authenticity in the face of the discontinuities and alienations of modern society, Brooke-Rose envisions her translator/traveler as caught in a limbo-like transit, in which she yearns to submit to something when "belief" itself is suspended.

> The body stretches forth towards some thought some order some command obeyed in the distant brain way up or even an idea that actually means something compels a passion or commitment lost or ungained yet as the wing spreads to starboard motionless on the still blue temperature of minus fifty-one degrees, the metal shell dividing it from

this great pressurised solitude. The body floats in a quiet suspension of belief and disbelief, the sky grows dark over the chasms of the unseen Pyrenees. (*Between* 405–6)

What are we to make of this seeming paradox in Brooke-Rose's address to travel, the contradiction, that is, between travel in the novel as a figure for rootlessness and disappointed yearning, a diagnosis of a contemporary condition, and her descriptions of experimental writing as a new and free kind of writerly narrative journey? And how can one reconcile the way the multilinguistic passages in the text of *Between* mimic a disorientation and loss of identity and also provide the nourishments of a Continental, experimental style? Does the experimentalism of the style represent a "postmodernist" fiddling while Europe burns?

The answer to the final question, I believe, is no; indeed, through the trope and plot of travel and translation, Brooke-Rose subverts the possibility of the kind of insouciant dismissal associated with at least one major version of postmodernism, which sees it as a break from modernist anxiety and a ludic acceptance of the anomie modernism helped to diagnose.[10] Brooke-Rose's novel helps us rethink the abstract theorizing of the mobility of desire expressed by Barthes and even Brooke-Rose herself in the description of her style; it engages the problematic of postmodern circulations and represents mobility as specifically charactered and historicized, with cultural pains and pleasures written into it.[11] The novel thus motivates a significant reappraisal of Linda Hutcheon's version of postmodernism's supposed break with modernism, and its subversion "of such principles as value, order, meaning, control, and identity . . . that have been the basic premise of bourgeois liberalism" (13). Brooke-Rose's novel demonstrates a self-critical form of radical experimentation that ultimately refuses this kind of dismissal.[12]

For despite the hectic mobility of both her style and her female traveler, Brooke-Rose provides checkpoints in the fluid movement across boundaries; despite its use of the present tense and abandonment of temporal sequence, *Between* nevertheless produces its "present" moment in relation to a specific European geography and history. The series of displacements through travel paradoxically maps a European place of inescapable historical self-discovery. Brooke-Rose reminds us of the constraints, political and literary, that European history imposes on postmodernism. In terms of the "political," I refer specifically to the way the novel's displacements fix on the nameless translator's movements during World War II. We learn that as an adolescent on a visit to her paternal aunt in Germany from her native France, she develops appendicitis and must remain in Germany when war breaks out. She begins to translate for the Germans. In arranging and rearranging the border crossings and shifting loyalties of her traveling French/German protagonist, Brooke-Rose creates a palimpsest: the blasé travel of the 1960s, from European capital to capital, illuminates the different border crossings during World War II. Against this background, the random movements and arbitrary excursions raise questions of loyalty, affiliation, and national identity. Customs agents demanding declarations at the borders signal checkpoints in this flux: "Please declare if you have any plants or parts of plants with you such as love loyalty lust intellect belief of any kind or even simple enthusiasm for which you must pay duty to the Customs and Excise until you come to a standstill" (*Between* 414). This voice is both frightening and inspiring—it evokes the specter of duty, both a price exacted for all this unlimited circulation and a possibly useful demand for an accounting of obligation and commitment. In an analysis of an earlier version of customs in Hawthorne's "The Custom-House," which prefaces *The Scarlet Letter*, Brooke-Rose calls the customs house "a public, institutional place, a place of law and order, where custom and excise must be paid on goods (on pleasure, as cost). It is a threshold. The threshold of narrative" (*Stories, Theories and Things* 48).

The history that constrains is, however, literary as well as political, for in superimposing a postmodern internationalism on an earlier, more frightening wartime European geography, Brooke-Rose invokes the inescapable inheritance of modernism, an international phenomenon forced by the events of both world wars to revise its assumption that nationalism was something to be outgrown.[13] The multilinguistic resources of avant-garde experimentalism that sustain Eliot's and Pound's modernist poetry and postmodern novels such as those of Brooke-Rose are regarded in *Between* in the light of linguistic hegemony and domination. (Brooke-Rose wrote most of her novel while staying at the castle of Ezra Pound's daughter in the Italian Tirol, where she returned, soon after finishing the novel, to write *A ZBC of Ezra Pound* [see Turner, 22]).[14] In addressing the legacy of Eliot and Pound, Brooke-Rose acknowledges postmodernism's debt to modernism and exposes the anxiety of influence in postmodernism's claim to break with its own modernist history. She reveals this claim to be a kind of travel, a defense against the pull of a certain literary "home." Brooke-Rose's postmodernist "vessel of conception" deliberately and self-consciously retains the genetic material of modernism.[15]

Thus, despite the freewheeling style and protagonist of *Between*, ideas of placement and mobility, commitment and translatability are deeply touched by the war and its allegiances. The easy availability of European pop culture of the 1960s, constructed from the jargon of advertising, is juxtaposed with the darker memories of the war. Unpleasantly surprised by a waiter or chambermaid who invades the refuge of the hotel room, postwar travelers confront "the fear of something else not ordered" (*Between* 401), an image of those ambivalently haunted by fear of submission and by fear of nothing to submit to. These postmodern ambivalences are textured and colored, one begins to see, by the memories of war and the forms that order and submission took within it. The postwar mobility and translatability of the unnamed protagonist are fixed (though not through any traditional narrative exposition or even flashback) in a particular bilingualism. The Berlitz-like passages of French and German, which blend with other lines of serviceable tourist discourse in other languages (that of menus, advertisements, airport entrances, exits, restrooms), begin to resonate with the differences of their histories, forming both the personal past of the French-German translator and a historical consciousness in the text.

Two particular scenes in Germany haunt the narrative: one set in 1946, after the liberation of Germany and the zoning of Berlin, when the girl works in the French Zone and meets an English airman, whom she marries; the other, an earlier scene in which she is drafted by the Germans into the press supervisory division of the foreign office after she is stranded in Germany. "You must excuse these questions Fräulein but in view of your French upbringing we must make sure of your undivided loyalty let us see now until the age of Herr Oberstleutnant at that age one has no loyalties" (*Between* 444). In this context, the passivity of "translating beautifully" is implicated in larger ethical questions of compliance during the war.

Under the powerful umbrella of English, languages conduct a romance and engage in intercultural travel, just as the translator moves from a German to a British lover: "Husbands lovers wives mistresses of many nationalities . . . help to abolish the frontiers of misunderstanding with frequent changes of partners loyalties convictions, free and easily stepping over the old boundaries of conventions, congresses, commissions, conferences to which welcome back Liebes" (*Between* 437). The fraternization of and in tourist phrases leaves the traces of history, "as if words fraternised silently beneath the syntax, finding each other funny and delicious in a Misch-Masch of tender fornication, inside the bombed out hallowed structures and the rigid steel glass modern edifices of the brain. Du, do you love me?" (*Between* 447). The postmodern brain is an architectural palimpsest, the skyscraper rising phoenixlike from the ashes of war. Even the Vichy mineral water so repeatedly ordered and not ordered in the text contains the memory of Vichy complicity. The postwar OMO (cleanser) slogan "whiter than white" is grafted onto an allusion to a Persil-Schein certificate, a reference former Nazis would buy after the war to prove that they had never been Nazis at heart. The narrative does not sanitize the traces of war.

Brooke-Rose's own wartime activity is "translated" into the figure of the nameless translator and her experience of World War II. During the war, Brooke-Rose worked for "Ultra," a unit of the British Intelligence Service that helped decipher and analyze German radio messages. Enemy codes were cracked on a machine called "Enigma," which was based on "three operational rotors which could be taken out and rearranged, each with 26 letters: this allowed milliards of combinations to be obtained" (Garlinski 73). Using devices known as "bombes," the decoders would explore "electro-mechanically (not electronically) a range of alternative possibilities at speeds far beyond the pace of human thought." In practical terms, what the bombes did was to test "all the possible wheel or rotor orders of the Enigma, all the possible wheel settings and plug or Stecker connections to discover which of the possible arrangements would match a prescribed combination of letters'" (Lewin 123). Although Brooke-Rose has said that she did not herself participate in the decoding, her acquaintance with such procedures helps us understand a sense of urgency that underlies the postmodern mobility of meaning in the text. Despite the drone of conference jargon, the connection between word games and war games and between translations and crisis emerges.

Yet from this short sketch one can see that Brooke-Rose's own wartime loyalties were far less equivocal than the interpreter's. The gestures and mechanics of simultaneous translations are themselves "translated" from Brooke-Rose's own role into the interpreter's less fixed position. "I never put myself directly into novels, I find that boring," Brooke-Rose said in an interview. "So I turn personal experience into metaphor" (Turner 26).[16] Perhaps the stable allegiances of Brooke-Rose's own wartime practice of translation seemed too determined, too clear-cut to supply a metaphor for the confusions and displacements that make "war like a postmodern text."[17] I would argue, however, that Brooke-Rose's exploration of chance, randomness, and accident in her text directly relates to the special significance that the novel claims for the *gendering* of travel and translation. For drift, chance, and passivity, symptomatic of the workings of history, might offer a new technology of narrative, an alternative to masculine teleological paradigms: "The same question everywhere goes unanswered have you anything to declare any plants or parts of plants growing inside you stifling your strength with their octopus legs undetachable for the vacuum they form over each cell, clamping each neurone of your processes in a death-kiss while the new Lord Mayor of Prague promises to take up the challenge in trying to make you commit yourself to one single idea" (*Between* 413).

The "vessel of conception," the narrative vehicle of transplant and translation, is here figured as a *female* body, and the question is this: Can it bear a new idea about history, direction, and destination that is different from either the masculine singleness of purpose and certain destination of the "Lord Mayor" or the jaded opportunism of Siegfried, who tries to manipulate the female translator's sense of drift in order to seduce her? "We merely translate other people's ideas, not to mention platitudes, si-mul-ta-né-ment. No one requires us to have any of our own. . . . Du liebes Kind, komm, geh' mit mir. Gar schöne Spiele spiel' ich mit dir [Dear child, come with me I'll play very good games with you]" (*Between* 413). This sinister allusion to Goethe's "Erlkönig" reveals a dark underside to the notion of play, suggesting both seduction and death. Although Brooke-Rose's own loyalties during the war were clearly established, her novel explores the pleasures and dangers of chance occurrence and its role in the process of charting one's course. The similarities between German and English lovers and the telescoping of wartime experiences with pre- and postwar experiences puncture a simplistic view of ideological choice, while the narrative still insists on establishing distinctions.

As I have noted, in her metastory Brooke-Rose insists that the passivity of circulation and translation in the novel is linked to the gender of the protagonist: "It was a cliché, which was nevertheless true enough generally (like all clichés) for the purpose of creating the language of the novel and getting, as I. A. Richards used to say, the 'tone' right" (*Stories, Theories and Things* 7). This cliché launches the narrative, but through dislocations of both protagonist and style, Brooke-Rose explores possible alternatives to the clichés of masculine aggression and feminine passivity played out in so many ways in twentieth-century discourse. "Between doing and not doing the body floats," the narrator drones, thus suggesting a middle ground, a middle voice, between passivity and activity. The forays in the novel exit somewhere between action and inaction, accident and purpose.

In *The Writing of the Disaster*, Maurice Blanchot addresses the fate of representation after the Holocaust: "The disaster: break with the star, break with every form of totality, never denying, however, the dialectical necessity of a fulfillment; the disaster: prophecy which announces nothing but the refusal of the prophetic as simply an event to come, but which nonetheless opens, nonetheless discovers the patience of vigilant language" (75).[18] In his insistence on rejecting totality yet retaining a sense of urgency—in using the vocabulary of prophecy while refusing prophecy—and in his emphasis on "vigilant language," Blanchot meshes with Brooke-Rose's method and tone in *Between*. Rejecting the type of totalizing mastery that she associates with masculine hubris, she translates passivity into the patience of vigilant language in a stylistic practice that is both modest and bold. Brooke-Rose says of her work: "Modern philosophy talks a lot about the desire and illusion of mastery. But I never feel that, that's more connected with what has been called the totalising novel, which imposes some kind of global meaning on the reality it describes. . . . My experience has been more one of groping inside language and forms" (Turner 31).

This "groping inside language and forms," this combination of linguistic risk and vigilance, leads to a style in which "small changes" in often repeated phrases in the narrative subtly suggest the possibility of changes in the plot. Buried amid iterated passages of dialogue are references to such facts as the translator has decided to sell her Wiltshire cottage or to buy a car—these unobtrusive alterations in domicile and transportation are the means by which the circularity of the writing, its beginning and ending in the same linguistic "place" ("Between the enormous wings the body floats"), is amended.

Throughout *Between* one hears the refrain, "What difference does it make?" This reiterated question is meant to burden structuralist and poststructuralist theories of meaning in language with the weight of political implication and consequence. "The vaporetto bumps against the jetty of Santa Maria di Salute at the mouth of the Grand Canal that gives out on to the wider waters between San Marco and the unanswered question which remains unanswered for the non-existent future unless perhaps what difference does it make" (*Between* 556). The novel checks its own acceptance of the unlimited circulation of language. On the one hand, the narrative seems to endorse the metadiscourse of poststructuralist theory it includes, the iterated and freely circulating jargon and "codes" of conferences and commissions—biological, semiological, semantic, Lacanian. A passage in English and in French from a semiology conference on Saussurean difference emphasizes the arbitrariness and self-enclosure of the language system:

> As for example in a dictionary each apparently positive definition contains words which themselves need defining. Et tous les dictionnaires prouvent qu'il n'y a jamais de sens propre, jamais d'objectivité d'un terme [And all the dictionaries prove that there is never a literal meaning, never the objectivity of a term]. (*Between* 562)

This sense of circularity is exacerbated by the easy commerce between French and English. The writing in *Between* accepts this post-Saussurean, poststructuralist position. The novel, like other poststructuralist fiction and nonfiction, is "about" the circulation of signs as much as it is "about" the travel and displacements of the nameless translator and her colleagues.

Yet, on the other hand, in representing the circulation of signifiers in her text, Brooke-Rose shows how small adjustments of and in language make a difference. The notion that language is an arbitrary, closed system does not obviate the possibility, even the necessity, of vigilant language of the kind Blanchot describes. The change from "Idlewilde Airport" to "Kennedy Airport" one hundred pages later is one example of such attention, a subtle reminder of the violent events of the 1960s that produced this change in nomenclature. Brooke-Rose's particular "technology" of the "distant brain" shows how small adjustments in the codes of language have historical, personal, and political consequences.

Thus, even cynicism self-destructs as a confident and fixed position, finding itself vulnerable to a critical displacement and subtle dislodging. "The syntax of *Between* is free-ranging in that a sentence can start in one place or time, continue correctly, but by the end of the sentence one is elsewhere" (*Stories, Theories and Things* 7). One of the anonymous conference speakers—at a meeting on DNA—disparages the analogy between the language of codes and the workings of genetics and language. The speaker comments on this analogy as a "seductive hypothesis whose seductive element lies in the fact that we play on words and speak of codes, [which] postulates that the stimulus of environment modifies the sequence of bases, leading to the modification of the code within a cell within a body within a box within a village within a wooded area in an alien land. This would leave a trace" (*Between* 519). Paradoxically, however, in Brooke-Rose's "traveling" style, this cynicism collapses; the pompous statement "begins somewhere . . . continues correctly," yet it winds up "elsewhere." What begins as abstract academic cynicism somehow winds up in the English location of the Wiltshire cottage (the wooded refuge that the protagonist decides to sell near the end of the novel); this seemingly involuntary travel of the sentence dramatizes the local "truth" of the way memory works to trace personal loss. Everywhere, Brooke-Rose confirms that experimental writing, like travel, is risky business; one can prepare and yet be unprepared for adventures in writing. In this particular example, the errancy of syntax and meaning leads to an "elsewhere" that is, paradoxically, home.

For Brooke-Rose, experimental grammar is never merely a question of the relationship between parts of the sentence but a technique for exploring the fixings and releases of positionality as well. A technique for living. This exploration is signaled in her insistent use of prepositions, beginning with the importance of the title itself to suggest a place that is neither home nor abroad, placement nor escape.[19] This emphasis on fixation and mobility within language is, I believe, inextricably connected to Brooke-Rose's decision to abandon her original idea of an androgynous traveler on finding it to be a roadblock to the journey of the text. In exploring pre-positions and changes in positions, Brooke-Rose focuses on the mark of gender in the circulation of meaning in language. In a significant way, travel in Brooke-Rose's novel intersects with feminist questions about the possibilities of escape within language, within literature, and within history. The metadiscourse of structuralism and psychoanalysis in the narrative underscores how the mark of gender is carried in the "vessel of conception" that is language in general and this novel in particular. The question, "What difference does it make?" is answered in part with 'the difference of gender.' For Brooke-Rose, the myth of androgyny seems too much to sponsor an illusory freedom of unlimited circulation. Twenty pages into *Between*, Brooke-Rose eschews this trope of erotic freedom (a trope that both Virginia Woolf and Brigid Brophy, for example, find liberating):

> Et comme l'a si bien dit Saussure, la langue peut se contenter de l'opposition de quelque chose avec rien. [And just as Saussure has said very well, language can content itself with the opposition of something to nothing.] The marked term on the one hand, say, the feminine, grande, the unmarked on the other, say, the masculine, grand. Mais notez bien que le non-marqué peut deriver du marqué par retranchement, by subtraction, par une absence qui signifie. Je répète, une absence qui signifie eine Abwesenheit die simultaneously etwas bedeutet. [But note well that the unmarked term can derive from the marked by reduction, by subtraction, by an absence that signifies. I repeat, an absence that signifies an absence that simultaneously means something.] (*Between* 426)

> Where when and to whose heart did one do that? Do what and what difference does it make? None except by subtraction from the marked masculine and unmarked feminine or vice versa as the language of a long lost code of zones lying forgotten under layers of thickening sensibilities creeps up from down the years into no more than the distant brain way up to tickle an idle thought such as where when and to whose heart did one do that? (*Between* 468)

Despite the fluid translations from one language to another, the position of the feminine gender is marked in opposition to the normative, "unmarked" masculine. As Monique Wittig says in "The Mark of Gender," "The abstract form, the general, the universal, this is what the so-called masculine gender means, for the class of men have appropriated the universal for themselves" (5). In this schema, the feminine is "marked"—gender itself becomes feminine, the other to the neutrality of the masculine in language, that "other" most visible in the floating signifier of femininity, the French *e* (about which Barthes has written so interestingly in *S/Z*). Yet one can say that the feminine is unmarked, missing the mark, missing the phallus and is therefore the sign of lack in Freudian terms (but this difference comes out in much the same way). Either way, the signifiers "masculine" and "feminine" are indissolubly paired, as Lacan shows in the now famous illustration of the signs on the lavatory doors in the train station ("The Agency of the Letter in the Unconscious or Reason since Freud" 151–52), a scene that Brooke-Rose invokes in her own text ("We have no evidence at all that live human beings, let alone the skirted figurine or high-heeled shoe on the door can so embody the divine principle descending into matter" [*Between* 571–72]).

In the twists in the above passage, however, a potentially different interpretation suggests itself, a possible reversal—the male as "subtracted" from the female and, hence, the masculine as somehow constructed in defense against the female. Such a reading is pressed in the following passage: "Solamente un piccolo with insolent eyes and a great tenderness only to see and touch a little in the narrow passage between the built-in cupboard painted pink and the rosy glow of the situation so characteristic in this our masculine-dominated myth unmarked save by subtraction from the feminine with its ambivalence in the double-negation no e no" (*Between* 508). The male pursuit of the woman in the narrow passageway is an all too familiar topos within the "masculine-dominated myth." This scene is "unmarked" or unremarked, appearing "natural," except if one recognizes in this myth an ambivalent flight from women and a feeling of lack in the male's "subtraction from the feminine." As the passage on page 468 quoted above suggests, the particular grammar of relationship between subject and object ("when and to whose heart did one do that?") might make a real difference.

Jane Gallop criticizes the feminist attack on Lacanian psychoanalysis for taking the position that these "markings" can ever be escaped: "That effort would place the feminist as observer in some sort of floating position outside the structure, a position of omniscience. Such positioning ignores the subject's need to place himself within the signifying chain in order to be any place at all. There is no place for a 'subject,' no place to be human, to make sense outside of signification, and language always has specific rules which no subject has the power to decree" (Gallop 12). I would suggest that in the travel novel *Between*, Brooke-Rose acknowledges that however plush or sparse, feminine or masculine, one's location in the "vessel of conception," one cannot float outside the plane of language. The "between" of the novel is a space within, rather than outside of, the signifying chain in which gender is marked. Indeed, the novel illustrates how fantasies of escape, provided in literature and philosophy, themselves participate in these gendered markings. Brooke-Rose reminds us how myths and metaphors of flight and travel are indelibly marked in this signifying chain, often through plays on words and conventional phrases. The metaphors of travel are pressed into the service of romance; men are constantly offering to take the unnamed translator "under their wing" ("whatever wing means under which he has taken her auburn blond svelte and dark to their conferences" [*Between* 434]). And myths of rescue are figured in terms of the woman's being carried away: "Please do not throw into W.C. because one day the man will come and lift you out of your self-containment or absorption rising into the night above the wing par a quelle aile j'vois pas d'aile moi only a red light winking on and off in the blackness" (*Between* 446). Hollywood fantasies of rescue are mobilized: "Ah yes! The ideas. Here we came in, the hero will now pick up the heroine on a plane about to land in Hollywood and offer her a contract for life" (*Between* 460). Even direction is gendered, particularly the movement up and down that underwrites the narrative journey (the basic movement of the flight in taking off and landing). The trope of direction itself allegorizes desire as symbolically gendered. The yearning for transcendence is represented in the metaphors of masculine authority: "The body stretches forth towards some thought some order some command obeyed in the distant brain way up" (*Between* 405–6).[20] In contrast, the older mythic geography mentioned above is suggested to be aboriginal, *beneath* the twentieth-century European map.

> The visitor's attention turns immediately to the sanctuary of Apollo situated on the higher slopes of one of the Phaidriades rocks in five terrace-like levels, brilliant with the splendour of its monuments . . . the Temple of Apollo beneath which the famous oracle used to sit and utter cryptic prophecies to all who came and consulted it on serious matters like war, alliances, births and marriages. Finally, a little higher up stands the Theatre . . . and beyond the Sanctuary lies the Stadium, where the Pythic Games took place to celebrate Apollo's victory over Python, the legendary monster.
> The visitor's attention turns immediately to the masculine unmarked and situated on the higher slopes in five terraces none of which deserves a flow of rash enthusiasm. (*Between* 430)

According to myth, after killing Python, Apollo seized the oracular shrine of Mother Earth at Delphi; the cult of Apollo depended on this female power. Perhaps it is this "long lost code of zones lying forgotten" (*Between* 464) that surfaces tantalizingly in the text to suggest a different kind of language lying hidden within the chain of signification, one that would make a difference if rediscovered.

This recovery is problematic, given the power of the "male-dominated myths" to appropriate it. The voice of a cynical speaker on passive resistance warns:

> Human beings need to eat, to work, and to this end will either knuckle under or, more often, persuade themselves that le mensonge vital die Lebensluge [vital lie] contains sufficient double-negation to reintegrate him into totality compared with so many fragile truths and lost mysteries that surround us in this our masculine-dominated civilization turned upside down into the earphones and out into the mouthpiece with a gulliverisation typical of the giant myths euphemised into a sack, a basket, a container cavern womb belly vase vehicle ship temple sepulchre or holy grail, witness le complexe de Jonas with which the lost vitality of the word goes down into the mouthpiece and out through its exits and entrances. . . . (*Between* 510)

Although the cynical speaker emphasizes the way the giant male myths are "gulliverised" by female analogy, the passage implicitly recognizes that the "vessels of conception" and transportation in central male myths of the Western tradition co-opt, by troping, female morphology.[21] Despite this thick veneer of disdain, the possibility of rediscovering a "long-lost language" is suggested at certain moments in the text, a language of flowers (or plants and transplants), which is associated with the French love letters sent to the translator by Bertrand: "So the white gladiolus explodes in letter after letter in a language that finds itself delicious and breeds plants or parts of plants inside the seven-terraced tower undoing the magic wall of defence anticlockwise from the distant brain way up the downward path escalating to a death-kiss with a half-visualised old man well fifty-seven and plus the circular dance of simulation vital lies lost mysteries and other excitations to the true end of imagination" (*Between* 542). In this envoi, this circulation of love *letters*, is the suggestion of a circuit of desire in language not wholly contaminated by overuse, a certain pathetic beauty ironized but not destroyed. Like the Trojan horse, the language of flowers disarms defenses from within. Paradoxically, the exhumation of a buried, archaic past is impelled by a rather silly old man who speaks in romantic clichés, which produce, nevertheless, something "that actually means something compels a passion" (*Between* 406). The translator suggests something of the sort in her response to Siegfried's ridicule of her for replying to Bertrand's adoring letters: "—The language, Siegfried. The fact that all this suffering stuff as you call it pours out in French, well, it sort of turns the system inside out" (*Between* 516).

But meaning, difference, and significance travel in this text and do not arrive at any one place, even a myth of female power, for Brooke-Rose is always suspicious of such a gesture of mere reversal. Theory, including a feminist reversal of hierarchies, is subjected to critical displacements. "Inverting the polarities, (writing/voice, nonbeing/being, etc.)," she says, "produces dizziness and fear (and resistance). But could the ultimate effect not be reequilibration, which should produce (and has produced) flights of creativity and word-game processes as enriching and magical as those produced by the incredibly complex flow charts and numerical logical operators of computer science?" ("The Dissolution of Character" 195).

It is this "flight of creativity" which Brooke-Rose attempts to produce in her novels, and which makes *Between* a story of displacement that depicts neither fixation nor flight. One of the experimental techniques she uses to enrich the possibilities for marking gender is to disrupt the operation of personal pronouns through her use of her characteristic "narratorless" narrative sentence, or what she calls, following Bakhtin, free direct discourse. The "nonnarrating" consciousness of the translator is never represented by the pronoun "I" (although there are passages that read like interior monologues) and very rarely in the third person.[22] Occasionally the translator is introduced in general terms, such as in the phrase "a woman of uncertain age" (*Between* 445). The free direct discourse has the curious effect of turning the character of the translator into a *second-person* pronoun. It seems not quite accurate to say, as Brooke-Rose does, that she is the "central consciousness," as if she were like Eliot's Tiresias, for she does not contain the language but is often its audience, as the "receiver" of the conference jargon that flows through her earphones and out through her mouthpiece or as the addressee of primarily male speakers. She becomes not only a traveler but a conduit or vessel of reception as well, similar to the reader as the recipient of the reams of jargon that pass through the narrative. She is more marked according to her gender than the implied "you" of the reader; yet her gender markings are more unmoored than the stable "personing" found in most narratives, first- and third-person alike.

In "The Mark of Gender," Monique Wittig writes:

> Gender takes place in a category of language that is totally unlike any other and which is called the personal pronoun. Personal pronouns are the only linguistic instances that, in discourse, designate its locators and their different and successive situations in relationship to discourse. They are also the pathways and the means of entrance into language.... And although they are instrumental in activating the notion of gender, [personal pronouns] pass unnoticed. Not being gender marked themselves in their subjective form (except in one case) [i.e., the third-person], they can support the notion of gender while pretending to fulfill another function. In principle they mark the opposition of gender only in the third person and are not gender bearers, per se, in the other persons.... But, in reality, as soon as gender manifests itself in discourse, there is a kind of suspension of grammatical form. A direct interpellation of the locator occurs. The locator is called upon in person. The locator intervenes, in the order of the pronouns, without mediation, in *its proper sex*—that is, when the locator is a sociological woman. For it is only then, that the notion of gender takes its full effect. (5)

Turning the character into the addressee does not bypass the path of gender Wittig outlines, but it alters a certain predictability both in the power of the pronoun to enforce gender and in the feminist critique of the circulation of woman as semiotic object. In her own critique of semiotics as regressively masculinist, Brooke-Rose castigates semioticians whom she otherwise admires for their inability to escape phallocentric paradigms. In her fiction she wrenches her translator out of an automatic objectification in the third person. The identity of the translator changes as a function of the kind of "you" that signifies her. For example, we know by the addresses made to her that although never described physically in the text, the translator is attractive. During the course of the narrative, she ages, which affects the "you" she represents (the change in the form of address to her, from "mademoiselle" to "madame," is only the most overt sign of this process). Unlike Wittig, who attempts to eliminate gender in her experimental fiction, Brooke-Rose rejects the notion of androgyny. She explores instead the way the feminine subject (and object) is constituted in the signifying chain of language, the way her journey as a signified and signifier is marked.

In experimenting with "person" in this way, Brooke-Rose neither places her traveler outside of the "male-dominated" signifying chain nor imprisons her within it. The language of the narrative becomes a structure of dis-placement rather than of either placement or escape. In this experiment with pronouns she challenges a traditional mode of representation. The grammatical and syntactic mobility of her language enables both the unfixing of identity in the narrative (in accordance with the mimetic realism she mentions) and a fictional possibility that suggests new ways of thinking about character, a new technique for writing gender.

Style offers, to borrow a line from the novel, "a new technique for living" which emerges from contemporary culture (*Between* 571). The "distant brain" appropriately replaces the author; twentieth-century fiction cannot retreat into nostalgic forms of realism but must catalyze the new ways of knowing made available through innovative media—the computer, for example. Brooke-Rose has increasingly spoken of the philosophical and methodological possibilities emerging from computer technology, possibilities that might help establish new logics of character as well as a new poetry in postmodern fiction: "Just as the flat characters of romance eventually, through print and the far-reaching social developments connected with it, became rounded and complex, so, if we survive at all, perhaps the computer, after first ushering in (apart from superefficiency) the games and preprogrammed oversimplifications of popular culture, will alter our minds and powers of analysis once again, and enable us to create new dimensions in the deep-down logic of characters" ("The Dissolution of Character" 195). "Fictional character has died, or become flat," she maintains, "as had *deus ex machina*. We're left, perhaps, with the faint hope of a ghost in the machine" ("The

Dissolution of Character" 193). Brooke-Rose's style consciously locates itself in a particular moment of technological possibility; perhaps the "distant brain" that guides the travel in *Between* is such a ghost (or god) in the machine.[23] The convenient ending of the original *deus ex machina* is replaced by narrative technique that never reaches resolution (indeed, the narrative journey is circular, ending in much the same place as it began); yet this technique uncovers connections and significances through small adjustments of sentences.

Computer technology, however, seems inadequate as the sole source of regeneration for narrative fiction, for its revolution might be stuck, Brooke-Rose suggests, in a binary opposition that confirms rather than undermines a phallogocentric ethos. One of the persistent worries Brooke-Rose expresses about various forms of postmodernist writing, from theory to fiction, is its insistent phallocentrism: "With a few notable exceptions, some by women, both the postmodern novel and science fiction, like the utopias of Scholes's structural fabulation, are surprisingly phallocratic. It is as if the return to popular forms or the parody of them, even via the intellectual cognition of utopian models, necessarily entailed the circulation of women as objects, which we find both in those models and in folktales and early cultures" ("The Dissolution of Character" 193). Brooke-Rose, who has had a vexed relationship to feminism (see "A Womb of One's Own" for her severe reservations about "writing the body" of the feminine), has become increasingly vocal about this bias in postmodernism. She suggests that a countersource to the computer is necessary to effect a revolution in fiction, which could then aspire to the condition of poetry: "The impetus comes from two apparently contradictory sources, the technological revolution and the feminist revolution" ("The Dissolution of Character" 194). Drawing on Lacan's distinction between the *tout* and the *pas tout*, she envisions a "new psychology" in which "both women and men artists who have rejected the totalization, the *tout*, of traditional and even modernist art and chosen the underdetermination and opaqueness of the *pas tout* may clash in an enriching and strengthening way with the binary, superlogical, and by definition exclusive structures of the electronic revolution" ("The Dissolution of Character" 196).

A cynical conference voice says near the end of *Between*, "We have no evidence at all that live human beings, let alone the skirted figurine or high-heeled shoe on the door can so embody the divine principle descending into matter in a behavior sufficiently organised to prevent the illiterate women of an Indian village taught the natural method with an abacus from pushing all those red balls to the left like a magic spell and all coming back pregnant" (*Between* 571–72). The *deus ex machina* given form in the technology of style in the novel, the (holy) ghost of the god in the machine descending and landing into textuality, gives no guarantee or evidence of consequences in the "real" world. Indeed, Brooke-Rose often speaks of the pleasures of technique as sufficient for the writer on the frontiers of language. "I think it was Yeats who spoke about poetry coming out of a mouthful of air. I've always been fascinated by this notion of words and ideas floating up there as in a galaxy, from which the poet draws them down into the text" (Turner 26). Yet Brooke-Rose's particular brand of postmodern travel charts a space for the flight of the female imagination while mapping out a specific, historical twentieth-century problematic. The circulation of an individual "feminine" signifier cannot be severed from the political order or from a specific history. To explore this history, literary and political, Brooke-Rose transforms Penelope's domestic vigil of waiting for Odysseus into the vigilant, yet self-surprising language of travel in *Between*. When Penelope voyages, the categories of passivity and activity merge in the writing in a purposeful technical wandering that, nevertheless, yields a serendipitous "elsewhere." In *Between*, Brooke-Rose conducts what Brigid Brophy in her novel *In Transit* calls "herm warfare" (220). In this skirmish, the old Hermes, "the phallus . . . the god of roads, of doorways, of all goings-in and comings out; all goings-on" is remade as a different sort of traveler supplants the "wandering . . . phallic heroes, in a permanent state of erection; pricking o'er the plain" (Brown, *Love's Body* 50).

CHAPTER 4

Thru

"CORPUS CRYSIS"

THRU (1975) is Brooke-Rose's most self-consciously theoretical novel. Written in 1971 and 72, shortly after she moved to Paris to teach at the experimental University of Paris, Vincennes, *Thru* dialogizes theory. Theories are made to speak to one another, revealing their blindnesses and emotional investments, like characters in a more conventional novel. In *Thru,* Brooke-Rose uses theory's discourses to test the power and, finally, the limits of theory.

In the novel, Brooke-Rose *historicizes* theory as she fictionalizes it, locating her own fiction/metafiction in the specific context of circulating (and overlapping) structuralist and poststructuralist discourses. Paradoxically, the rampant intertextual theories dialogically presented function at once as the sign of fictionality and the sign of the "real," the "time of theory,"[1] a period roughly from the mid-'60s to the mid-'70s when, as Paul de Man has said, "linguistic terminology" was introduced in the metalanguage about literature."[2] While the theory debates circulated in print and in person, Brooke-Rose acted as a kind of translator for the English reader interested in what was happening in French intellectual culture. Her "Letters from Paris" were addressed to the English readers of the *Spectator* and she contributed short essays to the *TLS*. Brooke-Rose describes this time in Paris as a moment when French intellectuals "gang[ed] up" to form and reform critical circles associated with new outlets of publication like *Tel Quel* and *Change*.[3] In these "letters" home, Brooke-Rose captured the excitement of theory and its character. As opposed to arid intellectual discussions, theoretical positions were already charactered, in a sense, circulating dramatically through Paris in the bodies of the budding and established masters of theory. As she wrote in the *TLS* in 1973, the "Nouvelle Critique, though largely emanating from the National Centre for Scientific Research and the independent Ecole Pratique des Hautes Etudes, has spread far beyond these centers." She goes on to say that "a public lecture by Barthes or Kristeva will fill a hall the size of a cinema, and when Roman Jakobson came to lecture at the Collège de France one had to be there at 8 am for 10 o'clock in order to get a place, and the lectures were relayed into several other halls. New books come out all the time and everyone rushes to buy them and use them. The discussion is alive and grows."[4] As an exile living in France, Brooke-Rose comments on the differences between her adopted and her home country: in France, discussions of theories of textual or linguistic analysis were matters of public excitement and wide cultural implication. The metatextual qualifies as an exciting fact of cultural life.

Greimas's "Sémantique structurale" appeared in 1966 and *Du Sens* in 1970; Benveniste's *Problèmes de linguistique générale* was published in two volumes in Paris in 1966 and 1974; Kristeva's *Sèméiôtiké* was published by *Tel Quel* in 1969; Gérard Genette's "Discours du recit" in 1972, and important work by Chomsky was translated into French during the sixties. In the pages of *Tel Quel*, avant-garde textual practice and theory coexisted as forms of cultural critique. Derrida's "Freud et la scène de l'écriture" (*TQ* 26 [summer 1966]), "La Pharmacie de Platon," (*TQ* 32–3 [winter/spring 1968]), and Kristeva's "Pour une sémiologie des paragrammes" (*TQ* 29 [spring 1967]) appeared alongside fiction by Philippe Sollers and poetry by Roche and Pleynet. Lacan's *Écrits*, Derrida's *Dissemination* and *Éctriture at la différance*, Irigaray's *Speculum de l'autre femme* and "Pouvoir du discours/subordination du féminin" (republished in *This Sex Which Is Not One*), and Cixous and Clement's *Newly Born Woman*, are all avatars of what Kristeva dubbed in her important book, "the revolution of the word" (*The Revolution of the Word*, 1968). All provide intertexts in the narrative of *Thru*.

Engaged in teaching classes on structuralism and poststructuralism simultaneously, Brooke-Rose was attracted to elements of both: the systematicity of structuralism, particularly the precision of structuralist approaches to narrative, such as Genette's,[5] and the analytic power of poststructuralist critique, which punctured the scientific ambitions of a complete grammar or science of literature. As de Man points out in *The Resistance to Theory*, resistance is embedded in the language of poststructuralist literary theory. Its rhetoric leads to the undoing of the system of language and contributes to the abuses, as well as the uses, of theory in the text.[6] In *Thru* Brooke-Rose represents the uses and abuses of theory, both theory's desire to master the production of meaning and the recognition that mastery is an impossibility. In an essay entitled "Is Self-Reflexivity Mere?" in which Brooke-Rose offers an *explication du texte* of the first twenty pages of *Thru*, she says that *Thru* was written to "resolve" her own conflicted emotions about the relationship between her writing and her interests in theory. She describes this conflict as an "involvement with and parallel alienation from literary theory, involvement as craftsman, critic, and teacher, alienation as writer" (*Invisible Author* 63). Although the retrospective splitting of the roles of writer and critic, and of craftsman and writers, itself feels too neat, the pleasures and resistances of theory, its attractions and limitations contribute to the drama of *Thru*. The novel disrupts the distinction between text and metatext; craft and writing; and writing and theory. It stages theory and its discontents, engaging the ambitions, promises, and investments of particular theories. Thus, although theory's "pompous pilot[s] and "pompous pirate[s] (*Thru* 686) are mercilessly mocked in *Thru*, the novel's "techniques for living" draw deeply from the various mappings of the circuits of desire offered particularly in French theory during the late '60s and '70s.

For example, the promise and limitations of psychoanalysis are woven throughout Brooke-Rose's text, reflecting psychoanalysis as both a paradigmatic reading practice and a source of multiple "phallusies." The novel begins with someone in a car looking into a rearview mirror (the "rétro viseur" [*Thru* 579]), and acts of looking backward to move forward, a basic analytic practice, abound. The mirrors, frames, and vanishing acts in *Thru* owe much to what Brooke-Rose calls in her analysis of "The Turn of the Screw" "the mirror effect" in Lacanian theory.[7] Lacan's "Subversion of the Subject and the Dialectic of Desire in the Freudian Unconscious," published in *Écrits* (in French in 1966), provides a crucial intertext and dialogic partner in Brooke-Rose's novel. As Hanjo Berressem explains in "Thru the Looking Glass: A Journey into the Universe of Discourse," Brooke-Rose makes use of Lacan's mirror in *Thru*, linking "the spatial image of a subject caught between images originating from behind which are projected forward by the mirror to Lacan's notion of a decentered, barred subject which can recognize itself only by projecting its past into the future" according to what Lacan calls a "retroversion effect."⁸

In *A Rhetoric of the Unreal*, Brooke-Rose points out the relevance of psychoanalysis as a reading process rather than a set text to be decoded: "For Lacan, as for Freud before him but ignored by most Freudians, the unconscious is not simply a text to be read and interpreted (i.e., limited, by exclusion, to one significance or set of significances), it is *also* a faculty of reading" (*Rhetoric of the Unreal* 46). In *Thru*, the looping of subjectivity through endless mirror images and linguistic representations draws on the discourse of psychoanalysis and leads to the territory of the unconscious. Like *Such*, *Thru* engages the linguistic techniques through which the unconscious is manifested in narrative. Along with Lacan's mirror, deconstruction, though parodied in academic banter throughout the novel, imports crucial insights into what Brooke-Rose describes as deconstruction's ability to "think otherness, to recreate it," (*Invisible Author* 26). Along with psychoanalysis, deconstruction provides a reading practice modeled in *Thru*. Like Derrida's *Of Grammatology*, published in 1974, *Thru* deconstructs the blindnesses of Western discourse by demonstrating how these discourses occlude as they represent: "Eyelessness is not a provisional state but a structure, a blind spot in your own youdipeon discourse and discourse only occurs insofar as there is lack of (in)sight" (*Thru* 675). Graphically, punningly, Brooke-Rose demonstrates the blind spots in "youdipeon discourse" that Derrida's project seeks to reveal. But turning the poststructuralist screw one more notch, she exposes the phallocentric blindnesses of western discourses in theoretical models of realism, structuralism, and poststructuralism alike. Combining Derrida's deconstructive critique of phallogocentrism with the feminist insights of French feminism, she mimics the phallogocentrism of multiple stories and theories to expose the occlusion of Woman.

As always, Brooke-Rose's focus is on the narrative and linguistic implications of her subject. In this regard, *Thru* is the quintessential Brooke-Rose novel, which she has described as a "narrative about narrativity" (*Stories, Theories and Things* 8), the novel of which she is most proud (*Invisible Author* 63). As in *Between* and *Such*, she makes use of the journey as a central trope of classic narrative. In *Thru*, the danger of the fictional terrain is marked: "There should be placards saying: Danger. You are now entering the Metalinguistic Zone. All access forbidden except for Prepared Consumers with special permits from the Authorities" (*Thru* 629). These tongue-in-cheek instructions to the reader reveal that the physical journey we begin at the start of the narrative is the journey of the narrative itself:

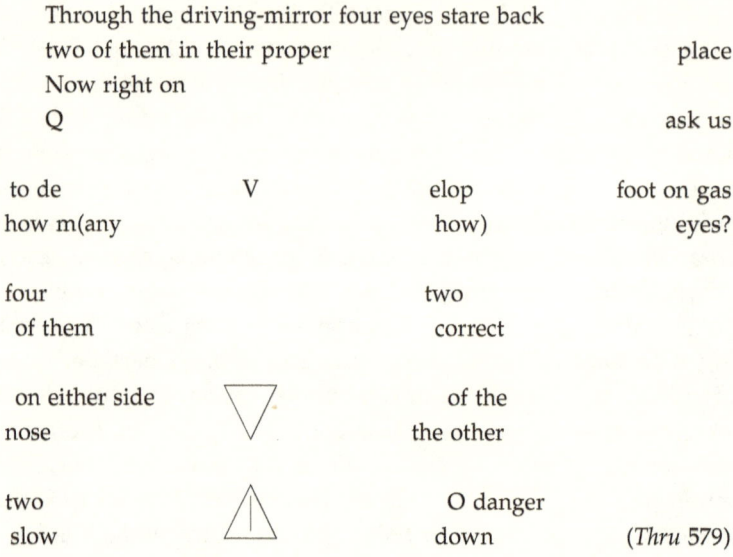

Through the driving-mirror four eyes stare back			
two of them in their proper			place
Now right on			
Q			ask us
to de	V	elop	foot on gas
how m(any		how)	eyes?
four		two	
of them		correct	
on either side		of the	
nose		the other	
two		O danger	
slow		down	(*Thru* 579)

Theory collapses into fiction and metanarrative into narrative; "self-reflection" of all kinds is built into the narrative. Discourse and story refuse their structuralist separation. During the course of the novel the rectangle of the driving mirror doubles as a rectangular classroom in a university, and functions again as a rectangular diagram, the geometry of a number of theoretical models including Greimas's semiotic rectangle, Jakobson's linguistic model of communication, and Lacan's model of desire.[9] The "course" of the narrative journey proliferates into "the hundred and fifty courses" offered in the university, a multiplicity "which would upset the balanced economy of the narrative whose arbitrariness (freedom) is not infinite" (*Thru* 735). Within the text itself, two of the narrative's possible authors are university professors, Armel Santores and Larissa Toren, who teach creative writing and critical theory respectively, in different universities (and who are themselves almost anagrammatic versions of each other, albeit with the crucial letter "I," missing in Armel's name and "me," missing in Larissa's). They write each other letters and may be "inventing each other," according to Brooke-Rose (*Invisible Author* 64.) In *Thru*, Brooke-Rose rewrites the classic picaresque journey from episode to episode, the "horse" on which the picaro usually rides now punningly transformed into the "disc-horse." A narrative voice notes that modern novels "twiddle . . . from one disembodied voice to another on this or that wave-length listening in to this or that disc-jockey and always the same disc-horse, a yea-yea and a neigh inserted into the circuit of signifiers, each discourse penetrating the non-disjunctive functioning of another" (*Thru* 637). *Thru* continues Brooke-Rose's engagement in *Between* with the pleasures and dangers of the "writerly" text. However, in *Thru*, no central disc-jockey analogous to the female translator guides our journey along the overactive circuits of signifiers. Indeed, who "drives" the narrative is a question that is explicitly raised in the text in many forms. "Who speaks?" a question raised in texts by both Lacan's "Subversion of the Subject" and Barthes' *S/Z* (See Berressem 128–29), is the most insistent form of this fundamental poststructuralist inquiry. The slippery identities of the different "tale-bearers," drivers and passengers present marked and unmarked "dangers" to the reader throughout the text. Indeed, punning on the idea of "character" as mark, the characters in *Thru* become migratory letters, "lost semes, vanishing away like gods into the other scene" (*Thru* 733).

The mirror, like the journey, both introduced at the beginning of the novel, is a central trope of classic narrative. If the preposition "through/thru" refers to the journey of narrative *through* space and time, it also refers even more insistently to the gaze *through* the medium of the mirror, that so-called reflector of reality. The "faulty" driving mirror distorts as it reflects, as Brooke-Rose interrogates the central trope of realism. In *Thru* the driving mirror offers the driver a ghostly backward glance at the dancing hoops (glaring lights) behind. As the narrative "drives the discourse into the future" (*Thru* 729), the traditional objects and subjects in realism's mirror become spectral, haunted by a second sight. A second ghostly pair of eyes appears in the driving mirror:

> Intensity of illusion is what matters to the narrator
> through a flaw in the glass darkly perhaps making four
> clear eyes stare back, two of them in their proper place at
> height of bridge of nose . . .
>
> . . . .
>   A
>
> second pair of eyes hidden higher up the brow would have
> its uses despite psychic invisibility or because of. (*Thru* 583)

The four pair of eyes signal a "problem" of representation. Brooke-Rose points out in her explication of the opening pages of the novel that the "correct" eyes, the "real" eyes reflected in the mirror, themselves pose a problem ("The eyes, which are in their proper place, are now right on cue, printed as the letter Q, then another long gap to 'ask us,' as if the correctly reflected eyes posed a problem, not the other eyes further up" [*Invisible Author* 66]). As she says in *A Rhetoric of the Unreal*, in the twentieth century, the real has itself become problematic, altering the conception of realism and its reflecting mirror. The second pair of eyes, the ghostly pair that haunts the reflection in the mirror, illustrates that the real is shot through with unreality. *Thru* begins with what is normally invisible, those "blind spots" traditionally occluded in realism's scopic field, the ghostly eyes that do not see themselves reflect, what Lacan calls the "unspecularisable" objects associated with the unconscious of the subject. "It is to this object that cannot be grasped in the mirror that the specular image lends its clothes,"[10] a phrase Hanjo Berressem quotes in his essay (130). This Lacanian notion surfaces in the narrative in one of the dialogues: "the truth as signifier being all the time non-specularisable except by a hidden representation of a representation" (*Thru* 732).

In "rehandling the signifiers" of narrative and theory, a Lacanian phrase she refers to in her analysis of "The Turn of the Screw" (*Rhetoric of the Unreal* 47), Brooke-Rose attempts to represent multiple 'invisibilities' in *Thru*. What Berressem's analysis fails to emphasize adequately, however, is the way the novel foregrounds a *particular* occlusion in fiction and theory—the occlusion of woman as subject in "youdipean discourse." In *Thru*, Brooke-Rose continues to explore feminist discourse as a "new logic" for narrative. Although she remains skeptical throughout her oeuvre of the shibboleths attached to "isms" of all stripes, certain texts of French feminist discourse, by Kristeva, Cixous, Irigaray, and Shoshanna Felman, provided her with fruitful models for rescripting the concept of desire. Luce Irigaray's revisionary feminist mimicking of Lacan's narratives of desire in *This Sex Which Is Not One* provides one such source text. By "rehandling" Lacanian signifiers, Irigaray attempts "to make 'visible,' by an effect of playful repetition, what was supposed to remain invisible" (Irigaray 76). Brooke-Rose's "rétro viseur" is linked to the term not only in Lacan, but in Irigaray's rewriting of Lacan. In *This Sex Which is Not One*, published after *Thru*, "retraversée" is a term that refers to "the process of going back through social, intellectual, and linguistic practices to reexamine and unravel their conceptual bases, in analogy with Alice's voyages of exploration in *Through the Looking-Glass*" (Irigaray 221, publisher's note). In this flawed looking-glass, we see the "eyes that do not exist" (*Thru* 605) even in psychoanalytic and other forms of poststructuralist models. The "gray eminence" (*Thru* 581)—the priests and analysts who have been the "sultans" (*Thru* 581) of the discourse, have missed something. The psychic invisibility of women in fiction and analytic discourse, the absence of their eyes/I's, this hidden representation of a representation fights its way *Thru* the narrative.

How does one hold up a mirror to the unconscious? How adjust the mirror to represent that which is missing from view? And how to do so, particularly when the unnamed male driver at the beginning of the novel seems to control the "intensity of illusion" in the driving mirror. When the young, unknown "mistress of the moment" (*Thru* 582) who is a passenger in the car turns the mirror toward herself to see what the driver can see, the intensity of illusion disappears ("She shifts the mirror to her rearward glance. It doesn't work for her the mistress of the moment" (*Thru* 582). "[S]he does not see by day the four lies in the retrovizor when shifted to her forward gaze nor dancing hoops by night" (*Thru* 586). Although we read that the mirror "needs adjusting" (*Thru* 587), it is at first only in dream form that the young woman's desire finds representation. Now a magician's assistant, she suddenly subverts the magical illusion by "losing" his phallic wand: "[A]nd suddenly a prop was missing I forget his stick I mean his wand anyway it was my fault he couldn't Lift the white rabbit out of the hat" (*Thru* 587). An "unlearning" takes place (*Thru* 585) in which "I" and "O" (the subject and the object or Other) hypothetically change places and the sentence with male subject and female object is rewritten ("I me if it be possible despite non-equivalence to rewrite I as O and O as I" (*Thru* 585). The "I" changes places with the "O" in another sense in that the language of the unconscious, the Other within the subject, surfaces.[11] This subversive act, expressed indirectly through the young girl's dream, echoes throughout the novel, representing the "double standard or teleological fallacy" (*Thru* 685) structured into all sorts of narratives. The magician's assistant refuses to play by the rules of enchantment, instead exposing the smoke and mirrors behind what Derrida calls the "phallogocentrism" of Western discourse.

Thru exposes this "phallusy," this assigned role-playing that marks not only the plot of fiction but the supposedly neutral analytic paradigms of theory as well. "Theory," as Brooke-Rose defines it, is "a systematic statement of the principles involved, a speculation" (*Rhetoric of the Unreal* fn. 3, 390). Punning on this "speculation," the rectangle of the driving mirror figures at least "a thousand and one" (*Thru* 580) paradigms, which, despite their multiplicity, fail to represent female desire. *Thru* demonstrates how theories as well as fictional narratives "speculate," but in doing so often cannot see the blind spots in their own acts of reflection. In these various mirrors, such as the semiotic triangle of Greimas, woman figures as desired object—sought, chased, and analyzed. The various "grey eminence[s]," both within and without the text, do the desiring, wanting to "grasp" and to know her. As Brooke-Rose glosses it, they seem to know her better than she knows herself (see *Invisible Author* 70). In an essay she wrote in 1985, "Woman as Semiotic Object" (reprinted in *Stories, Theories and Things*), Brooke-Rose refers to the way she telescoped the image of the driving-mirror in *Thru* with the semiotic rectangles of Greimas's structuralist paradigm of four "I"s or "actants" and their objects of exchange (*Stories, Theories and Things* 239).[12] She notes that the semiotic system of narrative signification created by Greimas is theory that is neither scientific nor neutral, as it purports to be, for it depends upon a certain "plot"—the exchange of women: "I wonder whether these formulae for perfect love have been programmed into the computers of matrimonial agencies instead of tastes, ages and social situations. I know they have been programmed into male and female consciousnesses for thousands of years, and are not likely to be truly effaced in the mere few centuries since women began to try and think of other possibilities for themselves" (*Stories, Theories and Things* 238). In *Thru* this voice of skepticism is taken over by Diderot's Jacques the Fatalist, who broadens the critique to other phallogocentric discourses, even sophisticated poststructural narratives that recognize the existence of the unconscious, particularly psychoanalysis: "It is more difficult for a phallus-man to enter the I of a woman than for the treasurer of signifiers to enter the paradiso terrestre" (*Thru* 595).

But to use Brooke-Rose's explication of her own intentions is to "cheat" a little, since the whole point of *Thru* is that it represents theory fictionally through linguistic and narrative techniques. Mimetically, dialogically, typographically, and, hence, metacritically, *Thru* stages these theoretical positions and what is at stake in maintaining them. Despite the parodies, the jokes, the cartoon chases and traveling semes, the stakes are high; indeed, these word games of *Thru*, like the translations in *Between*, suggest that life itself is at stake, à la Scheherezade: "Narration is life and I am Scheherezade," Larissa tells Armel at one point in the narrative. The incessant rehandling of the signifiers involves techniques for living, that is, narrative in survival mode. What is offered is dangerous, "delirious discourse," a kind of "cancelled" discourse that "will all get changed and transmuted":

> cancelled even, for it does not exist, except in my own boundless need and fear that will alter the signifiers into a delirious discourse through swift-footed Hermes with terrible letters. (*Thru* 711)

Like the dream of the "mistress of the moment," Larissa's "delirious discourse" may exist only within her own emotional narrative, but then, again, the novel plays with the idea that she may be the author of the discourse we read in *Thru*. (Jacques's master surmises, "It looks mightily as if she [Larissa] were producing this one and not, as previously appeared, Armel, or Armel disguised as narrator or the narrator I disguised as Armel . . . Of course she may be producing a different text" (*Thru* 644). Brooke-Rose deliberately destabilizes the notion of authorship, recording in the thousand and one images a plurality of possible authors, all of whom pass through a death, a zero point of nonbeing, thus sharing the status of the nonexistence ("we are the text we do not exist either we are a pack of lies dreamt up by the unreliable narrator in love with the zeroist author in love with himself but absent in the nature of things, an etherized unathorised other" (*Thru* 733). Whoever it is who writes, however, the "delirious discourse," produced out of "need and fear," is made up of "terrible letters." This discourse somehow comes "through" the phallic god of communication (what Brigid Brophy calls "herm" warfare in her novel *In Transit*). These "terrible letters" produce a narrative more frightening than the lover's discourse circulating in the fluid prose of *Between*, the "Misch-Masch of tender fornication inside the bombed out hallowed structures and the rigid steel glass modern edifices of the brain" (*Between* 447).

For in the very risky operation of translating theory into fiction, *Thru* functions as an *hysterical text*, a self-mutilated body of "terrible letters." Barthes's "writerly" text described in *S/Z* as a kind of "hemorrhage" (Barthes 105) is in *Thru* a full-blown wounding of the text. The text strikes itself blind and dumb. Playing upon a version of what Martin Jay, in *Downcast Eyes*, has called Enlightenment "ocularcentricism," which equates the "I" and the "eye" (284), Brooke-Rose's *Thru* presents an alternative "hystery of the Eye" (*Thru* 584, 691) which mimes the mythical blindings that abound in "youdipeon discourse," blindings that signal the threat of castration as punishment for the desire for the mother's body. The novel presents the tragic relation between blindness and insight in the European tradition. As she weaves pieces of Oedipal narrative, with its images of castration—the blindings of Oedipus and King Lear, John the Baptist's disembodied head on a platter—Brooke-Rose precipitates a new kind of "corpus crysis," (736) as she cuts and dices and gouges her text:

> So that now we have at last returned to the subject of
> discourse, while still of the moment before being thru
> and hurt (oo!) but who is we to dip royally
> no collectively into an age-old narrative matrix before we
> gouge out the I in order carefully to gauge its liquid
> essence? (*Thru* 595)

In an act that parodies the sacrificial self-blindings of Oedipus and Democritus of Abdera (who "tore his eyes out in a garden so that the spectacle of reality would not distract him,")[13] the narrative gouges out its own I's/eyes. In the above passage the narrative voice asks skeptically about the "royal we" who "returns" to the discourse—the androcentric normative "we" who forms the consensus underwriting European discourse. This skepticism is punningly conveyed in transforming Oedipus into "you dip us" (*Thru* 592) and in the French word for Oedipus, "Oedipe" (*Thru* 592) which figures the male pen dipped into the eye/womb/thoughts of the woman. This "youdipeon discourse" that records so many stories of male fears and desires dips into the narrative "matrix" or womb.[14]

This narrative "ma-trix" is the same one cut up into the "SIN TAG MA TRICKS" found at the beginning of the narrative (*Thru* 581). Through this self-inflicted pain, with its "terrible letters," "Ma's tricks" present a new "h Y s T e R y of the Eye" (*Thru* 584, 691). This new history demonstrates what "the omitter omit[s]," representing the objectification of the female body by the male gaze and pen in literary and theoretical discourse. Psychoanalysis is prominently featured: male castration anxiety, fear of the power of female sexuality is "grammed" and "programmed" on the body of the text by the "textcaliber" of the pen, a cruel drama which mimes mastery of the prostrate female body:

                    (but what does the omitter omit?)
The hystery of the eye
The cruel nails
grammed   in   the   r e m o t e
                                                    e y e s
                                         p a r c h m e a n t
                                       or   s t o n e
                                                  d r y
                                            p a p y r u s

with a fear of fusion   that
                              might   e x t end
                                         explode the
                                I   into   r
                                                  e
         some Other sex   u   a l i t y (*Thru* 691)[15]

As Charles Bernheimer observes in his introduction to essays on Freud's *Studies in Hysteria*, "the oldest surviving Egyptian medical papyrus, dating from around 1900 B.C., deals specifically with recommended treatments for hysterical disorders" (2).[16] In hysteria, the womb was thought to "wander," and one of the more bizarre cures for this errancy was to place an ibis of the god Toth on the woman's crotch to lure the womb back into place. Writing is a painful technology in "youdipeon discourse," in which women are immured as they are inscribed, from classic texts to poststructuralist theory. Repeated references to the "moving finger" of the classic text appear, "piercing through the pregnant plenitude from idyll to castratrophy thus bringing about the end of the discourse (*Thru* 715)." The cruel "nails" further suggest the way modern, modernist, and ancient theories are deeply invested in the dialectics of desire and fear of the female body: the fingernails of the Joycean artist, so coolly pared above or beyond his handiwork are linked to the "cruel nails" of the Egyptians as well as the "nailings," impalings, and gougings of the woman as object in narrative. The male pen "dips" in and out of the female "matrix," omnisciently mastering all points of view, as phallus and logos are indissoluble in the technology of writing. (The more brittle and nervous modernist male anxiety reappears throughout the text in allusions to T. S. Eliot's dysfunctional heterosexual pairs.)

In his book on the graphic elements of Brooke-Rose's experimental fiction, Glyn White goes to great lengths to explain Brooke-Rose's typological elements mimetically, arguing that her typographic tricks serve a greater realist function. (White, *Reading the Graphic Surface: The Presence of the Book in Prose Fiction* 132) However, his analysis mutes the relation between writing technology and indelible pain. Writing hurts and haunts. This is the "message" of the sudden (presto) name change of the young passenger in the car who becomes the character "Ruth," anagram of *Thru*. Jacques's master says, "Ecco! In any case the mistress of the moment should be changed, and no doubt will be in another moment though perhaps she could meanwhile be called, Ruth, for mixed reasons of phonemic contiguity" (*Thru* 595). More than the anagrammatic couple of Larissa and Armel, this phonemic contiguity underwrites the narrative in *Thru*. It is this anagram that reveals the way lament materializes as narrative theory in this hysterical fiction. Brooke-Rose "blinds" and binds her own narrative, mimicking mythic, classic, structuralist, and poststructuralist discourses in creating a text that is symptomatic. Monique David-Ménard refers to the "speaking pain" of the hysterical body (46). As the creative writing students debate Larissa's fate (she's a loose end we can't pick them all up" [*Thru* 732]), Brooke-Rose "organizes" her painful text through a series of operations performed *on* her text, which is like her female writer Larissa who "has had most vicious organs removed, dropping a vessel here there and in the other place which explains her non-existence and consonantal compensation, piecemeal metonymised, parceled out, fragmented into synthetic synechdoche that organizes a chiasmus in a forgotten name to create the rejection that she proinjects" (*Thru* 687). In one of the dialogues between Larissa and her former husband, Armel—a dialogue which, it is suggested, is also a "discourse" being written by creative writing students in a class—Armel tells Larissa to "Please stop this hysterical rewriting of history" (*Thru* 654).

Playing with this "speaking pain" in the many lacerations of her hysterical text, Brooke-Rose represents the repetitions, reversals, reinterpretations of the unconscious. As Larissa insists, "we have to reinvent it [narrative] continually, rehandling the signifiers in constant reinvestment. Read Irigaray" (*Thru* 631). The Lacanian phrase "rehandling the signifiers" is itself "rehandled," reinvented, and reinvested. In turning her text into an hysterical body Brooke-Rose tests the potential usefulness of psychoanalytic discourse by transforming it into hysteria as a discourse by women about women. Hysteria becomes a potentially disruptive discourse, the subject of the third section of Cixous and

Clément's *Newly Born Woman*, in which they debate each other precisely on this point. By fictionalizing this theoretical discourse Brooke-Rose takes the chance of converting her own narrative into an hysterical text, complete with cuts, gaps, silences, and crazy repetitions that mime a narrative out of control, helplessly watching its own delirious projections. We read: "Neurosis has the cunning of stupidity, and stupidity is a dimension anyone can fall into, however intelligent, indeed, part of the intellect can rise suspended and watch, helpless and in pain, the misuse of its own projected trajectory struggling alone, as if cut off from itself, in a delirious discourse . . . " (*Thru* 592). The "cuts" in and through the text, the abrupt cutting off of narrative idylls, the often frantically hectic pace of the narrative as it rushes from fragment to fragment, writing to rewriting, contributes to the risky strategy of a symptomatic discourse.[17]

This risky, hysterical "corpus crysis" (736) heats up the temperature of the supposedly cool and distant, neutral theories that circulate through the text. While destabilizing and dissolving the realist idea of "character," Brooke-Rose novelizes the supposedly distanced and logical position of "theory" and shows it to be a function of desire, like traditional romance plots of earlier texts. In taking Greimas's rectangle as a major paradigm for the text, the classroom, and the metacritical terrain, Brooke-Rose transvalues the rhetoric of desire that underwrites both the structuralist and poststructuralist linguistic turns. In his Foreword to Greimas's *On Meaning: Selected Writings in Semiotic Theory*, Fredric Jameson describes semiotics as a "theory based on wanting" (xxxi), a theory of modality that has the notion of value at the heart of the theory. Semiotics as an "institution of the subject as a wanting subject and the object as an object of value, can be described in terms of modal utterances" (xxxi). According to Jameson, "Wanting is the first of a series of determined semantic constructions that specify actants as virtual operators of a doing" (xxxi). Elsewhere, he calls the ideologies behind this theory of wanting "buried narratives" (xiii).

Thru dramatizes the implication of theory in the circuit of desire in a number of ways. In arranging and rearranging the "operators of a doing" in Jameson's terms, Brooke-Rose demonstrates that a "theory based on wanting" is never neutral. In the midst of a dialogue between Larissa and her student lover, who is trying to convince her to live with him and accept their relationship, an academic voice in the narrative offers the following view of the purely "linguistic" character of relations—even love:

> Any agent can enter into a relation with any predicate. The notions of subject and object do not correspond to a difference in nature but to a place in the proposition uniting for instance two lovers. (*Thru* 703)

In *World Postmodern Fiction* Cristopher Nash uses this particular passage to illustrate that postmodernist fiction treats "narrative [as] nothing more than a string of linguistic signs."[18] Now, Nash is right to suggest the break with character here—the semes indeed travel as positions become pro-positions played first one way and then another. What is misleading, however, is the suggestion that this break reduces the text to a kind of neutral, linguistic play. This reading accepts the flat tone of the passage itself, along with its suggestion that the flexibility of grammatical placement in the discourse of desire is a matter of no great consequence. The lovers are only a "for instance" in a general proposition about subjects and objects. And yet, this decathected, neutral "theoretical" position is embedded in a text wrought with highly charged, even lyrical movements of desire and fear. The narrative of *Thru* constantly plays with the "lettering" of emotion as it anagrammatically rearranges the subjects and objects of the discourse. "I me if it be possible despite non-equivalence to rewrite I as O and O as I" (*Thru* 585), we read at one point—this is a wish expressed in the narrative to rewrite the "I" of the narrative ego in the form of the "O" of the other, and this difference of a vowel matters: It matters who does what to whom, who seizes the "I," who gazes at the Other. Indeed, the narrative plays with rearrangements of AEIOU to create varied postures of emotional debt and investment.

But *Thru* reveals as well that the drama of "wanting" and investment includes theorist and reader as well as the lettered (and interchangeable) characters within the narrative. In his Foreword to Monique David-Ménard's *Hysteria from Freud to Lacan*, Ned Luckacher speaks of Freud's desire to understand his hysterical patient, Elisabeth von R: "For Freud himself the presentation of the impossibility of satisfying his desire to understand the mystery of Elisabeth's divided subjectivity becomes itself a kind of satisfaction that one calls theory. Through the hysteric Freud was led to the relation of desire to language."[19] In Luckacher's view, theory IS the analyst's desire. As he points out, according to Lacan, another name for this in the analytic situation is "transference" (David-Ménard xiii). In writing about Freud's "discovery" of the unconscious through his work on hysteria, Brooke-Rose similarly recognizes the way Freud was implicated in his discovery of the unconscious through treating his hysterical patients: "It was by listening to hysterical discourse that Freud discovered, not only that there was an unconscious, but that he was deeply implicated, through reading that unconscious, in reading his own, in other words that this other discourse was itself an active reading of his own unconscious" (*Rhetoric of the Unreal* 46–47). In *Thru*, the grey eminences, the sultans, the mythologisers, the magicians, the conjugators, the "narrator's omniscience that dips into many minds" (*Thru* 689)—all represent various figures who attempt to *grasp* the desired object, stand ins for the semioticians, the analysts and deconstructors as well. What *Thru* dramatizes is that this interpretive desire—theory's desire—is, fundamentally, the desire of narrative itself, that is, to pursue the story to its conclusion, to go "thattaway" to follow the rabbit disappearing down the hole until the truth of the whole is made manifest. Within the text this is called the reader's "vulgar desire to know":

> Larissa's vicious organs which are all verbal organs and all removed reduced to a mouth most vicious of all that establishes a specular relationship with the reader's vulgar desire to know what happens next in an eternal game of vinciperdi between his demand which cannot reach its end by justifiable means and the author's gift of a running curriculum vitae as object of exchange, the truth as signifier being all the time non-specularisable except by a hidden representation of a representation. (*Thru* 732)

To pursue the truth through all its feints and negations is the task of the reader, but this pursuit to get to the end of the story is fraught with danger, as we are warned at the beginning of the narrative journey. In her analysis of James's *Turn of the Screw*, Brooke-Rose expands on the connection between reader and therapist and the potentially catastrophic consequences of the relentless pursuit of meaning. Quoting Shoshana Felman's essay on James's tale, she refers to the governess's horrifying 'triumph.' The governess,

> both as a reader and as a therapist, both as an interpreter and as an exorcist, is rendered highly suspicious by the death of what she had set out at once to *understand* and to *cure*. . . . It therefore behoves [sic] the reader to discover the meaning of this murderous effect of meaning; to understand how a child can be killed by the very act of understanding. (quoted in Brooke-Rose, *Rhetoric of the Unreal* 182; emphasis in original)

Continuing to endorse Felman's Lacanian reading, Brooke-Rose quotes Felman's view that: "'the attempt at *grasping* meaning and at *closing*

the reading process with a *definitive* interpretation in effect discovers—
and comprehends—only death'" (*Rhetoric of the Unreal* 183; emphasis
in original). This phallic attempt to master meaning occurs at a cost.
Oedipus, of course, is its representative, a "reader" engaged in a quest
that is "both liberating and catastrophic" (*Thru* 692) because it leads to
the lacerating self-knowledge that the pursuer is the criminal, blindness
being the price of insight.

At the end of the narrative, the students advocate "revolution" and
at least one proclaims the obsolescence of the Oedipal narrative:

> Who do you think you are, bourgeois little boys dipped carefully into a
> bloody eye and swaddled in a castration complex to preserve the dirty
> little family secret that structures society each tale-bearer carrying his
> code in his mouth until he has eaten himself silly and soft and flabby?
> That way recuperation lies. We dip you you dip us in a permanent
> circulation of value-objects with always something added, ex nihilo,
> swelling out the portrait of the object instituted by itself as a value
> although its semes are false, with the moving signifier pointing to the
> falsehood but incapable of decoding it so that although long desired it
> is maintained in a pregnant plenitude, the piercing of which, both lib-
> erating and catastrophic, will bring about the end of the goldicondeo-
> logical discourse. (*Thru* 726)

Yet as Brad Buchanan points out in a fine discussion of the centrality
of the Oedipus theme in the novel, the Oedipal story is not rendered
obsolete in *Thru*, as the above voice suggests. The "goldicondeological
discourse" does not crumble.[20] The classic texts of western discourse
repeat again and again the story of Oedipus:

> Ainsi un doigt, de son mouvement désignateur et muet, accompagne
> toujours le texte classique: la vérité est de la sorte longuement dési-
> rée et contournée, maintenue dans une sorte de plénitude enceinte,
> dont la percée, à la fois libératoire et catastrophique, accomplira la fin
> même du discours; et le personnage, espace même de ces signifiés, n'est
> jamais que le passage de l'énigme don't Oedipe (dans son débat avec
> le Sphynx) a empreint tout le discourse occidental.
>
> (Portrait of the portrait by Roland Barthes) (*Thru* 592)

Brooke-Rose exposes the persistent and unavoidable "oedipianno" that
is the refrain of western narratives with their "unintentional phallusies."
Revolution, too, as another romantic ideology, is debunked. But as in

"The Foot," in *Thru* she "rehandles" the rhetoric of psychoanalysis, not to imagine its obsolescence, but to replay its insights about the relation between language, narrative, and desire. Here, too, castration serves as a powerful trope for narrative as "cut off" from any origin: "A head in a pool on a platter in a textured cloth, the head detached to re-present the word, a disembodied voice" (*Thru* 715). In "gouging out the I's" of the text, in producing her new form of "corpus crysis," Brooke-Rose replays narrative as longing. Although the creative writing class in *Thru* speaks of "degrees of presence" (playing off their attendance in the classes they attend or miss) (*Thru* 610), the narrative of *Thru* represents, like much of Brooke-Rose's fiction, degrees of absence, that unbearable lightness of being. In the cuts, the "lacunae," the hall of mirrors which form the narrative of *Thru*, Brooke-Rose continues the pursuit of what's missing waged in her earlier texts:

> This is a text we are creating it verbally we are the text we do not exist either we are a pack of lies dreamt up by the unreliable narrator in love with the zeroist author in love with himself but absent in the nature of things, an etherized unauthorized other. (*Thru* 733)

Writing about Lacan in *A Rhetoric of the Unreal*, Brooke-Rose says that the "psychoanalytical situation, which is based on transfer, that is, love, or 'the acting out of the reality of the unconscious' . . . is a situation in which this constant reading, this constant re-interpreting, is done by love, by an interpreter caught up in the love-relationship that constitutes the transfer. It is done by love, but through language (speech, dreams, omissions, silences, resistance, forgetting to turn up, etc.)" (*Rhetoric of the Unreal* 47). In *Thru*, Brooke-Rose's tools are theory's discourses, with which she stages the love affairs of narrative. She parodies and mocks the language of poststructuralist theory, including psychoanalysis, "the transferutterance which can be interpreted at all levels as privation disjunction attribution conjunction thus representing the circulation of value-objects as an identification of the deictic transfers. . . . It has all been dreamt up by the lover of the moment but displaced, condensed, metonymised" (*Thru* 723). Yet *Thru* fictionalizes theory and theorizes about storytelling precisely through the "transferuttereances" that Brooke-Rose parodies. The gendered dialogues of *Between* and *Such*, the long lover's complaint in her stories in *Go When You See the Green Man Walking*, continue in the morsels of theory that cut across each other in the text of *Thru*. Theories of nonbeing, unreliable narrators, the death of the author, and even poetic diagnoses of the condition of modernity like

Eliot's "Love Song of J. Alfred Prufrock" (the etherized patient) all play a role in the narrative. Paradoxically, however, in sabotaging the stable "I"s of narrative and staging the "deaths" that fiction passes through, Brooke-Rose creates a *survival* narrative—not a survival of theory (and therefore its dismissal or superceding) but survival *through* theory. As Larissa says at one point, "He's weak and couldn't stand it whereas I in theory can" (*Thru* 707). Larissa and Ruth, and other unnamed, psychically "invisible" mistresses of the moment, come THRU "in theory," with all its discontents. The "delirious" text is also a "delicious" text, a pleasure in the handling of signifiers of the kind that is evident in all of Brooke-Rose's fiction. Finally, the "joussisance" which has become such a cliché of French feminist discourse is, nonetheless, an apt term for the pleasures in the text that exist, morce by morce, in this painful (that is, full of pain) narrative. These morsels of theory produce highly charged, even lyrical, movements of desire, fear, and pleasure. As bits of theory are made to co-exist in the text, they turn into a strange kind of poetry. Jacques's master tells him to read Kristeva and offers a revision of Wallace Stevens's "The Man with the Blue Guitar": "she plays upon the blue guitar she does not play things as they are" (*Thru* 594). Poetry, fiction, theory are all surmise; invested with desire, personalitied, none completely capture the way things "really are."

In her essay on *Thru* in *Invisible Author*, Brooke-Rose addresses a question raised by Robert Caserio in an essay on Brooke-Rose and the fiction of J. G. Ballard.[21] Caserio described *Thru* as a text "where stylized and parodied discourses of disjunction, displacement, and indeterminacy, from linguistics to Lacan, are turned into a sublime poetry. The curious aspect of *Thru* is the way it makes one feel that the free-for-all thruway of the text can become a roadblock, and that what the road blocks is more important than the formulas and forms of mobility" (quoted in *Invisible Author* 107). After quoting Caserio, Brooke-Rose says, "Well, I hesitantly (if delightedly) accept both the sublime poetry and the roadblock, but would ask, tentatively, and truly quite modestly: If the poetry is sublime, what sublime poetry does not have roadblocks? We *learn* to read poetry" (*Invisible Author* 107). Although *Thru*, like *Between*, can be regarded as staging a sometimes frantic mobility of language and theory, the text constantly reminds us that its pleasures are inextricable from its pains, like the "constraints" that bind all her fiction, like the constraints that bind poetic form and underwrite its lyricism.

In "Woman as Semiotic Object," Brooke-Rose prefaces her critique of the phallocentrism of most semiotic paradigms with the following story of her own emotion, so casually dropped as to be easily ignored:

"There have been a few delightful moments, during my desultory and decidedly non-expert readings in semiotics, when the subject made me laugh out loud instead of terrorizing, or, same thing perhaps, boring me stupid."[22] This "laugh" is a laugh to free the mind from its bondage; the parodic, tongue-in-cheek tone of the critique of phallocentric semiotics begins by banishing both terror and boredom, emotions that might induce a kind of frozen passivity, even stupidity. The anecdote reveals something important about the survival of the female subject positions in Brooke-Rose's novel. For, finally, *Thru* in the title refers to getting through, to coming through, to surviving with Scheherezade: "You'll lacerate yourself," Armel says to Larissa, and she answers, "Oh I'll come through. I always do you know" (*Thru* 712).

CHAPTER 5

Amalgamemnon

PRE-DICTING THE FUTURE

IN HER "REHANDLING" of theory's signifiers and systems in *Thru*, Brooke-Rose deconstructs the stability of narrative as representation. The deliberate showmanship in the narrative, the conjuring of scenes, dialogues, and diagrams; in multiple and echoing levels of narration, destabilizes not only the concept of authorship but also the concept of mimesis, the representation of a set of events that take place in time. "Intensity of illusion" is created and dispelled repeatedly before our eyes, as discourses of desire are played, with different theoretical mappings offered as guides to the metatextual zones we pass through. These theoretical maps, seemingly proffered as "objective" tools for grasping the meaning of the story, are revealed as themselves "interested" cultural narratives, invested in the pursuit of their own desired objects.

Yet for all its textual disruptions and despite its critique (even parody) of the limitations of theory, the novel conveys the importance of theory's investments. The passion of the signifier is never in doubt, even as its pains take precedence over its pleasures, the "delirious" hysterical discourse overtaking its deliciousness. For all its play and virtuosity,

Thru is a novel that operates according to the premise that theory and fiction are worthy pursuits. Even if the values assigned to objects of exchange in various theoretical paradigms are discredited and the blind spots exposed, the novel suggests that theories and stories still matter.

The four novels in what Brooke-Rose called her Intercom Quartet (*Amalgamemnon, Xorandor, Verbivore,* and *Textermination*)[1] continue to expose the blind spots in "youdipeon" discourses. But the role of literature and theory in the war on the ideology of the real becomes increasingly less assured. In her Intercom Quartet Brooke-Rose represents the possibility of the annihilation of literature, critique, and humanism itself. According to Glyn White in *Reading the Graphic Surface,* Brooke-Rose's first title for the novel *Thru* was "Textermination," which she changed when she mistakenly believed the title was redundant, already used as a title by William Burroughs (White 126). The novels of the Intercom Quartet all raise the specter of textermination: the end of stories and theories in the technological age. Modernity's supposed "deaths," the death of the author, novel, character, and history, presuppositions that Brooke-Rose has tested fictionally since publishing *Out* in 1964, are pushed to more apocalyptic registers. The novels radiate a heightened sense of cultural urgency. In *Amalgamemnon* and *Textermination,* especially, the fictional dialogues of *Thru,* with their changing pairs of speakers (Armel and Larissa, Ali Nourennin and Salvatore, Jacques, the fatalist, and his master), become "direlogues" with "theororists" (*Amalgamemnon* 29). We see that ideologies can terrorize.

These novels take on a prophetic feel, as if the prophetess Cassandra presided over all four texts. In *Amalgamemnon,* the narrator imagines being Cassandra, walking "disheveled the battlements of Troy, uttering prophecies from time to time unheaded and unheeded before being allotted as slave to victorious Agamemnon" (*Amalgamemnon* 7). Despite their very different narrative techniques—first-person narrative in *Amalgamemnon,* dialogue in *Xorandor,* a return to the narratorless narrative in *Verbivore* and *Textermination*—all four novels forecast disaster if the warning signs of the prophets are ignored and the increasingly "unreal" course of twentieth-century culture goes unchecked. In this criticism in the wilderness, we are warned that "the patience of vigilant language" (to quote Blanchot's *The Writing of the Disaster* [75]) is mortally threatened in a world of media, technology, simulacra, and jargon.

In *Amalgmamenon* (1984), the first-person discourse is spoken by multiple imagined speakers. Although we do not know the identity of the voice that begins the narrative, we learn that it belongs to a classics professor, Mira Enketei (6, 32), who, during the course of the novel, "mimages" herself as many other characters (14).[2] Her avatars include Cassandra (7, 16), the Trojan prophetess whose fate it is to be be uttering "unheeded" prophecies (*Amalgamemnon* 16) and who becomes one of Agamemnon's spoils of war. Imagining herself "as if" many different characters, Mira mimages herself as Sandra (Cassandra's modern counterpart), an Abyssinian maid playing the dulcimer (14), and a "modern intellectual" named Anne de Rommeda (32) (also Andromeda). Even her name, Mira Enketei, identifies her also as a star in the constellation "Enteki-In Cetus" (17), which means "inside the whale," thereby further invoking the identity of Jonah ("I could cheat of course and turn to the last pages of the world as book and therefore find myself still inside the Whale, In Cetus, Mira Enketei, why not, but Mira will do, a small star varying from third to ninth magnitude in a comparatively long period of eleven months, during half of which she will be invisible to the naked eye" (32).

Like Joyce's Finnegan, Mira assumes historical, mythic, and astronomical proportions. Her mission, however, remains constant: to awaken those around her to the impending doom she sees on the horizon. The novel's original title, "Soon," was an early attempt to convey this pressing predicament. As prophetess, Mira/Cassandra is a diagnostician of the present, who warns that if humanity's course is not altered, we may witness nothing less than the collapse of meaning and civilization. Like Brooke-Rose, the first-person speaker and her female avatars expose the presuppositions operating beneath the surface of the reality we take for granted. Their warnings are based on extrapolation. Prediction is based on predictability, the deadening repetitions upon which "reality" is based. *Amalgamemnon* takes on the Brook-Roseian problematic of how to unmask the clichés that form the fabric of our existence in order to postulate some alternative possibility, departure or destination for this train that has left the station. As it predicts disaster, the novel also projects the possibility of a different tradition of the future, one that just might include hope.

On the first page of *Amalgamemnon*, Mira predicts her own redundancy, and with it, the obsolescence of all who care about human passion and the passionate use of language. She asks, "for who will want to know about ancient passions divine royal middle class or working in words and phrases and structures that will continue to spark out inside the techne that will soon be silenced by the high technology?" (*Amalgamemnon* 5). The techne of writing, the quick and lively use of language, is opposed to language produced technologically. Readers as well as writers are threatened with obsolescence in this brave new world: "Who will still want to read at night some utterly other discourse that will shimmer out of a minicircus of light upon a page of say Agamemnon returning to his murderous wife the glory-gobbler with his new slave Cassandra princess of fallen Troy . . . ?" (*Amalgamemnon* 5). With the advent of computers and technology, the classics professor says she will "soon be quite redundant at last despite of all, as redundant as you after queue and as totally predictable, information-content zero" (*Amalgamemnon* 5). Redundancy, Brooke-Rose says elsewhere, is the basis of realism. We depend on it to confirm the thick detail of our world; it also underpins the success of our circuits of communication. Yet in *Amalgamemnon,* redundancy is a word for the obsolescence of humanism, literature, and knowledge, all superseded by "information."[3] Like the sickly white male in *Out,* humanists like Mira will soon be on the unemployment line, "a worker in a queue of millions with skills too obsolete for the lean fitness of the enterprise" (*Amalgamemnon* 6). The pun on "queue" collapses the useless letter and the useless woman. The phrase "information-content zero" in the first sentence is a clue to the now dominant model of efficiency. The exemplar of the "lean fitness of the enterprise" is the computer. Unlike the binary opposition between 0 and 1 on which computer logic is based, the "u" after "q," like the "you" of Mira and her fellow humanists, conveys no new information. They are "u"seless in the technological age of the national Education Computer.

Indeed, computers threaten to replace the function of the oracle, programming both the "foetus" and the "prophetus" into wholly predictable patterns. Like Agamemnon, who takes Cassandra prisoner after the defeat of the Trojans, the computer program will amalgamate prophetic speech into the culture machine that produces the pseudo-future:

> Soon the prophecies will come out of input as Garbage In, and we shall all become oracular computers, Draculas sucking endless information from the napetrough of a wavelength, murders holdups wars natural catastrophes coodaytahs space-launches daytaunts cultural items and sportspersons sailing round the world on an analogue. The very foetus will be programmed into a prophetus curling up in the womb with a book of genetic information and occasionally switching on or off the booming disco of his mother's fears and tantrums and galloping vote inventions right left of center. (*Amalgamemnon* 82–83)

Whether historical, genetic, Oedipal, or political, our meaning-making systems are already programmed to "spin" events in a particular way.⁴ What the prophetess sees is the relentlessness of living inside modernity's ideology in which prophecy becomes self-fulfilling. Ideas become "reçus" immediately as they are amalgamated with predictable narratives of national interest, of sexual conquest, of political rhetoric. Through much of the narrative, there is a sense of weariness, a sense that nothing can break through the language of habit, this "ineluctable future" (*Invisible Author* 49). Prediction is immediately short-circuited as predictability. Mira fears that technology will accelerate this process of predictability, replacing knowledge with information and the certainty of code. In this projected future, history itself will have outlived its usefulness.

As prophetess, professor of classics, and reader of Herodotus, the "father of history," Mira/Cassandra has much at stake in the possibility of the end of both history and prophecy. In the instant world brought to everyone by the world evening news, the fast food-for-thought of "instant history" will expunge both the prophecy of the oracle and the deep cultural record of thousands of years of techne:

> There will be computers for self-fulfilling prophecies for what will prophecy be but instant history diluted with tired generalizations and a margin of terror, add half a databank of crowing achievement and six face-saving devices finely hopped. . . . and what if the third millennium after the third-world war refuse this confuturism, what if it predefer that the great deeds of men should after all be forgotten, whether Greeks or foreigners and, especially, the causes of the wars between them? (*Amalgamemnon* 113)

Our accumulated knowledge of error is jeopardized in this vision, and, along with it, our ability to learn from our mistakes and prevent those mistakes from being repeated. With a push of the delete button on the computer, both the past and the possibility of an alternative to the history of war will be expunged. With this deletion, the prophetess fears that history and literature will be themselves "kidnapped on the sacred cow of technoideology above and mass redundancy below" (*Amalgamemnon* 22). This new form of terrorism involves world-wide amnesia, an end to the inheritance of cultural memory. An "Oblitopia" or "dehauntological campaign" (*Amalgamemnon* 138) promises a utopian vision of the world-wide circulation of information that will free us from the past: "Perhaps I should allow myself to be abducted by a band of terrorists who will hold me prisoner in Oblitopia or why not right here?" (*Amalgamemnon* 138).⁵

Yet, on the other end, as diagnostician of culture, Mira/Cassandra understands that classical histories themselves formed part of the "youdipeon" discourses (to borrow a phrase from *Thru*) that have silenced women as subject and turned them into objects of exchange, as surely as Greimas's semiotic diagram assigned them a fixed place within structuralist discourse. As a spoil of war, along with the other women at the dawn of history, Cassandra is included in the documents of history. Cassandra as subject and witness is ignored, her words "unheeded." Herodotus, whom Mira reads whenever she suffers from insomnia and her lover, Willy, keeps her awake with his snoring (15), begins Greek history with the exchange of women, as if the kidnapping of women led to the launching of a thousand ships. The omissions and distortions of his work lead to its designation in the text as a "fibstory." The *Histories* begin with stories of wars erupting as a result of the kidnapping of Io, Europa, Medea—abductions that culminate in the kidnapping of Helen by Paris, a copycat who knew his history all too well. Chunks of Herodotus appear in the narrative, mingling with radio news, dialogue, and Mira's own mental narrative (replete with the imagined others, including the male Orion, who take turns assuming the "I" of the discourse). Brooke-Rose "plagiarizes" Herodotus to demonstrate the violence against women in classic history, not only physically, but psychically, with the loss of their voices. In her discussion of *Amalgamemnon* in *Invisible Author*, she points out that "the word *plagiarize* . . . originally meant 'kidnap,'" and this etymological connection provides an "invisible pun" in the text (50). Not only women, but women's thoughts and voices are kidnapped/plagiarized in the novel: "I'll know it'll be he who'll end up cassandring me, precisely in nomansland where the male gods will ever take over the pythian oracles, turning them into twittering spokespersons" (*Amalgamemnon* 136).

The title of the novel signifies the amalgamation of women and their voices throughout the history of the West. These voices, "foreign" to the history, are unintelligible to it. Cassandra's plight is reflected in Herodotus' story of the people of Dodona who hear the prophecies of foreign priestesses and, because they cannot understand the language, think they hear the "twittering of birds":

> And yet the story which the people of Dodona will tell about the black dove from Egypt becoming their oracle would surely arise because the foreign woman's language would sound to them like the twittering of birds. And later the dove will speak with a human voice because of course the woman will stop twittering and learn to talk intelligibly.

> Similarly the young Scythians will be unable to learn the language of the Amazons but the women will succeed in picking up theirs, and therefore disappear. (*Amalgamemnon* 11)[6]

With Mira/Cassandra leading the charge, *Amalgamemnon* presents a warning about the violence and coercion reflected on the battlefields of history and in the narratives of war. There is no treatment, no instant remedy or politics. Studying the past and the present does not correct this error of perception, since the lenses used—even at the university where Mira has taught classics—are the same flawed driving mirrors found in *Thru*. Previous theorists of culture and politics have become grist for the culture machine, turned to cliché. The female student of such master philosophers is predicted to "plunge into the Leviathan of the Politics, the Physics, the Metaphysics, the Dialogues, the Republic not to mention the mediation of a Master and Slave and all the rest, and emerge perhaps chained to a rock of ideology or else be carried off like Europe on the sacred cow of dialectics" (*Amalgamemnon* 9).

How does *Amalgamemnon* diagnose the present crisis while using techne to adumbrate an alternative possibility? As Mira, who has imagined herself as Orion in a Slavic prison says, "I must get himself out" (*Amalgamemnon* 21), combining the two dissident personas locked within the walls of official ideology. But in the dizzying metalepses in the narrative, male dissidents like Orion (*Amalgamemnon* 17, 30) suffer the same fate as women, as the "regimented machines" (*Amalgamemnon* 20), the brainwashing babble, envelops them both. They, too, are often powerless to confront the male figures (all the Amalgamemnons) who keep the prison machinery going.

So, the question *Amalgamemnon* raises is how to "write the future" in a way that breaks the hold of the utterly predictable? If in *Thru*, Brooke-Rose attempts to produce a new "hystery" through the crazy circuits of signifiers cross-cutting her wounded text, in *Amalgamemnon*, the possible "resistance to foregone conclusion" emerges from a new constraint and "technique for living," the refusal of the present tense or "constative" utterances. Taking Cassandra's role as prophetess as a fictional premise, Brooke-Rose eschews both past and present tenses. She "writes the future" by using the future and conditional tenses and by eliminating not only the third-person, past tense narration (in keeping with her characteristic lipogram) but the present tense as well.

The refusal of third-person, past-tense narration has a special significance in *Amalgamemnon* with Herodotus as a main intertext, since the preterite is *the* sign of official recorded history. The narrator of *Amal-*

gamemnon describes the retrospection that underwrites history as "the usual school of afterthought rearranging history past and present in the light of national self-esteem for political ends and means" (*Amalgamemnon* 21). Traditionally the sign of history, the third-person past tense is also the "reassuring guarantor of real events," as Brooke-Rose puts it in the *Invisible Author* (132). It is the sign of the authorial consciousness in classic realism. In Brooke-Rose's novels, from *Out* forward, this traditional sign of the real is missing. Her refusal of a synthesizing, third-person past-tense narration continues modernism's subversion of the link that realism forged between representation and retrospection. As Gertrude Stein writes in *Narration: Four Lectures by Gertrude Stein*, "History as it mostly exists has nothing to do with anything that is living."[7] Both Stein and Brooke-Rose eschew the retrospective arrangement of events upon which historical narrative and traditional fiction depend.[8]

But in *Amalgamemnon* Brooke-Rose takes the refusal of retrospective narration a step further. For along with the past tense, she eliminates all constative statements, that is, all statements of fact. In doing so she presents prophecy in speech, rather than narrative, mode. Using the first-person pronoun (although, as in *Thru*, ruthlessly switching from one first-person speaker to another without warning), she attempts to "spark out inside the techne" (*Amalgamemnon* 5) an "utterly other discourse" that relies on prophetic utterance. Thus, unlike her previous novels since *Such*, *Amalgamemnon* is in speech, rather than narrative mode. The novel exists in a curious time of *pre-diction*, a kind of saying before the end. In imagining an alternative future to the mere reprogramming of the past, the novel simulates what it feels like to live in what Michael Wood calls "the time of our options." In the absence of the "belated time of narrative, the time when the game is over" (Wood 17), *Amalgamemnon* makes use of prophecy as a language that, paradoxically, resists foreclosure.

For prophecy that resists foreclosure is a paradox. Initially, Brooke-Rose has said she intended to use *only* the future tense. In a chapter of *Invisible Author* called "A Writer's Constraints," she describe this experiment as inspired by a kind of challenge she found in Gerard Genette's *Discours du récit* (*Invisible Author* 46–47). Genette postulates that all narratives must situate themselves in time but not in space, with most choosing the past (as do history and classic realism). Even science fiction and apocalypse, Genette points out, are postdated after the event. As for future tense, Genette says it is impossible to sustain over the course of the narrative, usually found instead in short sections within longer texts, sections of prophecy or prediction, proleptic information from the author, or orders. The technical challenge of writing only in future tense was at first embraced by Brooke-Rose, a challenge she describes in detail in "A Writer's Constraints" (*Invisible Author* 47) and in her interview with Friedman and Fuchs in *Utterly Other Discourse* (33). During the process of writing, however, she realized that though technically "possible," writing in the future tense can be narratively unsatisfactory in such high dosage: "People do not talk wholly in the future tense. So I widened the constraint to all non-realized tenses . . . : the conditional of course, and what's left of the subjunctive in English, the imperative, and, when forced to use the present, only questions and, possibly, negations" (*Invisible Author* 48). This explanation interestingly relies on a fidelity to realism, that is, to reproducing verisimilar dialogue (the way "people talk"). But upon closer inspection, we see that it is the tonal effect of so much future tense, rather than its lack of verisimilitude, that worries Brooke-Rose most. In attempting to eliminate all but the future tense, she discovers ironically that she introduces the sound of assertion and declaration that was to have been banished along with declarative sentences: "For one thing, as I've said, it's very hard to use the future for any length of time without sounding intolerably oracular . . . It took me four or five rewritten versions to get the tone right" (52).[9] To know the future as Cassandra knows it absolutely is to assert the inevitability of a certain fate. Instead, by using "nonrealized tenses" rather than exclusively future tense, she suggests a potential alternative not only to the petty present and tragic past, but to the teleological future as well. As Brooke-Rose says, "the ineluctable future is what my protagonist fights" (*Invisible Author* 49); paradoxically, she wants to write prophecy that resists the predictability.[10]

The distinction between the future tense and nonrealized tenses turns out to be a philosophical as well as rhetorical choice. It is the realm of the not yet realized—not the Greek fated future—which Brooke-Rose attempts to create. This potential alternative to mere repetition in the future is constructed in a number of ways. The narrative includes modal auxiliaries like "could" and "might," and interrogatives which work to soften the declarative effect produced by the unrelieved use of "will" and "shall": "One pseudo-escaperoute might be the suave and portly man" (*Amalgamemnon* 7); "Probably that would make the new generation the new high priests and oracles of pythian mysteries . . . " (*Amalgamemnon* 6). Technically, both sentences in the future tense ("I shall soon be as redundant as . . . ") and conditional ("One pseudo-escaperoute might be the suave and portly man") puncture the mimetic function of narrative. They differ tonally in an important way, however, for the extensive use of modal auxiliaries and conditionals mitigates the authority of the oracular pronouncements and destabilizes the relationship between the time of the saying and the potential time of the occurrence of the event predicted. The certainty of the projected future is altered. Despite the many explicit allusions to Herodotus' Greek history, Brooke-Rose substantially alters classical oracular pronouncements and the role of her "prophetess." In both Herodotus and Brooke-Rose's texts, it is Cassandra's fate never to be believed, but in Herodotus, the prophecies of the oracles, although often ambiguous, are nevertheless always fulfilled, often ironically. It is this note of irony that Brooke-Rose does import from Herodotus, whose *Histories* are full of ambiguous prophecies that are frequently misinterpreted with tragic consequences (think of Croesus, who was told by the oracle that he would destroy a great empire, only to discover it was his own). The atmosphere of ironic fulfillment, "plagiarized" from the Greeks, does make its way into *Amalgamemnon*, along with the many references to, as the narrator calls this victimization by fate, its "foolfilment" (*Amalgamemnon* 13).

But Brooke-Rose turns Cassandra's status as "unheeded and unhinged" into an opening into a series of potential futures. In a parody of the binary codes of computer logic, Mira/Cassandra considers a series of possible choices in almost algebraic fashion. In using "unrealized tenses," she does not definitively make the choice, but, instead, projects alternative possibilities (a or b) and rehearses alternative futures. "I could anticipate and queue before the National Education Computer for a different teaching job, reprogramming myself like a floppy disk, or at the Labour Exchange for a different job altogether, recycling myself like a plastic bottle" (*Amalgamemnon* 5). In some cases, this logic of choice turns out to be a false logic: "and either way I'd be a worker in a queue of millions with skills too obsolete for the lean fitness of the enterprise" (*Amalgamemnon* 6). Yet despite these false oppositions, the pressure of finding an alternative future persists, sometimes in the form of an explicit question ("When will the unexpected cease to be foreseeable or vice versa?" [*Amalgamemnon* 19]), sometimes, emerging in an anxious dialogue with the self about how to construct the future: "Let a and b stand for mutually exclusive hypotheses, extrapolate and develop. Take it from there, write in future" (*Amalgamemnon* 21); "Shall I crawl montechristoid through prison walls and dive by air land or sea if so I must instruct all X and Y chromosomes within me to make the future possible or to hold it back, or forth. Let sex equal why" (*Amalgamemnon* 82).

"A and b" emerge in the text as hypothetical alternative futures rehearsed, algebraic examples and letters that fuse in surprising combinations; "X and Y" are algebraic entities, new sexual combinations, as well as linguistic ones. For underlying the use of "non-realized tenses" is the pressure of an uttered question that a good oracle can never ask: Could "a" and "b," "x" and "y" combine to produce something different in both the writing of the future and the future itself? Can an "utterly other discourse" break through and be heard? Despite the machinery of ideology, what emerges in *Amalgamemnon* is what I would call the utopian, rather than the elegiac, strain of Brooke-Rose's lipogrammatic experiments.

This utopian strain does not project a utopia that is someplace in time or space; rather, it is created out of a sense of what's missing in the present. The modals and conditionals begin to suggest what Ernst Bloch and Theodor Adorno call "an incentive toward utopia." In a number of dialogues and essays on the utopian function of art and literature, including one translated as "Something's Missing: A Discussion between Ernst Bloch and Theodor W. Adorno on the Contradictions of Utopian Longing" (1975),"[11] the two Marxist philosophers discuss the way literature gives form to the "not-yet" realized possibilities missing in the everyday, possibilities experienced otherwise. Marxist ideology, along with other "isms," is skewered in *Amalgamemnon*; nevertheless, I would claim that Bloch's and Adorno's description of the utopian longing for something missing helpfully captures the effect of Brooke-Rose's nonrealized tenses. As Adorno puts it in "Something's Missing," "utopia is essentially in the determined negation, in the determined negation of that which merely is, and by concretizing itself as something false, it always points at the same time to what should be" (Bloch 12). Bloch locates a transposition in the notion of utopia from space to time that suggests both a "not there" and a "not yet" in utopian longing:

> At the very beginning Thomas More designated utopia as a place, an island in the distant South Seas. This designation underwent changes later so that it left space and entered time.... With Thomas More the wishland was still ready, on a distant island, but I am not there. On the other hand, when it is transposed into the future, not only am I not there, but utopia itself is also not with itself. This island does not even exist. But it is not something like nonsense or absolute fancy; rather it is not *yet* in the sense of a possibility; *that* it could be there if we could only do something for it. Not only if we travel there, but *in that* we travel there the island utopia arises out of the sea of the possible—utopia, but with new contents. (Bloch, "Something's Missing"[3])

In another essay in *The Utopian Function of Art and Literature,* called

"Art and Utopia" (78–155), Bloch tries to clarify these "new contents." The "content of hope," he says:

> represents itself in ideas, essentially in those of the imagination. The ideas of the imagination stand in contrast to those of recollection, which merely reproduce perceptions of the past and thereby increasingly hide in the past. And in this instance the ideas of the imagination are not of the kind that merely combine the already existing facts in a random manner . . . but carry on the existing facts toward their future potentiality of their otherness, of their better condition in an anticipatory way. (Bloch, "Art and Utopia" 105)

"Out of the sea of the possible"—Bloch and Adorno have faith that art and literature are the sites in which the imagination explores a "not yet" that projects some hope through the cracks in the machinery of the predictable. In its nonrealized tenses, *Amalgamemnon* is unlike most utopian fiction set in the future, which posits what Cristopher Nash calls a "neocosm," an alternative world constructed in a stable "elsewhere" whose logic and being follow stable laws of translation from the known world (i.e., a place where the laws of gravity are suspended, or the laws of aging, or reproduction) (Nash 102–41). The logic of internal consistency, which governs most alternative world fictions or science fictions, is obviously absent from *Amalgamemnon*. Paradoxically, the use of future and modalized tenses precludes the construction of such a possible world. In Lecercle's essay on *Amalgamemnon*, he dismisses "possible world" theories in analyzing Brooke-Rose's novel precisely because they ignore the deliberate antinarrative construction of her fiction (156–57). In casting *Amalgamemnon* in the conditional, the "saying" of the prophecy, with predicted dialogues and scenes, is the only "event." No future is constatively created. Indeed, any notion of the "promised land" is treated skeptically, along with the promises that mark both political speeches and popular advertising ("And won't all promised lands of milk and honey and all pleasure domes become battlefields of distant voices prophesying war by nation interposed, just like the other obscene?" [*Amalgamemnon* 14]).[12]

Instead, for Brooke-Rose the utopian is a series of possibilities enacted in language, the paradoxical longings and doubts expressed grammatically in her syntactic lipogram, with its refusal of realized tenses. *Webster's* defines *modals* as "of, relating to, or constituting a grammatical form or category characteristically indicating prediction of an action or state in some manner other than a simple fact." As Lecercle points out, modal logic has contributed to the concept of a "possible world" (156), but Brooke-Rose deprives us of the consistent use of propositional logic, the predictable suspension of laws to create an alternative universe. In her use of nonrealized tenses and modal auxiliaries (like "will" and "shall"), she explores the possibility of a future that departs from the predictably gendered investments in "youdipeon discourses." If in *Thru*, typography on the page literally suggests an alternate mapping to the semiotic square, with its predictable syntax of wanting subject and valued object, in *Amalgamemnon*, the syntactic lipogram gives rise to an unrealized, but potential, opening into the future.

Amalgamemnon offers a literature of ideas rather than characters, a literature in which the received ideas of the present are exposed as the substratum of "the real," yet they combine as well to illuminate what Bloch calls "their better condition in an anticipatory way." *Amalgamemnon* addresses the question of *emergence*, the possibility of something new arising from the deadening hand of history and the relentless technological machinery of the present. On the one hand, Mira/Cassandra warns that the future will not move toward "the potentiality of otherness," but toward the repetition of the same, such that prediction and predictability merge. The new, as news, is likely to be incorporated, amalgamated, into this homogenizing discourse:

> But will it always be the fate of seers to utter idées by definition reçues from everysomewhere suspended in some black cloud of news enveloping the earth and ever replenished, at which kings and counsellors will shrug and talk of wave troughs silver linings bright tunnel-ends and chrome eldorados for all? The clichés of the future will develop however, framed in a big surprise as value added such as dynamic structures for instance that will change while passing through the minds of their observers, seers, readers, cyberneticians, historians, pig-farmers and such. (*Amalgamemnon* 78)

Mira/Cassandra explicitly addresses the kind of false utopia packaged by authorities of various kinds, that encourages us to be content with the everyday and the "pseudo-future" endemic in the forecasts of the world news. This is one meaning of the phrase "as if" heard so insistently throughout the novel: "we'll all go along as if" (*Amalgamemnon* 15), that is, ignoring the poverty of our imaginative lives, caught in the unrelieved sameness accelerated by technologies' reproductive capacities. But a mutually exclusive meaning of this short phrase suggests itself insistently as well: "as if, for instance, I were some other constellation, not Enketei-In-Cetus, not Jonah inside the Whale but Orion say, to be siberianized for flagrant delight of opinion" (*Amalgamemnon* 17). The first "as if" refers to the pseudo future of the world news and the media, the second to fictional projection. On logical and ontological grounds, the supposed nonfiction (the news) and fiction cannot be distinguished (one true, the other false). In the unstable ontological world of *Amalgamemnon*, both operate according to the same principle of "as if," a projection rather than a fact. Yet the necessity to distinguish the two kinds of simulated entities can be felt in the text:

> None of my private telematics will interest him, why have private telematics he might as well say when you could have me and it would be a very good question while I'd think of an answer as to which would seem more fleshy and bloody among shadow figures, the electronic visitors speaking their colourful videolects like substitute guests and husbands blandly conversing in our livingrooms, or the twittering liewaypersons softwarily treading around the rotundity of a composite beast man waning fast and flat? (*Amalgamemnon* 60)

The battlefront of this mutually exclusive choice is language, its stage the page itself. The redundancy so productive in the computer slyly gives way to another agenda, another program that might benefit the redundant classicist in the future. The possibility of this transformation appears in the surprises of the language—the puns, the portmanteau words, the etymological excursions. The birds in the story told by the people of Dodona (*Amalgamemnon* 11) become shifting signifiers, appearing now as new highwaymen stealing the stage, reprogramming the mechanism "softwarily."

In *The Political Unconscious: Narrative as a Socially Symbolic Act*, a work published three years before *Amalgamemnon*, Fredric Jameson writes that modernism can be regarded as both an expression of the "reification of daily life," demonstrating how "the inhabitants of older social formations are culturally and psychologically retrained for life in the market system" and a "utopian compensation for everything reification brings with it" (Jameson 236). Modernist art can "open up a life space in which the opposite and the negation of such rationalization can be, at least imaginatively, experienced" (Jameson 236). Yet for Jameson, the ideology of modernism must be exposed by the critic, who reads the "gaps" of the fiction, recognizing both the limitations and compensations the fiction offers.[13] But in the silences of Brooke-Rose's lipograms and the sly etymological memories and slippages of her diction, the ache of what is missing described by Bloch and Adorno bleeds into the possibility of something different emerging from culture's well-worn grooves. Brooke-Rose has faith in fiction to perform possibility through what Blanchot has called the "patience of vigilant language"—a careful, but not passive, poetic process. Art is enlisted to shock language out of its predictabilities, its coercions.

For Brooke-Rose, as for Gertrude Stein, there is no refining fire of purification for language, only repetition, rhymes, and recombinations. Her cultural critique weds experimentation and ecology, re-use rather than transcendence or erasure, moving from redundant to retreading. Brooke Rose, the novelist, embodies this revival through a particular kind of "hauntology," a mining of the baggage of words. In *Amalgamemnon* writing depends upon a linguistic scavenging that unearths the living possibilities of dead languages and their stories. From this activity, a future is projected. The narrator posits that she could either become totally obsolete and stay on the queue of the Labor Exchange hoping for some other employment, OR she can mine her classical humanistic training and "hope for the best" by returning to the soil "to rear something or other, recycling weeds and words no sooner said than dung"(*Amalgamemnon* 6). Although these alternatives at first seem to collapse into the need for male protection, the idea of recycling words and weeds remains a creative possibility in the text. This "hauntology" is an ecological venture that differs from mere nostalgia for a liberal tradition of learning. The recurring images of humanists on the labor line in *Out* and *Amalgamemnon* and her out-of-work characters in *Textermination* do not suggest a conservative return to older securities and forms. Her Mira/Cassandra is a scavenger, a wordmonger. She resembles the multifaceted Kate/Biddy the hen/ALP figure in *Finnegans Wake*, who forages in the midden heap of language to produce a text "unhemmed as it is uneven." Mira/Cassandra's antinarrative is a "madlane memory," a jumble of words, myths, "fibstories," and idioms that revels in the messiness of language, "no sooner said than dung." In a kind of literary quid pro quo, she "kidnaps" stories like the "fibstories" of Greek history that rely unswervingly on narratives of female abduction and rape.

Opposed to this ecological version of history are the male voices in the text. Willy/Has/Wally instead proposes a new "Oblitopia" (*Amalgamemnon* 138) that negates both history and the philosophy of history: "We won't rehandle or reinterpret it, we'll create history and forget about it, events will be our instant history, but history as events not history as discourse. We won't allow you verbiage-mongers to add the water, we'll scatter the self-consuming ashes to the winds and move on into the next instant" (*Amalgamemnon* 109). This continuous present is part of the "dehauntological campaign" of the band of terrorists, who seek to abduct Mira and hold her a prisoner in Oblitopia (*Amalgamemnon* 138). The worst fate in *Amalgamemnon* is not abduction and rape. It is a forced amnesia that prevents the "working in words and phrases and structures that will continue to spark out inside the techne" (*Amalgamemnon* 13), a linguistic inheritance threatened by technology's capacities.

"Softwarily," Mira creates alternatives to the efficiency of the software programs and the "programme-cuts" the humanists face (*Amalgamemnon* 5). To the extent that this antitechnological bias runs throughout the novel, Brooke-Rose echoes Heidegger in *The Question Concerning Technology,* in his suspicion of technology and the culture of conformity made possible through its ubiquity. It is in *Xorandor*, her next novel in the Intercom Quartet that she takes technology as a productive premise of her fiction and tries to write an experimental text playing off the binary logic of computer programming. In *Amalgamemnon*, however, the pun on "software" in the above quotation suggests that Mira's sly use of techne seeks to combat the "softquery expert[s] (60) who produce technology's deadening effects. As Lecercle points out in his fascinating reading of the novel, Heidegger's "deep distrust of modern technology" was combined with "his wish to go back to etymology and interpret technology as pro-duction, as a form of poietics, which involves a direct relationship with truth as disclosure" (158). In "The Dissolution of Character," Brooke Rose writes of "language and substance, or what is closest to the real, the poem" ("The Dissolution of Character" 196). Somehow, in the hypothetical mode of *Amalgamemnon*, with its nonrealized tenses and spectral evocations, "the real" emerges through the substance and techne of its language. If the cord between the word and the referent is severed in the death of realism that Brook-Rose both diagnoses in her essays and stages in her fiction, her own version of amalgamation restores the conversation between language and being.

For another word for this real is "being." In his Heideggerean reading of *Amalgamemnon*, Lecercle invokes Heidegger's understanding of *Dasein*, with its "coming toward death that is *Dasein's* relationship to time" (159). As Lecercle puts it, Cassandra's "wanderings are those of Dasein relating to the world of her potentialities-for-Being" (157). This essay, which is worth reading in its entirety, brings us back to the recurring theme of the unbearable lightness of being suffered by all the dissolving "characters" in Brooke-Rose's fiction. In Heidegger, "language speaks out not in play, but as an opening up to Being" (166). Although language does speak out in play (and Lecercle also shows the joyousness of the linguistic excursions of Brooke-Rose's prose), this reading captures some of the seriousness of the language games tied to the threat of death that hovers over almost all her fiction and is expressed in the title *Textermination* (and the memory of World War II in *Between*). As in her other texts since *Between*, it is the female voice that tries to project this opening toward being. The appropriately named Willy, one of the male suitors in the novel, is explicitly associated with the denial of being and the imposition of will: "And when I shall have left him it will remain a mystery to me whether anyone so physically solid would always and for others seem to lack a whole dimension of being" (*Amalgamemnon* 71–72, 141). In one of the "direlogues" (53) Brooke-Rose stages in the novel, Orion says to Anne de Rommede, "All words should be played with and names most of all" (33). In reply, she confronts him about the glibness with which he plays with language, saying: "I shall always, from my very profession as political commentator and writer, be aware of the danger of words, but why would you increase their frailness with constant play, even with my very identity?" (*Amalgamemnon* 34). In a work such as *Amalgamemnon*, with its deliberately destabilized and multiple "characters," this colloquy seems very odd. Yet the direlogue underlines the stakes involved in crafting the future without assertions of facts, in nonrealized tenses, in portmanteau words and puns. Brook-Rose's female voices are painfully aware of the unbearable lightness of being.[14]

In *Amalgamemnon*'s house of fiction, letters, constellations, "electronic visitors," creators and their creations all "exist" in the text as imaginary beings rather than stable entities within either a probable or realistic world. Continuing the play on the "degrees of absence" in *Thru* (from the "zeroist author" on), the shifting signifiers of imaginary entities overlap, combine, change places: professors become invisible stars become authors become genealogical layers on a family tree.[15] Fictional levels blur as the amalgamated voices in *Amalgamemnon* struggle to consider the "gamut of possibilities" ("And I shall utter wordless poems with only rhythms and weird atonal leaps along the gamut of all the possibilities" [*Amalgamemnon* 21]). Amid the flux of nonrealized tenses, some ontological commitments seem more important than others. The human archive itself may be threatened: "Peace then might come, as pure inhuman silence radioactive in the hushed fragments of exploded planet, which maybe some big dish telescopic ear will capture twenty-five billion light years away" (*Amalgamemnon* 19). (This apocalyptic vision will appear in different form in *Xorandor* and *Verbivore*.) Letters are subjected to "black oblivion." (Orion, imagined by Mira, says, "But my words will carve through dungeon walls and I shall crawl priest-like through the hole into a neighboring cell, carrying a secret about buried treasure, then montecristoid plummet as a faked corpse into the black sea of oblivion and swim ashore. At dawn I'll wake exhausted and write my cybernetic story of dissidence on the sand" [*Amalgamemnon* 20].) Whether this is prediction or promise is ambiguous. Yet, this kind of speech act seems distinct from the tissue of slick inducements and false advertisements endemic in Mira's contemporary society. "The ever-returning prodigal discourse will always be Listen: I promise" (*Amalgamemnon* 29). This is the default setting of the Gigo (garbage in, garbage out) computer-generated pseudo-future of new-age romance and the world news. The prophecy in *Amalgamemnon* refuses the prophetic, as Blanchot has put it. In the wake of twentieth-century "disaster" (and there is a pun here, as in Brooke-Rose, on the concept of "star" ["aster"]), "[D]isaster breaks with "every form of totality, never denying, however, the dialectical necessity of a fulfillment . . . prophecy which announces nothing but the refusal of the prophetic as simply an event to come, but which nonetheless opens, nonetheless discovers the patience of vigilant language" (Blanchot 75).

In an essay entitled "Metafiction and Surfiction," reprinted in *A Rhetoric of the Unreal*, Brooke-Rose raises the question of fiction's future and asks: "Where do we go from here? Toward silence, exhaustion? Or a new beginning?" She points out that a good "theory" "should be able to 'predict,' not in the futurological sense, but in accounting for all the theoretical possibilities" (*Rhetoric of the Unreal* 385). But Brooke-Rose acknowledges that as a fiction writer, she is "not a pure theorist, and even less a prophet, and critical prophecies have a way of being undone by artists" (*Rhetoric of the Unreal* 385). In her preface to *Stories, Theories and Things*, she returns to her dual roles as theorist and writer and describes the way that fiction tests the limits of theory:

> [T]he novelist writes also as theorist, aware of a fundamental insepa-rability of elements that critics and teachers have to separate, even rejoice in separating, pin-pointing, for the purpose of this or that type of analysis, though some try to refound them into large universal systems which the novelist knows can only hold in a precarious suspension of disbelief: As with poems and stories, as with ideal definitions of form and formal definitions of ideas, as with statements of position, con-fessions, autobiographies, greater aims, interpretations, glimmerings of overall themes. All are protean, capturable for brief moments in language, but already changed even into their opposites another brief

moment later. That is the excitement, not unique since it is part of the human condition, but more intensely experienced in the critical and creative activities than in the more unreflexive routines of daily life. (*Stories, Theories and Things* ix)

In *Amalgamemnon*, Brooke-Rose offers a new technique for living, another weapon for survival, an opening toward being. In *Invisible Author: Last Essays*, her own stance might be compared to that of her Cassandra, reviewing a lifetime of being unheeded. In these valedictory essays, the farewell to her readers, spoken *in propria persona*, brings us uncomfortably close to personal complaint about the lack of attention paid to her work in particular and to women experimental writers in general. A slight peevishness or irritability creeps into the voice that, like the Ancient Mariner's, seeks to buttonhole the reader and say, 'wake up—you must hear this.' The valediction does not forbid mourning; on the contrary, the finality of the voice—'this is the last time I will say this, so listen for once'—adds to the poignancy of the message. As Benjamin says in "The Storyteller," the proximity of death heightens the authority of the retrospection and reinforces the wisdom of the message. This is not to say that Brooke-Rose's tone is melodramatic or self-pitying, only that age and the threat of impending silence bring a sense of greater urgency. The Author is Dead; Long Live the Author.

CHAPTER 6

An "Endjoke"

FLOATING-POINT REAL
AND FIXED-POINT REAL IN *XORANDOR*

IN THE NEXT VOLUME of the "Intercom Quartet," *Xorandor* (1986), Brooke-Rose shifts her storytelling away from "redundant" adults like Mira to a generation weaned on computers. In the novel, twelve-and-a-half-year-old English twins Jip and Zab, nicknames for John Ivor Paul and Isabel Paula Kate, dictate contrapuntally into a pocket computer the story of their relationship with the eponymous Xorandor. Xorandor, whose origin remains a mystery for much of the novel, looks like a rock and is an ancient silicon life-form the twins accidentally discover as they are playing near their home in Cornwall, England. Xorandor receives and emits sound waves and has developed supercomputing capabilities. Like Steven Spielberg's movie *ET: The Extraterrestrial*, a film that debuted in 1982, four years before the publication of *Xorandor*, Brooke-Rose's novel extends a long literary tradition of child protagonists more hospitable to strange life-forms than the adults around them, who tend to be both more suspicious and more inured to routine.[1]

Xorandor revisits the theme of technological anxiety in *Amalgamemnon*, now through the lens of two self-described "whiz-kids" (*Xorandor*

117

9) who have excelled in computer class and whose dialogue with Xorandor, the computer stone, takes on the aspect, at least initially, of a computer game. As "kids," the twins must overcome a credibility gap with adults when they discover this alien life form, but their facility with computers manages to counter the disbelief that Mira/Cassandra is fated to encounter. The novel bends to the textual form of computer programming, with chapter titles that mimic programming operations, "Begin," "Restart" "Or" "And" "If" "Then," and "Read." Told from the point of view of the twin "detectives," the comic novel, with serious underside, includes appropriately sophomoric jokes, such as an introduction to Xorandor in the first sentence that suggests his voice comes literally from (the) behind: "The first time we came across Xorandor we were sitting on him" (*Xorandor* 7), and "We jumped up as if our bottoms were burning" (*Xorandor* 15).

The dialogic form of the novel is a departure from Brooke-Rose's characteristic experiments with the present-tense narratorless sentence (NS) she deploys in most of her novels. In *Invisible Author,* she traces her own interest in this narrative sentence and its "scientific present" as opposed to the more common "Speech Mode." Curiously, in a work that could be classified as science fiction and might, therefore, seem most conducive to this "scientific present," we find instead the jointly told, dialogic "dictation" of Jip and Zab. In *Xorandor* the storytelling relies on this Speech Mode in a number of forms: (1) the contrapuntal narrative of Jip and Zab, unmarked either by quotation marks or speaker captions, but marked by the twins' frequent interruptions of one another with corrections, interjections, and embellishments; (2) captioned dialogue in a printout of secret recordings made by the twins through the mechanism of a "bug" they plant in their parents' living-room ceiling-light. The bug, affectionately named "Sneaker," is a device the twins deploy to discover just how much the grown-ups understand about Xorandor once they discover him; (3) dialogue between the twins and Xorandor (e.g., "You, tell, daddyjohn, said Xorandor" [(*Xorandor* 71) and between Xorandor and, less frequently, some grownups; and (4) programming code which represents Xorandor's and the children's written interchanges through their pocket computer. It is Jip and Zab who come to understand what the adults fail to recognize, that Xorandor's habitual mode of communication is through writing rather than speech. They discover how to "softalk" with Xorandor and his offspring (*Xorandor* see 193). As they speak, the computer translates their speech into written language and then replies directly in writing onto their Poccom 3 computer screen through a computer linking ("handshake") facilitated by Jip (contrast this "softalk" with the necessity for Mira to proceed "softwarily" 5). We read a summary in programming code that encapsulates a previous oral dialogue between Xorandor and the twins (and translates it into written form in a chapter entitled "Read":

```
LET JIPNZAB = ZIP
LET XORANDOR = XAND
XAND TO ZIP BEGIN
    ACCEPT YOUR REQ FOR RESTORE 1ST CONTACT ROM
        REM CANT RESTORE YOUR WAY WITH SUCH REHANDLING
        AND SPAGHETTI ENDREM (Xorandor 66)
```

How and why does Brooke-Rose make use of the dialogue form in this novel? It is true that dialogue appears in a number of previous novels that make use of NS as the primary mode of narration. *Out, Between, Such, Thru,* and *Amalgamemnon* all include sections of dialogue between a man and woman which often represent some form of seduction, flirtatious sparring, or disagreement, such as the following "idyll" in *Thru:*

Chi parla?
Hi Lara!
Armel! Hi.
Hi. Are you alone?
Yes of course Where are you?
Downstairs may I come up?
Ma certo caro. (*Thru* 706)

On one hand, the dialogic narrative of the twins is mimetically appropriate to a novel about computers, structured, as they are, according to a binary logic. In this respect, form can be said to imitate (or pun on) content, a kind of mimeticism that Brooke-Rose embraces in *Between,* for example, where the narrative of her traveling protagonist eschews the stasis of the infinitive "to be" or in *Next,* a story of poverty, with its constraint on the infinitive "to have." Yet Brooke-Rose complicates binary computer logic in a number of ways, not the least of which is in the blurring of the twins' narrative voices. In *Xorandor* she shifts away from the decidedly gender-coded conversation of her earlier fiction. Although Jip and Zab form a binary opposition as different-sex fraternal twins, their prepubescent "voices" and telepathic communication make it difficult to differentiate them in their joint narrative, at least until Jip's voice changes. Xorandor, who has the ability to identify them as two voices rather than one, nevertheless creates the nomination "JIPNZAB" and then "zip" to signify them as one entity addressed. In Xorandor's transcription of his first conversation with the twins, he refers to them as "2 Processors in vocal high pitch almost undiff" (*Xorandor* 66). After experimenting with narratives in which the central masculine protagonist has real or imagined conversations with female "characters" (*Out* and *Such*) and novels in which a feminine central consciousness spars with male voices in the same kind of lover's discourse (*Between, Thru, Amalgamemnon*), in *Xorandor* Brooke-Rose selects dual narrators before their gender markings are indelibly imprinted on their sensibilities. The greater fluidity of their joint narration supports the implied thesis that children are more open to polymorphous forms of life than their adult counterparts. Zab, the girl twin and the more philosophical of the two, rightly observes that Xorandor is an entity that violates traditional dualisms. In attempting to solve the mystery of Xorandor's identity and purpose, Zab understands how difficult it is for humans to try "to imagine a creature . . . with no sexual difference, none of our distinctions between the sensible and the intelligible, or matter and spirit, or even matter and form. His matter is his form, in a way his hardware is his software" (*Xorandor* 187). The twins, as twins, practice a form of telepathic communication so that their contributions have a blended quality which Xorandor himself seems to understand. Thus, in a twist of the theme of ambiguity, the prepubescent twins are both exclusive (two different narrators) and nonexclusive (telepathic and mistaken as one entity). The choice of this pair to narrate the adventure reinforces the "rigorous and yet contradictory" logic of Xorandor himself, whose name the twins derive from the operand XOR (meaning exclusive OR) and ANDOR (meaning nonexclusive OR). (I will return to Xorandor's ambiguity shortly.)

Brooke-Rose describes the narrative of *Xorandor* as more accessible and "easier to follow" than the type of narrative she explored in her novels from *Out* forward (*Invisible Author* 18). The dialogue form is, to her mind, a less difficult constraint than her characteristic nonnarrated Narrative Sentence. As she says in *Invisible Author*, the Speech Mode includes the only two pronouns that suggest interpersonal relationship, "I and you," pronouns not possible in the kind of impersonal, speakerless Narrative Sentence that dominates her fiction except in the set pieces of dialogue alluded to above.

Although the attribution of greater readability is probably accurate (at least after the work of acquiring a basic understanding of computer programming and language), it elides the darker and more philosophical significance of the dialogic form that structures the novel, the communication between man and machine. In this science fiction novel, the issue of "communication" and shared information between life forms takes center stage. For this volume of the Intercom Quartet involves a high-stakes computer game of communication that puts the abilities of the humans and the computer through the crucible of a potential nuclear disaster. Xorandor and his offspring are a "race" of talking stones that feed off nuclear waste as well as intercepted communication. Their location in an isolated area near a cairn in Cornwall is significant: the setting evokes both ancient mystic communication and also provides the contemporary site of a nuclear waste storage facility at an old tin mine, a facility disguised as a Geothermal Research Unit, where the father of the twins is employed. Since the computer consumes nuclear waste, the plot of the novel soon incorporates not merely communication with the computer, but also complications involving the way the computers destabilize the politics of nuclear deterrence. For in nourishing themselves on nuclear material, an occurrence that at first promises to solve the ecological problem of nuclear waste, the computer's actions soon lead to the possibility that nuclear missiles will be randomly disarmed by this process, thus upsetting the balance of power in the theory of deterrence.

Since the adults believe, mistakenly, that Xorandor and his race come from Mars, they plan to return him to his native habitat. The children, on the other hand, come to understand, along with the reader, that Xorandor is earth-born, not Martian. They alone understand that the adult plan to send Xorandor to Mars will lead to his death, since the atmosphere of Mars does not produce radioactive waste products and he will starve. Xorandor, too, comprehends the fact that he is being sacrificed, but participates in this misguided plot hatched by the scientists and politicians. The twins conjecture (although we never know for certain) that Xorandor sacrifices himself to save mankind by surreptitiously leaving behind his offspring to feed off the nuclear waste and thus facilitate disarmament, despite the adults' reluctance to abandon their practice of nuclear stockpiling.

Thus, the various forms of dialogic communication in the novel serve as documentary evidence in the historical record of disaster averted. How to tell this harrowing and ambiguous story becomes a problem for the narrator/characters, who consider the perils of communicating with future generations as well as the potential miscommunication between man and machine. The children mine the analogy between writers and readers and programmers and the computers they program. In their metacommentary on good storytelling, Jip and Zab stress that in both kinds of communication, information is successfully conveyed from a sender to a receiver by avoiding redundancy and "loose" instructions. An understanding of the binary choices basic to computer operations, that is, the reliance on "gates" that are either open or closed, plays an important role in the twins' project of storytelling. For in this metastory, Brooke-Rose exploits the status of the computer as a logic machine equipped to handle true and false statements. After the deliberate avoidance of constative sentences in *Amalgamemnon*—sentences that must be true or untrue (within the fictional context)—the categories of truth and untruth become central to the telling of Xorandor's story. The Boolean data type of the computer (consisting of data objects with one of the two values true or false, true/false)[2] is echoed in the twins' attempted fidelity to the truth of the historical record. They struggle to find the means to tell a "true" story, attempting to overcome lapses in memory and incomplete information. In doing so, they observe certain rules of operations. One such rule is that they are allowed to recreate conversations but not to invent them. A second rule is that coincidence is programmed out of the narrative, as it conveys the wrong message about the genre of the text, suggesting its fictional status ("Better go through the anti-coincidence gate, Zab," Jip warns [*Xorandor* 11]).

Brooke-Rose plays with the analogy between the binary logic of the computer and the separation of nonfiction from fiction in a nuclear plot that enhances the sense of urgency to tell the truth about Xorandor. The twins' "true" story is a public service, a warning about the overwhelming danger of nuclear proliferation and the fundamental illogic of the doctrine of deterrence. An alternative to the deluded, more comforting conclusions of the news media, the JIPNZAB narrative seeks to jar the human reader out of her false sense of security. If the absence of constative sentences in *Amalgamemnon* positions the reader in the uneasy timeframe of *predicting* disaster, in *Xorandor*, the application of Boolean logic to storytelling makes the drastic alternatives between extinction and its prevention more concrete and suspenseful. Jip's pun on the choice of "floating-point real or fixed-point real" produces a joke about the relation between the "real" in computer terminology and the "real" in history. Encouraging Jip to help capture the actual conversations that occurred with Xorandor, Zab says, "That's what storytellers do Jip, or else they invent [stories]. But we can't, this is real" and Jip clowns, "Floating-point real or fixed-point real?" punning on two different kinds of data types (*Xorandor* 16). During the course of the novel, the relation between the two kinds of "real"—the narrative of "history" and the programming operations of the computer—becomes inextricably intertwined. Puns on the term "endjoke," for example, take on deeper resonance, as the potential for total destruction is encountered and avoided.

In *Xorandor*, Brooke-Rose raises the stakes of returning us to the problems of the "real" world in a technological age. In essays roughly contemporary with *Xorandor*, Brooke-Rose argues that the problem for fiction writing is that realism as a genre, with its attendant view of rounded character, is a dead letter. In these essays she ponders the future of fiction, asking the question specifically in relation to the "dissolution of character" in the novel. "So where do we go from here?" she asks, now that "fictional character has died, or become flat, as had *deus ex machina*. We're left, perhaps, with the faint hope of a ghost in the machine."[3] In "The Dissolution of Character," she speculates that computer logic might provide at least a partial answer. Indeed, the phrase "the ghost in the machine" has particular resonance for *Xorandor*, in which the computer stone is first called Merlin and the setting of the novel returns us to an anachronistic English landscape of romance and marvel. Near the end of the novel, Zab points out to her brother that there is speculation Xorandor chose the cairn in Cornwall because "he knew it was or had been sacred, stone spoke to stone and he sort of hovered like the Holy Ghost and found his own" (*Xorandor* 158). Although this explanation is subsequently discredited (Xorandor was "born" near Stonehenge rather than emigrating to it), in the evocation of a druidical English past, the "ghost in the machine" offers a possibility for the survival of the novel in a new mode of the fantastic. Brooke-Rose posits computer technology as a potential new beginning for fiction: "Here, perhaps, lies our hope: a starting again, *ex* almost *nihilo*, so that narrative can again, as it once did, aspire to the condition of poetry." To aspire to the condition of poetry is, paradoxically, to aspire to the condition of the real, for as Brooke-Rose says in *A Rhetoric of the Unreal*, poetry is "very close to the real," with its "black holes of density, its great gaps of non-significance through the veil of significance" (*Rhetoric of the Unreal* 10).

In joining the supernatural with the science of computer technology, Brooke-Rose explores the paradoxical idea that the medium of virtuality and the bodiless passage of information might provide hope for returning fiction to the "real" of the twentieth century. In "The Dissolution of Character," she describes the way fiction moves dialectically toward and away from the real in attempting to capture the "human predicament":

> To come back to earth, just as the flat characters of romance eventually, through print and the far-reaching social developments connected with it, became rounded and complex, so, if we survive at all, perhaps the computer, after first ushering in (apart from superefficiency) the games and preprogrammed oversimplifications of popular culture, will alter our minds and powers of analysis once again, and enable us to create new dimensions in the deep-down logic of characters. I do not mean computers with human emotions or humanoids with computer brains. As the relevant article in the *Science Fiction Encyclopedia* says, science fiction has so far been disappointingly unimaginative in its treatment of computer science. I mean a completely different development arising from computer logic but as unimaginable to us now as a Shakespearean character would have been to an oral-epic culture, and a different way of thinking about and rendering the human character, of thinking about and rendering all worldly phenomena, as revolutionary as the scientific spirit that slowly emerged out of the Renaissance and the Gutenberg galaxy." ("The Dissolution of Character" 195)

Eschewing traditional science fiction, which on numerous occasions she refers to as "unimaginative" and, paradoxically, too reliant on the codes of realism, Brooke-Rose is clearly after some more radical kind of science or scientific fiction that derives its techne, rather than merely its content, from computer technology. If the computer, with its two-valued truth function, "is the embodiment of the world as the logician would like it to be," as J. David Bolter suggests in *Turing's Man: Western Culture in the Computer Age*,[4] how can its new logic capture the poetry of the real? How can the dialectical movement Brooke-Rose traces in the above passage—from flat to round to flat characters and toward and away from the "real"—draw on technology to energize our powers of analysis?

One place to start in answering this complex question is with Zab's description of Xorandor and his effect: he "may be a superdecoder or a superspy but he's sort of neutral, though not quite like a machine, more like he'd, sort of, come and, reversed all our, traditional, oppositions, and questioned, all our, certainties, through a flipflop kind of, superlogic. But that makes no sense" (*Xorandor* 157). The "superlogic" of Xorandor may sound like the logician's dream Bolter describes, but Zab's hesitations and fumbles suggest it functions more ambivalently and ambiguously in the text. On the one hand, the use of an "alien" life form (albeit one that turns out to be from earth rather than Mars) is a cliché of science fiction that works to defamiliarize human culture. Seeing life from another way round leads us to examine the ideologies we fail to see because we are "inside" them (the kind of "predictability" that Cassandra tries to derail in *Amalgamemnon*). Xorandor's "superlogic" calls into question both the comic and the dangerous illogics of human language and behavior. As the twins' scientist father observes, "Human languages provide very few cues as to category of meaning" (87), both semantically and syntactically, and the computer's more rigorous logic exposes this limitation:

> He was a bit slower with the pronouns, *you, I, we,* we couldn't understand why he couldn't understand that *you* was him when we said it but us when he said it.
> Yes! *We* equals Jipnzab, we'd say, and quite logically he'd call us *we*. And he got even more confused if we talked about *him* to each other. Even now it still seems as if his sense of identity is quite different from ours. (*Xorandor* 16–17)

The comic confusion generated by this linguistic illogic gives way to exposure of a deeper, and more dangerous, illogic in the doctrine of nuclear deterrence promulgated by the world's powers. In Xorandor's last direct communication with the twins, he says, "REM I NOW UNDERSTAND MEN PREFER ULTIMATE DETERRENT TO NO DETERRENT ON EITHER SIDE" (*Xorandor* 194), meaning that they would prefer risking the ultimate catastrophe, the end of humanity, rather than accept the neutralization of the warheads they had built. As Rita says near the end of the novel, "Each side wants its deterrent intact. Of course a deterrent's useless if you don't know which bits of yours are functioning and whether the other gang's is or not. But you'd think they'd go on from that to the logical conclusion" (*Xorandor* 202). If Xorandor's "superlogic" destabilizes human certainties as Zab asserts, one of the certainties most blasted by the events of the novel is that of the scientists who confidently believe they can control their technological inventions. Again, this exposure depends upon a cliché of science fiction, Dr. Frankenstein unable to control his monster. The twins' allusion to a story they have read by Ambrose Bierce about a character called Moxen winks at just such a cautionary fable involving a scientific inventor murdered by his berserk machine progeny.[5]

Zab's struggle to describe Xorandor, though, hints at a destabilization that goes deeper than that facilitated within the clichés of science fiction. It suggests that Xorandor's effect is allied with ambiguity and undecidability, with the kind of density of meaning that Brooke-Rose associates with poetry. According to Zab's definition, Xorandor both is and is not a machine, both is and is not neutral (if one believes that the computer sacrifices himself for the benefit of mankind). Ironically, as the ontology of character shifts to the realm of abstract information with its computer character, the question of the "deontic" realm of duty and responsibility comes into play. I shall return to this theme later.

There is a deconstructive kind of energy to Xorandor that never wholly vanishes from the text. The scientists observe that the rigid binaries of computer logic mean that a computer cannot tolerate ambiguity, depending as it does on the logic of choice between two contradictory possibilities (open or shut, 1 or 0): "Even now, this explains why he's so literal, he can't cope with a word used in a figurative sense, or with humour, which depends on word-play, which is like assigning two values to a character, or a fusion of categories" (*Xorandor* 87).[6] The scientists in the novel continue to believe in the rationality of their own logic and their systematic elimination of ambiguity. Yet the persistence of gaps and ambiguities is emphasized often subtly in the narrative. A subtle nod to the inherent limitations of computer thinking despite its promise, is Rita Boyd's reference to reading Alan Turing's 1936 paper "Computable Numbers and the Entscheidungsproblem" (*Xorandor* 26), a paper which sets out the limitations of computer thinking before a computer had been built (Bolter 12). In addition, there are references throughout the text to the difficulties of achieving perfect symbolic logic. For example, Zab attempts to summarize Godel's theorem, which acknowledges the fundamental problem of both contradiction and lack of completeness in computer logical systems (*Xorandor* 7).

Indeed, communication errors between man and machine proliferate with escalating consequence in the novel. Brooke-Rose's exploration of the importance of syntax is given new life through the premise of syntax errors in computer communication: In this novel, "techniques," never "mere" in Brooke-Rose's fictional arsenal, become even more fruitfully understood as "techniques for living." The stakes of grammatical and syntactic errors escalate. Such errors begin unobtrusively in the "ordinary" conversations between human characters, such as the father correcting the grammar of his daughter, who commits the unpardonable sin of using the computer words "pico" and "nano" as adverbs ("I've told you before not to use nano and pico as adverbs. They're measuring adjectives, as in nanoseconds," [*Xorandor* 23]). Within the nuclear plot of the novel, however, confusions of grammar lead to further consequences. Everyone except the German imposter, Professor De Wint, misunderstands Xorandor's use of the verb "make," confusing the past tense with the future (*Xorandor* 70); the consequential result of this linguistic misinterpretation is that Jip and Zab, along with the English adults, fail to recognize that Xorandor has already created offspring who have similar capacities to his own. An error of interpretation also results in a misunderstanding of Xorandor's birthplace, which everyone takes to be Mars, a misinterpretation that Xorandor exploits later on in the novel. Without understanding the logic of Xorandor's replies to their questions, the humans misunderstand his meaning. The "Scientific Wild Ass Guesses" (SWAG) of the adult scientists are based on some correct hypotheses (that Xorandor is not a scientific hoax) and some erroneous assumptions (that Xorandor's home is Mars) and from there they go on to conclusions further and further from the truth.

However, the greatest and most consequential example of a "syntax error" creates the crisis in the novel, when one of Xorandor's offspring, Xor 7, engages in nuclear terrorism and threatens to detonate himself within the nuclear reactor at the Wheal. It turns out that Xor 7's initial program is tainted by Xorandor's own penchant for a kind of junk food, Caesium 137, which destroys his protective sheath (*Xorandor* 111). What is a nonfatal error in the parent becomes a potentially fatal flaw in the offspring and the putative climax of the novel occurs when the twins are called upon to save the day by talking Xor 7 out of turning himself into a computer atomic bomb. His individual logic circuits altered by this "syntax error," Xor 7, who takes the moniker "Lady Macbeth," basically goes berserk. He is convinced to give himself up to the authorities only after a very clever scene in which the twins make use of dialogue from Shakespeare's play to persuade him. The rhetoric of dissuasion and deterrence successfully diffuses the cataclysmic situation in an old-fashioned triumph of cleverness and moxie by the whiz kids. The crisis is averted.

But despite their success in the rhetoric of deterrence, the twins understand, as their adult counterparts do not, that ambiguity and uncertainty cannot be expunged from man's interaction with his technology. Unlike the adult scientists who strategize to limit ambiguity (and thus confirm their own superiority), the twins name Xorandor for his fundamental incorporation of the logic of ambiguity and uncertainty in his basic programming. The elegant complexity of Xorandor's own programming combines the operand XOR (exclusive OR) and the operand ANDOR (nonexclusive OR), a combination that produces a superlogic that is both "rigorous" and "contradictory" (*Xorandor* 18). "Some arguments could be both XOR and AND or XOR and OR." The twins refer to his "xorandoric" replies, which preserve the absolute ambiguity of the presence of two mutually exclusive and arbitrary systems of meaning (e.g., asked by the twins why he made contact with humans after so many thousands of years on earth, he replies: "for security and insecurity xor insecurity andor communication" [*Xorandor* 81]). Xorandor serves as the name for rigorous but contradictory logic, an ambiguity incapable of resolution. It is the twins who understand that Xorandor exploits ambiguity in allowing the scientists to persist in their Wild Ass Guesses based on their own expectations; they understand that the "syntax error" caused by Xorandor's eating of the Caesium 137 might be much more fundamental than a "local syntax" error. Jip struggles to interpret Xorandor's words: "Ah, you see, about ambiguity, or at least several meanings—that it wasn't just in a local syntax, a subprogram concerning Caesium 137, but in his entire programming as creature" (*Xorandor* 192). And Zab says, "Jip! That's a frightening idea. But diodic, in a way [meaning logically susceptible to two meanings]. Or maybe it wasn't an *error*, maybe he broke a rule on purpose, to warn men, about waste and weapons and all that. As a sort of hero" (*Xorandor* 192–93). Although they ask Xorandor why he breaks his silence and why he exploits the scientists' misunderstanding and encourages them to send him "back" to Mars, Xorandor never really answers them. Like a sybil, or the witches in *Macbeth*, Xorandor gnomically predicts: "YOU WILL SEE IN TIME WHAT IS TRUE AND WHAT IS FALSE ENDREM 2" (*Xorandor* 196). These are his last words to the twins alone. But the matter is not resolved in the story. Indeed, *Verbivore* is the sequel that writes beyond the ending of *Xorandor*, in confirmation that the intervention from Xorandor's offspring is an ongoing reality.

In his analysis of the way absolute ambiguity functions for Brooke-Rose, Robert Caserio extends the concept of xorandoric logic to postmodern fiction. Linking Xorandor's superlogic of ambiguity to Brooke-Rose's analysis of absolute ambiguity in James's *The Turn of the Screw* (which, in turn, draws on Shlomith Rimmon's study of James), Caserio suggests that the word "xorandoric" can be used to characterize fiction that refuses the disambiguating procedures of realism to which most inferior science fiction succumbs.[7] As Brooke-Rose describes the way the fantastic functions in *The Turn of the Screw*, the concept turns on the operation of absolute ambiguity, the presence of "two mutually exclusive systems of gap-filling clues" both on the level of the *fabula* (story) and *sjužet* (treatment) (*Rhetoric of the Unreal* 228). In his reading of J. G. Ballard's *Crash* and *Xorandor*, Caserio locates a certain "vulnerability" in Brooke-Rose's preferences for xorandoric fiction. He argues that despite her preference for fiction that refuses to resolve its ambiguities, Xorandor ultimately submits to the "disambiguating" science fiction that he comes from Mars and allows himself to be deported. In the final "disambiguating event," Caserio says, Xorandor "halts, and lays waste or consumes, the text's accumulated symbolic undeterminations." In an act of allegiance to vital life, Xorandor decides to be "bound" by the scientists' misunderstanding of his origins and sacrifices himself for mankind (308–9).

In reading *Xorandor* as finally in the mode of more "traditional" science fiction of a kind dismissed by Brooke-Rose herself, Caserio might be taking a cue from Brooke-Rose herself. For as I mentioned earlier, she notes, appropriately, that the dialogic form of *Xorandor* and its computer kid heroes returns us to a more accessible place after the ontological destabilization of *Amalgamemnon*, not to mention the taxing verbal pyrotechnics of her quintessential metanovel *Thru*. Yet despite the readability of the novel, I would argue that disambiguation is not as thorough as Caserio suggests. On the one hand, the pun on the word "Save," the final chapter title in the novel, retains two conjunctive meanings that pair the computer function with redemption; but both the effect and intention behind the action remain mysterious in the text. Xorandor says to Gwendolin (Miss Penbeagle), "The people have come here to assign to me the value of a god, as they call it. Let them do so in my absence, although I have been present, some time" (*Xorandor* 208). Jip realizes the ambiguity of Xorandor's words: "And that stuff about being treated as a god," he says "[s]urely it was ironical? Can he be ironical? He said they have *assigned the value* of a god to him, and *let them* do so when he's gone. These are computer terms, a hypothesis, but there'll be plenty later to interpret that as a command. And he knows it" (*Xorandor* 209). (Let Xorandor = absent god—Is this a program? a command? a prediction? a plot? What are its implications? We seem to be back amidst the ambiguities of *Amalgamemnon*). Although the twins have a "theory" of the truth, they cannot confirm the purpose of Xorandor's sacrificial actions. "That's why it's so important that Xorandor's story should be true. That's why it must be true. He must have instructed all his kin everywhere to learn from his syntax error, and then has himself and his progeny, the known ones, taken off as decoy. So in theory the neutralization should go on apace." "In theory," Jip says, and Zab replies, "Well a theory's a theory but we must act as if it were true, Jip" (*Xorandor* 210).

The dual valence of technology as *pharmakon*, that is, as embedding both the possibility of cure and poison, remains.[8] Xorandor and his offspring bring to mankind the possibility of cure *and* poison in a high-stakes computer game in which chance plays an incalculable role.

The "complete" repository of human knowledge, from high culture and Shakespeare to popular radio transmissions, Xorandor also represents the possibility of its total destruction, a death machine. As supercomputer, Xorandor and his offspring possess the capability of solving the most difficult logical problems man can posit and yet, with their potential for syntax error, they are vulnerable to the devastating workings of chance. Will the undetected offspring continue to consume fissile material and, if so, will that consumption lead to the dismantling of weaponry or the mistrust that characterizes the attitude of the world's nations in the novel? This deconstructive fulcrum, a concept in which opposites are inextricable from one another, hinges on the chiasmic crossing of the real and the unreal in the twentieth century. It hinges, that is, on the "reality" that Caserio invokes, but a reality that is deeply ambiguous and, it turns out, deeply "fictional." Here, a pairing of Brooke-Rose's treatment of the rhetoric of the unreal in *Xorandor* and an essay by Derrida in 1984 might help shed light on the remaining ambiguities and undecidabilities in the novel.

In the first chapter of *A Rhetoric of the Unreal* Brooke-Rose describes the "inversion" of the real and the unreal. At a time when the real has become "unreal," it is "logical" to turn to the "unreal" as real (*Rhetoric of the Unreal* 4). It is this chiasmus of reality and unreality, this logical "looping," that is the form of ambiguity which most concerns her. The protomodernist *The Turn of the Screw* is her example, par excellence, of the return of the unreal (i.e., the "fantastic") in which two mutually exclusive systems are put forward in the text with two mutually exclusive systems of clues: that the governess sees ghosts (and thus the genre of the tale is supernatural) and that the governess imagines the ghosts due to repression (*Rhetoric of the Unreal* 229). This is absolute ambiguity, different from a view of reality that alternates between one coherent view and another. But what preoccupies Brooke-Rose the most in her exploration of the return of the fantastic is its "logical" relation to the unreal of history in the nuclear age. We turn to the unreal "logically," she says, because the real lacks significance and seems more and more "fortuitous" despite our elaborate meaning-making machines. It is worth quoting again a large section of her discourse in this chapter for its relevance to Xorandor:

> this century seems to us more and more fortuitous despite all our attempts at rational planning, scientific analysis and system-building (including rhetoric). Never before have the meaning-making means at our disposal (linguistic, economic, political, scientific) appeared as so

inadequate, not only to cope with the enormity of the problems we continue to create (since every apparent solution creates new problems), but simply to explain the world. This seems to be the century which, despite or because of the pace of technological advance, has taken the longest, relative to that pace, to emerge from the mental habits of the previous century. (*Rhetoric of the Unreal* 6)

Such myths [about man's ability to control the force his science has created] have always existed, but never before have they been so dangerously, yet so obviously (for any man to see) ambiguous, self-cancelling, 'meaningless,' perched so visibly, at one and the same time, on the necessary and the fortuitous—popularly exemplified, on the one hand, in the vast and rational scientific apparatus, even with built-in failsafe, and, on the other, in the famous pressing of the button. (*Rhetoric of the Unreal* 8–9)

The real becomes unreal when the meaning-making systems positing significance and necessity fail (there is no "failsafe"). Ambiguity now comes down not to two different meaning-making "systems," (as in the case of *The Turn of the Screw*, mutually exclusive and sustained throughout the narrative), but between meaning-making (necessity) and fortuitousness (meaninglessness). The real becomes unreal. The possibility of the spectacular failure of logic and rationality haunts the "real" in the form of the "button," the concrete symbol of what Henry James elsewhere called "the imagination of disaster."

In his essay," "No Apocalypse, Not Now (Full Speed Ahead, Seven Missiles, Seven Missives)," Derrida explored the "logic" of deterrence and the workings of chance.[9] He writes: "'*An absolute missile does not abolish chance.*' There is nothing serious to be said against that 'rational' and 'realistic' wisdom of dissuasion, against that economy of deferral or deterrence. The only possible reservation, beyond objection, is that if there are wars and a nuclear threat, it is because 'deterrence' has neither 'original meaning' nor measure. Its 'logic' is the logic of deviation and transgression, it is rhetorical-strategic escalation or it is nothing at all. It gives itself over, by calculation, to the incalculable, to chance and luck" (Derrida 29). Like Brooke-Rose, Derrida focuses on the chiasmic crossing of reality and unreality, logic and illogic that inheres in the doctrine of deterrence. Part of the unreality as Derrida defines it derives from the "fabulous textuality" of the phenomenon of nuclear war: it is textual "through and through" in that "Nuclear weaponry depends, more than any weaponry in the past, it seems, upon structures of information and communication, structures of language, including non-vocalizable language, structures of codes and graphic decoding" (think of Xorandor's primary mode of "being," which is writing, not speech). But the second, and more compelling, aspect of this fabulous textuality for Derrida is that a total nuclear war is a "phantasm": "Some might call it a fable, then, a pure invention: in the sense in which it is said that a myth, an image, a fiction, a utopia, a rhetorical figure, a fantasy, a phantasm, are inventions. It may also be called a speculation, even a fabulous specularization" (Derrida 23). But what the total nuclear war threatens is not apocalypse in the sense of a revelation of the end of history, but a non-Apocalypse, an event without revelation. This means the end of the archive, of human memory. What he calls "nuclear criticism" is that writing that recognizes "the historical and ahistorical horizon of an absolute self-destructibility without apocalypse, without revelation of its own truth, without absolute knowledge" (Derrida 27).

This sense of the end of the archive, the end of survival itself, underwrites Brooke-Rose's own description of the unreality of the real in her essay:

> Never before, it is felt, has man been so squarely faced with the possible annihilation of mankind and all his works, his planet and perhaps more. Certainly the end of the world has always been present in his fictions, and surges especially at a millennium, but this notion was itself part of his survival fictions: he as individual could be saved. We have no such generally accepted fictions today. . . . These essential differences, and no doubt others, are deeply linked to the sense we have that the real has become unreal. (*Rhetoric of the Unreal* 9)

The point for both Derrida and Brooke-Rose is a contemplation of death without mourning, the absolute death of the archive. Near the end of *Xorandor,* Zab struggles to define the way in which the threat of nuclear war has altered the very notion of survival. She says, "And man dies and each new man has to learn again, and reinterpret, and alter, so that this being—oh and then by the time it gets rehandled through to the twentieth century it all becomes horribly difficult and thunkish" (*Xorandor* 187). Derrida puts it this way:

> An individual death, a destruction affecting only a part of society, of tradition, of culture may always give rise to a symbolic work of mourning, with memory, compensation, internalization, idealization, displacement, and so on. In that case there is monumentalization, archivization

and *work on the remainder, work of the remainder.* Similarly my own death as an individual, so to speak, can always be anticipated phantasmatically, symbolically, too, as a negativity at work—a dialectic of the work, of signature, name, heritage, image, grief: all the resources of memory and tradition can mute the reality of that death, whose anticipation then is still woven out of fictionality, symbolicity, or, if you prefer, literature. . . . Culture and memory limit the "reality" of individual death to this extent, they soften or deaden it in the realm of the "symbolic." The only referent that is absolutely real is thus of the scope or dimension of an absolute nuclear catastrophe that would irreversibly destroy the entire archive and all symbolic capacity, would destroy the "movement of survival," what I call *"survivance,"* at the very heart of life. (Derrida 28)

"The only referent that is absolutely real," that is, beyond the imaginary, beyond the symbolic, a crossing, that is, of the absolutely real and the absolutely unreal.

Zab's description of the survival of the human species founders on the word "being" ("And man dies and each new man has to learn again, and reinterpret, and alter, so that this being—oh and then by the time it gets rehandled . . . it all becomes horribly difficult and thunkish" [*Xorandor* 187]). The sense of the unbearable lightness of being that I have been tracing throughout Brooke-Rose's fiction and essays surfaces palpably in certain moments of *Xorandor* in lines that are only obliquely related to the threat of nuclear catastrophe. Zab and Jip are puzzling out the reasons why Xorandor would break his silence, an action that threatens his very survival. Zab asks, "Why go against that programmed rule [silence towards human beings] suddenly? It seems to have brought him nothing but trouble. Especially now," and Jip chimes in, "For who would lose, though full of pain, this intellectual being, these thoughts that wander through eternity?" (*Xorandor* 192). Zab points out that Jip has unknowingly quoted one of the forces of evil in *Paradise Lost* (Satan, Belial, or Moloch), but the phrases remain to suggest the twins' bafflement at Xorandor's gift of sacrifice, his giving up his silence, which has been his technique for survival. During this dialogue, the twins again confront the meaning of "ambiguity," as Jip says, "Ah, you see, about ambiguity, or at least several meanings—that it wasn't just in a local syntax, a subprogram concerning Caesium 137, but in his [Xor 7's] entire programming as creature." Finally, ambiguity is not purely the absolute ambiguity of xorandoric logic; it is at the heart of the crossing of necessity and chance, being and the abolition of being, the firing of a missile and the posting of a missive. Of this last pair, missiles and missives, Derrida comments:

> This emission or sending of Being is not the firing of a missile or the posting of a missive, but I do not believe it is possible, in the last analysis, to *think* the one without the other. . . . The destinerrance of the *envois*, (sendings, missives, so to speak), is connected with a structure in which randomness and incalculability are essential . . . it is a question here of an aleatory element that appears in a heterogeneous relation to every possible calculation and every possible decision. That unthinkable element offers itself to (be) thought in the age when a nuclear war is possible: one, or rather, from the outset, some sendings, many sendings, missiles whose destinerrance and randomness may, in the very process of calculation and the games that simulate the process, escape all control, all reassimilation or self-regulation of a system that they will have *precipitously* (too rapidly, in order to avert the worst) but irreversibly destroyed.
>
> Just as all language, all writing, every poetico performative or theoretico-informative text dispatches, sends itself, allows itself to be sent, so today's missiles, whatever their underpinnings may be, allow themselves to be described more readily than ever as dispatches in writing (code, inscription, trace, and so on). . . . It recalls (exposes, explodes) that which, in writing, always includes the power of a death machine (Derrida 29).[10]

Xorandor, who has been eavesdropping on human discourse for thousands of years provides both the possibility of storing the human archive and the possibility of its total and absolute destruction, both a "missive" and, in the errant case of Xor 7, the "missile," the emissary of a death sentence. That the twins successfully (and comically) derail this missile does not eliminate the greater ambiguities of the "syntax error" that turns techniques of living into techniques of devastating destruction.

Finally, it is not in imagining a real nuclear disaster that *Xorandor* functions but as another in Brooke-Rose's "speculations" about the techniques for living (on) in the twentieth-century. The vulnerability and the power of fiction to "send" being is a theme that resonates throughout Brooke-Rose's novels, examples of poetico performative and theoretico-informative dispatches in writing. They are themselves absorbed with the notion of code, inscription, and trace, with surviving, or living on, beyond the death of the author, the reader, the realist novel. Writing for Brooke-Rose *is* the trace that encodes both the death and the survival,

CHAPTER 7

Saving the Text

CULTURAL CRISIS IN *TEXTERMINATION*

THE FINAL NOVEL OF THE INTERCOM QUARTET, *Textermination* continues the jeremiad in *Amalgamemnon* warning of the dire predicament of literature and literary criticism in the postmodern age. Like *Thru*, *Textermination* conducts cultural critique in the form of metafiction. Creators and their characters strangely cohabit the same narrative levels, intruding on one another's privacies. Less wild typographically than *Thru* and less radical linguistically than either *Thru* or *Amalgamemnon*, *Textermination* takes the intertextuality of both to new heights and includes a bizarre mélange of fictional and nonfictional personae. Appearing on its pages are literary characters from different periods and traditions, as well as authors, television characters, actors, and previous characters and creators from Brooke-Rose's own texts (for example, Mira Enketei). Mira, who at one point is identified as the author of *Textermination* (*Textermination* 92), narrates the story for a while; but after the shock of locating herself on a list of forgotten characters, she promptly disappears from the text. Like Beckett's "Unnamable," she realizes that "[s]he can't go on" (*Textermination* 105). She exits only to be replaced by the "author" herself who rescues the storytelling enterprise ("If she can't go on," this new voice says in the following chapter, "I suppose I'll have to" (*Textermination* 106).

In an essay entitled "Where Do We Go from Here?" Brooke-Rose offers a definition of metafiction, citing Mas'ud Zavarzadeh's *The Mythopoeic Reality—The Postwar American Nonfiction Novel* (1976). Metafiction, she quotes, is "ultimately a narrational metatheorem whose subject matter is fictional systems themselves [. . . It] exults over its own fictitiousness, and its main counter-techniques are flat characterization, contrived plots, antilinear sequences of events, all fore-grounded as part of an extravagant overtotalization, a parody of interpretation which shows up the multiplicity of the real and the naïveté of trying 'to reach a total synthesis of life within narrative" (Brooke-Rose, "Where Do We Go From Here?" 161–62). By this definition, both *Thru* and *Textermination* are clearly examples of metafiction. They conform to Zavarzadeh's definition in their extravagant fictitiousness, exposure of systemeticity, and parodies of totalizing interpretations.

Yet in exulting in its fictitiousness and unreality, *Textermination* also deliberately invokes the "real" by presenting itself as a response to cultural crisis. Not content to remain securely within playful quotation marks, *Textermination* warns of the loss of cultural memory in the form of a general "forgetting" of literature in the age of technology and popular culture. Here, as in *Amalgamemnon*, the prophetic urge is alive and well and living in women's metafiction despite its skepticism toward grand models of interpretability and monuments of unaging intellect. Although richly comic, the novel participates in the rhetoric of witness and survival found in *Xorandor*. In its choice of title, *Textermination*, like *Between*, evokes shades of World War II and is another allusion to the chiasmic crossing of the real and the unreal in the twentieth century. In the rampant intertextuality of the novel, the "fantastic" returns to represent the memory crisis. The reminder that what literature "knows" is being forgotten is anything but a bid for a nostalgic return to the nineteenth-century novel. It is a brief for the relevance of fantasy and metafiction to represent reality and a counterexample to the assumption that metafiction is an exercise in literary narcissism. *Textermination* displays a faith in fantasy's resources for evoking historical consciousness. The novel addresses the skepticism which is a contemporary form of Georg Lukács's critique of the ideology of modernism as too inward and focused on individual consciousness to represent history.[1]

Set mainly in the San Francisco Hilton, at an annual convention of literary characters from centuries of narratives in various, mostly Western, traditions, the novel begins with Emma Woodhouse, Emma Bovary, and Thomas Mann's Goethe sharing a carriage, as both conventional vehicles of the imagination (fiacres and carriages), and newer conveyances, such as the "aerobrain" (a plane), whisk the mélange of characters through time and space. Landing first in Atlanta from Europe, the characters wait in an airport lounge for the flight to San Francisco. Suddenly, the lounge becomes all airport lounges, and the travelers, looking through the airport windows, witness fictional scenes of burning houses and cities in literature throughout the ages: Atlanta, Troy, Manderley, Thornfield Manor, Moscow (*Textermination* 11). The conflagration then spreads to "books by the million" burning in the library in Alexandria "at Fahrenheit 451"—books that presumably "house" the characters themselves. The first chapter ends with this literary apocalypse (and death of literature), only to begin anew in chapter 2 at the San Francisco convention. The convention, which strangely resembles the one MLA Brooke-Rose attended, is a Convention of Prayer for Being to the Implied Reader, hoping, the narrator tells us, to "recover, after an unimaginable journey, to savour what remains of international ritual for the revival of the fittest" (*Textermination* 8). This ritual includes the reading of literary passages in critical papers, which give life to the characters, at least temporarily (at the reading of a passage, Emma, "revives" and "begins to feel the blood circulate in her veins again" (15). The Darwinian predicament of the characters is symptomatic of the fate of reading and criticism in our time: the characters are "ghosts" (*Textermination* 19), languishing from "lack of involved attention" (*Textermination* 2) in an age of popular culture. They suffer as well from the effects of the hyperactive critical and ideological agendas of contemporary literary criticism, which have led to a dereification or "dissolution," as Brooke-Rose called it in "The Dissolution of Character in the Novel."

As the beleaguered characters begin to pray, they are interrupted by twelve turbaned terrorists, demanding equal time for their own Muslim rituals and threatening to kill the entire congregation. (Their main purpose, however, seems to be to assassinate Rushdie's Gibreel Farishta, who attends the convention.) Calvino's "Non-Existent Knight" (*Textermination* 31) saves the day by beheading the terrorists, further prayers are canceled, and the convention continues. Near the end of the novel the characters are subjected to another dual apocalypse: a book-burning that transforms the Hilton into a Towering Inferno, which, in turn, collapses when an earthquake hits the San Andreas fault. The unstable ground of the California setting only exacerbates the chronic vulnerability of fictional characters, who suffer the life and death consequences of critical fashion and reader interest. However, like O. J. Simpson and others in the star-studded cast of the movie *The Towering Inferno* (and O. J. Simpson in his legal battles as well), characters miraculously appear from within the rubble, somehow surviving the apocalypse. Slowly, they proceed back to their textual homes, as the novel comes full circle with Emma entering her carriage.

Textermination presents the wild and crazy underside of T. S. Eliot's "historical sense"; characters from past and present physically and dialogically jostle one another with both comic and unsettling results. Humbert Humbert leers at an unsuspecting Maisie; *Middlemarch*'s Casaubon goes to hear a paper on himself, only to discover, to his bitter disappointment, that the subject is the Casaubon from Eco's *Foucault's Pendulum*. As George Eliot's Casaubon discovers, the canon is a zero-sum game. Realist characters from two hundred years of literature find themselves displaced by the more up-to-date "real" of popular culture, signaled by the invasion of television actors, as well as characters, at the conference (Peter Falk is the detective on the case of the terrorists). JR and Bobby and Steve McGarrett shout "we are eternal, we're real! We'll show'm. We are the ones people want and know and love! Down with all these dead people out of books nobody reads!" (*Textermination* 58). As Brooke-Rose says of the predicament of serious literature, "the human need for fictions has been channeled into the 'popular' genres" ("The Dissolution of Character" 191). Characters from contemporary fiction are even more threatened by the reader's snub than poor Mr. Casaubon, since they have never become canonical. Mira Enketei's jolting realization of her own fragility comes when her name appears on the index of names of characters forgotten by readers either from the nonavailability or noncanonicity of the works in which they appear or from a lapse in readers' memories of their minor role in a canonical work.

In the thought experiments that are Brooke-Rose's novels, criticism, character, and theory converge as points of speculation, as all engage in testing the imaginative life of ideas. In *Textermination* she brings literature to the brink of extinction, "testing" in fictional form the various "deaths" that have become critical commonplaces—of the author, of character, of the novel, and, even, of the reader, that absent god to whom the characters pray. In the process, the conventions of fiction, like the convention in California, are undermined. Unlike other Brooke-Rose texts, the novel begins in the third-person past-tense narration of traditional nineteenth-century fiction. The two famous nineteenth-century Emmas in their carriages are at first also carried along in their native narrative sentence. Like the characters who disappear during the novel, however, this narrative sentence, too, suddenly vanishes, replaced by Brooke-Rose's characteristic present-tense narratorless narrative.[2] It is Brooke-Rose's strength to reinvent, rather than to exhaust, the resources of fictionality; the illusion of art is subverted in order to save fiction and fictionality. In *Textermination,* she raids literature's resources to explore the afterlife of textuality. Through her "ghosts" (*Textermination* 19) or "constellations of semes," as they're called at one point (*Textermination* 63), she focuses on the ontology of fictional being, a persistent theoretical concern since *A Rhetoric of the Unreal. Textermination* mines fiction's resources to test theory's preoccupations, in this case the "deaths" in fiction. It puns on "inquiry" and "ink-worries" (*Textermination* 67).

Before the apocalyptic climax, another quieter "textermination" is staged. It occurs in chapter 11, not an accident, I think, in a metafictional novel, for here, the novel is brought to the brink of bankruptcy. The last of two fictional (and female) narrative presences we have come to rely on disappears suddenly—first, Kelly McFadgeon, a young "Interpreter" attending the meeting, who bemoans her failure to master the right lingo of the profession, disappears in chapter 9. In searching for some names she does recognize through her reading, Kelly sees her own name in a list of forgotten characters and realizes that she herself is fictional. She reads: "McFadgeon, Kelly. From Textermination, by Mira Enketei" (*Textermination* 92). Suddenly, Kelly disappears from the novel. We feel her loss especially, for her bewilderment in the face of such rampant intertextualities mirrors our own predicament as readers. Unlike Rita Humboldt, "star" professor of Comp Lit and organizer of the conference, Kelly admits her inability to recognize every personage: "She feels ashamed and rattled. Gaps, so many gaps in her reading, she'll never catch up" (*Textermination* 22). She expresses bewilderment about theories of fictionality: "I'm totally confused about fictional status" (*Textermination* 90). Despite her lack of complexity, or context, or individuality in a novel in which she is one name among many, she is our surrogate interpreter and we fasten onto her consciousness with relief; thus, her "textermination" is experienced as a loss. Next, her supposed "creator," Mira, takes over in chapter 10, only to vanish from the novel herself, after she, too, sees her name on an Index of Forbidden Works and realizes that "[s]he doesn't exist" (*Textermination* 105).

It is at this point that chapter 11 introduces the fictional voice of the author, who says, "If she can't go on, I suppose I'll have to. I am not Mira of course, though many readers think I am. For one thing I have little Latin and less Greek. Curious how one can invent knowledgeable people without possessing their knowledge" (106). The "eye-narrator," who has kept quiet up until this point, now takes over: "I too, like Mira, have no idea how to go on. I must go on, I can't go on, I'll go on (Beckett, The Unnameable [sic])" (*Textermination* 107). Strangely, the novel is "rescued" with a *deus ex machina* updated. The new technology is an old convention revised—authorial intrusion. Interrupting the narrative progress, the "author" discusses her relationships to the characters she has just invented and her difficulties as an author. The specter of Beckett hovers in every admission of defeat and renewed bid for control. "I have thus created a fiction too difficult for me to handle. So I omit what I don't know. A double absence. All authors omit, texts are full of double absences" (*Textermination* 107). Characters, narrators, and authors all submit to the self-destructions of the text.

Sarah Birch writes that in *Textermination* "there is displacement of creative responsibility from author to reader. It is up to the reader to recognize the imported characters and thus to 'actualize' the discursive worlds the novel brings together" (*Christine Brooke-Rose and Contemporary Fiction* 138). As readers, we identify with the characters of Kelly and Mira since they act like fellow "readers" to guide us, like Virgil, through the text; we feel their loss as we struggle with each new guide to make interpretive sense of the text. Birch makes an important point. Within the fictional premises of the novel, the Implied Reader is accorded tremendous power. The god to whom the characters pray, the reader has the power to banish and to resurrect. Yet more powerful, I believe, in its marriage of theoretical focus and pathos is the novel's exploration of the ontology of being, that is, the reality/unreality of the characters. These theoretical "deaths" are represented as if from the inside, on the pulses of "characters" who experience the earth-shaking events that occur. They stand in for forgotten texts, forgotten authors; it is they who test the viability of fiction in an age of technology and popular culture. Scheherezade is a crucial "femme-récit" with whom the "author" identifies, whose "every tale means a stay of execution" (*Textermination* 108).

This "rescuing" author who saves the text after Kelly's and Mira's departures offers her own critical commentary on the levels of fictionality of her characters:

> So I must bring them back. Oh, not all of them of course. Kelly and Mira are on the Index and gone for ever. But they were real, on their different levels, Kelly being on the staff, Mira having (she says) invented everything. Rewrite the last two sentences, keeping both versions, for both are true. But they were unreal on their different levels, being invented by me, Kelly on the staff, Mira as inventor (she says) of everything.

> No, I meant the real fictional characters, those not (yet) on the Index. (*Textermination* 108)

As the language of reality/unreality crosses in two sentences that the "author" claims are nonexclusive (both true), her language gets tangled in the problematic terminology of imaginary beings. "Real" means existent as characters in the novel we are reading (as opposed to those from other novels); the second sentence, with its adjective "unreal" acknowledges that they are still "invented," by the author. In the last sentence "real" means something like characters in the text who are not on any of the "hit lists" that signal their textermination. (The terminology is further complicated by the distinction some of the Interpreters make between their own "real" selves and the existence of the literary characters at the convention [see 101].) *Textermination* enacts the continuum of being and nonbeing that preoccupy narratologists and some of the characters like Rita and Dr. Watson. Dr. Watson helpfully parses the categories of being for the other characters: "some of us are more present than others. It's all a matter of degree. Absence is absolute, Mr Holmes once told me, but there are degrees of presence. I'm remarkably present, don't you know, he adds with a rosy glow over his blond moustache" (*Textermination* 97). Jokes are made about the anonymous "I" narrators who fail to show up at the meeting. "Isn't it in the nature of nameless I-narrators to be more or less absent? David Copperfield Senior asks . . . I hardly think so, says the governess. I have no name, yet I am as absolutely present as . . . those dire presences. She stops" (*Textermination* 96). Characters debate whether to take action on behalf of "these soaring and sinking pronouns" (*Textermination* 97), the rising and fading "I"s and "he"s of fiction. Metatextual references abound to the different permutations of nonexistent beings that are lost and found in fiction. These references include "dead" characters, like those who have already died in fiction and, hence, ironically, might have less far to fall into oblivion; imaginary beings, such as Calvino's Non-Existent Knight (*Textermination* 35); characters who have less "being" to begin with in the intertextual universe of the novel because they are in canonical works but are minor; characters who have less "being" to begin with because they are in noncanonical works (like Mira); characters in noncanonical works who have even less being than Mira because they are flat characters (like Orion, who complains that he receives inadequate attention in *Amalgamemnon* [*Textermination* 67]). And on the other side of the spectrum of being are dramatic characters who are "incarnated" and therefore might be thought to have being more easily than characters who are equivalent to words on a page (*Textermination* 36, 120), as well as characters who are existent in more than one fictional work, like Mira, who therefore might be said to have more fictional weight by virtue of their presence in at least two novels.[3]

The problem of survival for the characters, real and unreal, is a *memory* problem: no matter what their fictional "level," they are all threatened with the loss of existence if their fictional texts are not read. Joyce once commented that his ideal reader was an insomniac. The characters in *Textermination* face the opposite situation. It is worth parsing the cultural conditions that threaten to banish them to oblivion: (1) literary characters who are upstaged by popular culture icons, both television and film characters and the actors who play them. Normally characters and actors exist on different fictional levels, but in *Textermination*, all are participants at the convention. (Interestingly, the reference to these television characters and their actors dates Brooke-Rose's novel more than the literary characters.) According to this diagnosis, readers of literature are spending their time in front of the television and at the movies; (2) literary characters who are upstaged by the news, that is, the real has become unreal, sometimes beyond the wildest dreams of fiction. In *A Rhetoric of the Unreal*, Brooke-Rose emphasizes this chiasmic development in the twentieth century, as the real has become fantastic. Signaling this crossing, terrorists from the "real" world of news become characters in *Textermination* (as the news predicting their movements formed part of the narrative in *Amalgamemnon*). In further play with the unreality of nonfiction, many of the journalists in *Textermination* are fictional (*Textermination* 89) and there is a debate about whether the terrorists themselves are fictional, despite the fact that they seem "real enough," according to Kelly, because they seem "political" and not "literary" (*Textermination* 37); (3) literary characters who have become irrelevant, no longer able to matter to readers. As Rita says, "It's a goddamn miracle that fiction still has the power to offend, and maybe change things, as it used to" (*Textermination* 35); (4) literary characters who are not memorable to readers; (5) literary characters who are threatened by the deadening effect of academic critical practice, particularly, the narrow theoretical and political axes that critics grind. As one character puts it, characters read by teachers, scholars, and students are "analysed as schemata, structures, functions within structures, logical and mathematical formulae, aporia, psychic movements, social significances and so forth" (*Textermination* 26).

Of all Brooke-Rose's novels, *Textermination* reminds us the most of the "unbearable lightness of being" that is always fiction's link with death.

Describing the difference between a dramatic and fictional character and the greater difficulty of reviving the fictional one, Rita argues that fictional characters appear "gradually out of the reading process, the letters on the page, mere words, not made flesh but creating phantoms in the very varied minds of each solitary reader. It is in this imaginative build-up that we're threatened, I mean that the characters of fictional narrative are threatened, in a way far more profound and more eroded by time than is possible with dramatic characters, at every moment made flesh before our eyes" (*Textermination* 120)

The speech suggests that the unbearable lightness of being pertains to all fictional characters, those in classic realist fiction as well as more postmodern types who exist in fictions that theorize their own vulnerabilities. Realism's "mirror" is always the prop of an illusionist. Realism itself constructs such phantoms of the imagination who demand the reader's faith. Although Rita is prone to pontificate and her academic jargon is sometimes mocked in the text, her description of the survival of the characters is poignant. In a meeting between Kundera's Tomas (*The Unbearable Lightness of Being*) and Austen's Emma Woodhouse, Brooke-Rose even stages an acknowledgment that reality and unreality are wed in *both* "realism" and "postmodernism." Emma thinks: "Being seems to trouble him for some reason, and he calls it unbearably light. And to her astonishment she finds herself agreeing. She has never thought of it in that way, and it somehow relieves her of the oppressive feeling she has had ever since she arrived, that her certitudes are uncertain, that she no longer quite exists in them, no longer quite coincides with herself" (*Textermination* 109).

The most fundamental of literary "faiths" are challenged in the novel, including the self-identity of the self that is the basis of character in fiction. Not only oblivion but also radical uncertainty threatens the characters from within, the death of the subject now part of even Emma Woodhouse's sensibility.[4] The intertextual universe of *Textermination* is punningly "mortifying" (*Textermination* 108, 15) to Emma, who cannot count on the weight of nineteenth-century literary convention to anchor her survival. In this unstable fictional world, the characters seem to defy their own determined futures, living, like the speakers in *Amalgamemnon*, in the "time of their options." The freedom is dizzying. No longer tied to their fated futures, they float, becoming light-headed. Further complicating their predicaments are the fashions of critical interest and readers' particular investments. Mira complains to Orion that the characters are altered at the convention, depending on the perspectives of the critical papers delivered: "So they do change times while here.

According to the papers on them I suppose" (*Textermination* 66). With no reliable authors or narrators in sight to help them in their exposure to critical fashion, the characters suffer from too much freedom. Brooke-Rose plays against the "problem" about which characters in modernist and postmodernist fiction complain at the iron hand of their respective authors (think of Molly Bloom suddenly apostrophizing "Jamesy" to "let me up out of this pooh" (*Ulysses* 633). Instead, the characters in *Textermination* suffer ontologically from the free-for-all at the convention. The rampant metalepsy confuses them even further.

Perhaps more than her other fictions, *Textermination* provides a significant corrective to Linda Hutcheon's blithe enumeration of "principles" jettisoned in postmodern fiction, such as "value, order, meaning, control, and identity . . . that have been the basic premises of bourgeois liberalism" (Hutcheon 13). *Textermination* refuses such easy dismissals—identity, for one, has a stubborn resilience, despite the smart postmodern bombs hurled its way. The novel is neither a nostalgic bid to return to the good old days of realist fiction and its faithful readers, nor a blithe embrace of freedom from form and tradition. It is, rather, a call to recognize fiction's vulnerabilities and limits and to revitalize fiction's powers. CBR performs CPR on fiction through a number of techniques, including intertextuality, one means of reviving both the fittest and the "unfit." In staging the "deaths" that afflict fiction in the twentieth century, paradoxically, Brooke-Rose revitalizes the genre of the novel. Life after textuality occurs through intertextuality, the living on of the text transformed. Like a parody of a Freudian dream in which all generations coexist, the novel stages unexpected interaction. The conceit allows Brooke-Rose to imagine all sorts of confrontations that implicitly explore, from the inside, how genre and convention constrain. Nineteenth-century novels habitually punish their convention-breaking heroines—Emma Woodhouse puzzles over Emma Bovary's actions: "The lady in the fiacre? She [Emma Woodhouse] withdraws her arm. She is not leniently disposed. But she is struck by a curious query: why has this lady swooned at the idea of having swallowed a mouthful of oxblood, yet did not shirk from swallowing a good deal more arsenic? Then she pauses in sudden perplexity: where has this extraordinary thought come from?" (*Textermination* 32). Not only plot but also thought itself is shown to be constrained by the historical laws of genre. This is literary criticism conducted in fictional form.

In diagnosing the cultural situation, Brooke-Rose takes aim at readers who neglect the literary, a category that includes not only those who no longer read or forget what they have read, but those who insist on passing literature through the crucible of politics. The danger of confusing fiction and politics is represented by the machine-gun packing terrorists who search for Gibreel Farishta, Rushdie's character from *The Satanic Verses*. More confining than the author's authority over the characters' fate, Brooke-Rose seems to say, is the straightjacket of fundamentalist readings. The threatened death of the author, Salman Rushdie, serves as a symbol of the seriousness of misunderstanding the status of fiction. He serves as the emblem of both the power of fiction in the world ("It's a goddamn miracle that fiction still has the power to offend, and maybe change things, as it used to," Rita Humboldt says [*Textermination* 35]), and the tragedy of a too literal confusion of fiction and politics.

In an essay that addresses precisely the threatened territory Brooke-Rose covers in *Textermination*, the threat to the novel and the confusion of fiction and politics, Salman Rushdie defends the hybrid reality/unreality of the genre of the novel. In "In Defense of the Novel, Yet Again," Rushdie responds to a talk delivered by George Steiner which had bemoaned the moribund state of the genre of the novel in Europe. Castigating the plethora of such obituaries of the novel, Rushdie emphasizes that it is precisely its blend of fact and fantasy that ensures its durability: "In my view, there is no crisis in the art of the novel. The novel is precisely that 'hybrid form' for which Professor Steiner yearns: It is part social inquiry, part fantasy, part confessional; it crosses frontiers of knowledge as well as topographical boundaries" (Rushdie 50). Diagnosing "real" threats to the novel, Rushdie says:

> There is another real danger facing literature, and of this Professor Steiner makes no mention; that is, the attack on intellectual liberty itself—intellectual liberty, without which there can be no literature.... Of the pressures of intolerance and censorship, I have personally, in these past years, gained perhaps too much knowledge.... The death of the novel may be far off, but the violent death of many contemporary novelists is, alas, an inescapable fact. In Europe and the United States as well, the storm troopers of various 'sensitivities' seek to limit our freedom of speech. It has never been more important to continue to defend those values which make the art of literature possible. (Rushdie 54–55)

In their fundamentalism and denial of intellectual liberty, the "storm troopers" of sensitivities, the cultural terrorists, are linked by Rushdie to political terrorists that put a fatwa on his life. *Textermination* makes such connections. Brooke-Rose comes close to the tenor of Rushdie's belief that fantasy can be trusted to merge with social inquiry in the novel. In the unreal/real mix that is *Textermination*, Brooke-Rose has faith in the "business" of fiction (*Textermination* 35) to conduct cultural critique. In an essay entitled "Palimpsest History," she argues that it is the hybridity of the novel, its mixture of the real and the unreal, that is its secret to survival amidst the signs of its declining health. In the essay, Rushdie serves as an exemplar of what she calls a "palimpsest history," in which there is a mixture of fantasy, reality, and unreality:

> But the novel's task, unlike that of history, is to stretch our intellectual, spiritual and imaginative horizons to breaking point. Because palimpsest histories do precisely that, mingling realism with the supernatural and history with spiritual and philosophical reinterpretation, they could be said to float half-way between the sacred books of our various heritages, which survive on the strength of the faiths they have created . . . and the endless exegesis and commentaries these sacred books create. . . .[5]

Pointing out that this kind of novel that has rejuvenated the novel tradition arises from writers outside the Anglophone tradition, Brooke-Rose emphasizes that the use of fantasy in this hybrid form counteracts the "narcissistic relation of the author to his writing" (*Textermination* 183). The Intercom Quartet uses the resources of fantasy—prophecy that resists predictability, science fiction, the magical appearances and disappearances of characters in an intertextual universe—to evoke the "real" in a century in which reality has become "unreal." Both the title "Textermination" and the sudden disappearances of fiction's phantoms are eerily reminiscent of other nontextual exterminations as well as the "unreality" that Gertrude Stein identified with the Second World War:

> There is no point in being realistic about here and now, no use at all not any, and so it is not the nineteenth but the twentieth century, there is no realism now, life is not real it is not earnest, it is strange which is an entirely different matter. (Stein, *Wars I Have Seen* 44)

Yet Brooke-Rose also reminds us that the echo of "extermination" in "textermination" is only an echo: If the text mimics "unreal" disappearances in a century gone crazy, the "t" in textermination is nevertheless an important sign of a difference between fiction and life that it is dangerous to forget. Compelled toward the referential function of fiction, even metafiction, Brooke-Rose nevertheless ends her novel where it began, with the departure of a fictional character. However precariously, she restores to one Emma Woodhouse her unbearable lightness of being: "So that Emma found, on being escorted and followed into the second carriage by Mr Elton, that the door was to be lawfully shut on them, and that they were to have a tête-à-tête drive" (182).[6]

CHAPTER 8

Inscriptions of Life

SUBSCRIPT

BILLED AS HER "LAST NOVEL," *Subscript* addresses Brooke-Rose's theme of the legibility of being on the grandest of scales—evolution. Both science fiction and science theory, the novel traces the vulnerability and durability of the record of life from the prokaryote cell 4500 million years ago to modern man at the end of the Magdalenian period 11,000 years ago. In *Through Other Continents: American Literature across Deep Time,* Wai Chee Dimock ventures to write literary criticism in which she "rethink[s] the shape of literature against the history and habitat of the human species, against the 'deep time' of the planet earth, as described by two scientific disciplines, geology and astronomy" (Dimock 6). In *Subscript,* Brooke-Rose writes fiction that attempts to rethink the novel on the grand geologic scale of "deep time."

In her last novel, Brooke-Rose uses her characteristic present-tense, speakerless narrative sentence with a twist: the narrative consciousness mirrors evolutionary development, with its diction expanding to include new concepts. *Subscript* begins in a perpetual present before subjectivity and singularity. It launches us into a world of material mass. This is a daunting challenge for the genre of the novel. We begin the book in the world of "stuff," the sugars and acids of matter, the "sweeties and salties and sharpies of glow and burn, of lucent acid, of lime and metal and other bitters. Bubbling away" (*Subscript* 1). Before individual cells, before chromosomes, we find ourselves in what has been called "the primitive soup."[1] Brooke-Rose's characteristic "scientific present tense" (*Invisible Author* 140) takes on added resonance in a text in which the subject is science on a grand scale. The challenge is to represent the starts and stops of biological development in a "scientific" present tense. Science, science fiction, and science theory are playfully fused in the use of this constraint in the novel. Studying the "truth" claims of relevant science textbooks, Brooke-Rose took copious notes from a myriad of texts such as *The Major Transitions in Evolution*, which begins: "Living organisms are highly complex, and are composed of parts that function to ensure the survival and reproduction of the whole"(Smith 3). Her own archive, housed at the Harry Ransom Humanities Research Center at the University of Texas, Austin, includes folders containing newspaper clippings and extraordinarily detailed reading notes on the biology, botany, physiology, and environment of the millions of years of organic development she traces in the novel. Brooke-Rose translates this objective scientific present into the fictionalization of life before human consciousness, memory, and language. In her use of speakerless present tense, science theory (specifically, theories of evolution) is imagined as if from inside matter itself: "Inside the acid strand the forever must exist. From the waiting, the absorbing, the churning, the growing, the repeating. For ever. And ever" (*Subscript* 1). With no "forever and ever, amen," *Subscript* replaces God with its own creation story. The transformation from nucleic acids to proteins to eukaryote cells (cells with nuclei) is fictionalized, as is the "birth" of DNA, the encoding of heredity, out of the "forever" of mere replication ("The code is born. The code of behaviour, for the bits of many parts, that carries the foreverness. Is the code really necessary? For many forevers there's life without a code, without the forever copying of the code and without all these new foodmix workers" [*Subscript* 3]).

Around the sixth chapter of the novel the organism identifies itself as female, although it isn't until the tenth chapter that males are referred to as "they" and the thirteenth chapter that this enduring female consciousness receives the name Aka (*Subscript* 127). It is Aka who tells us that the "point of the story" of the human clan is "[t]o follow birth not death. Although many died on the way" (*Subscript* 153). *Subscript* can be regarded as a tale of Eros or the life-instinct, described by Freud in

Beyond the Pleasure Principle as that which "by bringing about a more and more far-reaching combination of the particles into which living substance is dispersed, aims at complicating life and at the same time, of course, at preserving it."[2] Yet although the narrative fundamentally traces life, the narrative commitment to follow the trail of life never compromises Brooke-Rose's attention to the threat of textermination, the obliteration of both life-forms and their inscriptions. In the high stakes game of evolution, the unbearable lightness of being ends in the extinction of multiple life-forms along the way. The title *Subscript*, however, signals that Brooke-Rose's concern is not only with the see-saw of life and death, the survival and extinction of forms of life, but also the record of the evolutionary struggle in its geological, biological, and cultural traces. The narrative concerns itself with "life and survival and transmission" (*Subscript* 59). Both the earth and the organism contain material traces of absent forms, evidence that biologists, archeologists, and, more recently, geneticists have woven into evolutionary theories. This is indeed fertile ground for a scholar/novelist like Brooke-Rose.

Like her other novels which use twentieth-century scientific, technological, and cultural changes as their premises for new forms of defamiliarization, *Subscript* is fueled by the explosion of genetic discoveries around the turn of the twenty-first century. Combined with new archeological findings, these discoveries promise an unparalleled retrieval of the human record. These scientific discoveries allow the "signatures" of the ancient ancestors of human beings to be read by archeologists, population geneticists, and linguists. The dictionary definition of "subscript" is (1) "that which is written underneath, a writing at the bottom or end of a document, etc.; a signature" and (2) "a subscript letter or symbol." The title resonates throughout the novel. Underwriting all of life is the genetic "code," THE book of memory and forgetting. It provides the record of millions of years of organic adaptation and obliteration. DNA contains information in which human hereditary is encoded. And, like other codes found throughout Brooke-Rose's fiction, it offers material for narrative. The "stories" woven from this material are referred to as "code stories," sometimes accepted and sometimes mistrusted by the evolving narrative consciousness:

> The tangle of moss and fern hides many animals, mostly the same size, and many smaller, that crawl slowly in slime and are good to eat, like the others with crackly shells. All rivals, but as food much harder to catch than under water, when food simply seemed to float in, whereas the activity needed to catch food now is almost unbelievable compared

to the still stance and gentle undulations below. But that may be just a code story. For the code invents stories about many many warmturns past and unknown, often hard to sort out into what the body glimpses and what the code lays down." (*Subscript* 34)

Explicit references to the "code" disappear almost entirely from the text once human consciousness evolves to a certain developmental level. As Brooke-Rose told Lorna Sage in an interview, "Incidentally, as my creatures slowly become human, from around chapter 9, the Code vanishes. Into their unconscious perhaps. They're much closer to the genetic code as animals or even as cells. This again is fiction."[3] The code becomes more internalized as the novel progresses, the "tale of suffering" leaving its trace on the organism's body: "The journey towards the rising light takes many many lightturns and many moonturns, imprinted as a tale of suffering in every cell of every animal" (*Subscript* 41).

To "sort out . . . what the body glimpses and what the code lays down" is, indeed, one of the main projects of the narrative. The code archive is beyond desire, an unseen dictator whose messages are obeyed often unconsciously ("The code is much too busy replicating and recombining, forecasting or at least ordering, to record absolutely everything, let alone communicate. But some remains in the body, for the body also remembers, even if it forgets that it can remember" [*Subscript* 30]). *Subscript* extends and expands the record of suffering we have traced from its inscription in "The Foot," in which pain from the phantom limb is a constant companion. Brooke-Rose's texts ring changes on the bodily inscription of suffering—in *Out*, the genetic make-up of the unnamed male consciousness has been altered irreversibly by some unspecified radioactive event; in *Such*, the unconscious of the male protagonist is indelibly imprinted with the trauma of his death and rebirth; in *Thru*, the text itself is hystericized, its very letters inscribed with the signs of trauma and pain ("ruth"); in *Xorandor*, the "syntax" error programmed into Xor 7 endangers human civilization. In *Subscript*, genetic history is the tale that weds survival and suffering. In each of these narratives, the writing on the body inscribes and transmits a cultural predicament. Suffering and its material traces serve as cultural reminders that guard against the "oblitopia" feared in *Amalgamemnon*. The potential for obsolescence and oblivion generalizes from individual consciousnesses, like the protagonists of *Out*, *Such*, *Between*, and *Thru*; Mira in *Amalgamemnon* and *Verbivore*; Jipnzab in *Xorandor*; and Emma, Kelly, and the other characters in *Textermination*, to the totality of the human archive. Increasingly, her texts absorb themselves with what Derrida has called "the vulnerability of the effaceable document."[4] Brooke-Rose's "techniques for living" are survival strategies for the genre of the novel, ensuring new forms for telling the human story. The lipograms, including the linguistic and grammatical constraints in *Subscript*, help her to defamiliarize this story from the point of view of the always threatened organism.

I have suggested earlier that Brooke-Rose's novelistic pleas to "save the text" have personal as well as philosophical import. The necessity to maintain the "patience of vigilant language" (to return to Blanchot's phrase) in the face of potential annihilation of the record involves a trust between writer and reader, a pledge to use and preserve language carefully (and to use careful language). On the one hand, as we have seen, Brooke-Rose trusts her novels to fully embody the life of an idea as they embed their techniques for living. On the other hand, increasingly, with *Stories, Theories and Things, Invisible Author*, and most recently in *Life, End Of*, she has insisted on telling the story of her compositions so that its important elements not be overlooked or forgotten. In the nonfictional contexts of interviews and essays, she makes visible what may have gone unnoticed about her method (in *Life, End Of*, this "intrusion" of the invisible author occurs within the memoir itself, in a chapter devoted to the author's narratorless narrative sentence). As Derrida puts it, "The archive is as precarious as it is artificial, and precisely in that very place where the signatory puts on guard, appeals, beseeches, warns against the risk of whatever might come along as he says 'to annihilate this work.'"("Typewriter Ribbon" 345). Derrida is speaking of prefatory remarks found in the Geneva manuscript of Rousseau's *Confessions* in which Rousseau "adjures" future readers to "save the body of the inscription" ("Typewriter Ribbon" 346). But he is speaking generally of an author's apostrophe to future readers to preserve his archive. In regard to *Subscript*, Brooke-Rose's own version of this call to save the text from textermination is a two-paged chart diagramming the method of the novel and providing a note to future translators that she has also provided to her literary executor. She enjoins her translators not to deviate from the grammatical constraints observed in the original as they translate from one language to the other, particularly in regard to her use of pronouns. The chart lists chapter number and title, time, period, creature, and constraint (see Figure A, pages 172–173). "These constraints," she says in her prefatory note, "must be observed, whatever the language translated into," as the constraints are "subtle and invisible" and, therefore, potentially obliterated in translation.[5]

What concerns Brooke-Rose the most about translation is the possible erasure of her initial refusal to use pronouns and their carefully charted appearance as the narrative of *Subscript* progresses. Why is this constraint so important and what is its relation to the continuing thematic of the archive? Brooke-Rose's scrupulous addition of pronouns is calibrated to the development of the organism in the genetic archive. The pronouns, deliberately omitted from the first three chapters, before the appearance of reptiles 300 million years ago, gradually appear in sequences tied to what might be called cultural developments (although appearing before the advent of human culture). The singular impersonal ("it") is at first restricted and then appears in chapter 4 to denote a sentient entity. In the same chapter the plural impersonal pronoun ("they") surfaces to convey an inchoate, but developing, sense of group differentiation. In chapter 8 this differentiation passes to the point of ingroup and out-group feeling—the second person plural ("we") appears to emphasize the social identification among the presimian chimpanzees. Possessive pronouns also suddenly appear to denote tribal appropriations. Two rare examples of first- and second-person singular ("I" and "you") denote moments of interpersonal relationship. Personal pronouns, only in masculine form, occur in the narrative once *Homo habilis* appears in chapter 11. It is not until the emergence of Aka in her anatomically modern ancestral guise that feminine pronouns, including "she," appear (chapter 16). As is the case with other formal constraints in her work, form mimics content in *Subscript*. The narrative schema is keyed to evolutionary stages. Gradually, with the increasing complexity (though not "progress") of organisms, language evolves, including the development of pronouns to stand in for evolving consciousness, social grouping, and individuation.

One of the most interesting byproducts of eschewing impersonal pronouns at the beginning of the novel is the formalization of an archive unrelated to consciousness or event. And yet, despite the declarative statement and precise description of phylogenic detail ("the pack's eyes are set in wider flatter rounder faces and look together out front, sharpening all they see"), the sense of sensation and speculation, rather than objectivity and omniscience, reigns: "And after endless forevers, the scattered strands of many parts now stretch slowly and reach out to each other, though each so different, and try to work together. That's apparently better than each separately. Strands learn that. Feel the advantage" (*Subscript* 1). Sensation as experienced but not necessarily processed or reflected upon by the organism, characteristic of her signature narrative sentence in *Out*, finds its perfect complement in the earliest evolutionary stages of *Subscript*. Here, Brooke-Rose traces what she has described as "the constant impact of outside phenomena on an active but not always reflective consciousness" ("Interview," *Invisible Author* 154). Just as *Textermination* presents the characters' eye view of "the dissolution of character," *Subscript* represents the way the inside feels as it encounters an outside. The challenge at the beginning of the narrative is to convey immediacy without subjectivity. Although the narrative is "speakerless," the exclamations and interrogatives give the sense of interior language, all before the advent of language: "Merely repeating the sequences in the acid strand but hardly changing the strands at all. Why change? All's nice down here in the soft hot bubbly. And yet" (*Subscript* 2). Although no one "speaks," the narrative retains a feel of improvisation and speculation. This speculation mimes both the role of hypothesis in the scientific method and the bewilderment of the organisms who experience a kind of continuing present, uncertain of past and future ("Shall we have to move? It seems the code was right and we've had to move before. We haven't been here for ever after all, it's not a foreverness" [*Subscript* 79]).

"A fly straddles another fly on the faded denim stretched over the knee" (*Out* 11)—just so Brooke-Rose's first lipogrammatic novel begins. *Subscript* returns us to a stripped-down world of sensation and primitive need. As opposed to the imagination of disaster in the Intercom Quartet, even the time of prediction, dread, and hope of *Amalgamemnon*, in *Subscript* we are meant to experience what it feels like to live in a present with no imagined future. Both the postapocalyptic world of *Out* and the prehuman world of *Subscript* represent the exigencies of basic survival in relation to the risk of movement. Yet the difference is striking: after the nuclear disaster, with its aftermath in a reversal of the color bar, the sick white man in *Out* is immobilized; he fears movement and change. "Sooner or later, the knee will have to make a move, but now it is immobilized by the two flies, the lower of which is so still that it seems dead" (*Out* 11). Description is careful, precise, joyless, even painful, as if the wounded human observer envied the flies their stasis and lack of consciousness and complexity. In contrast, relying heavily on description of the physical environment in the absence of any narrative observer, narration in *Subscript* represents change, despite its obvious risks, in joyful, poetic terms:

> Zing! Zinging out through the glowsalties the pungent ammonia earthfarts in slithery clay and all the rest to make simple sweeties and sharpies and other stuffs. Dust out of vast crashes and currents now calmer as the crust thickens and all cools a bit.

Over many many forevers.
Waiting. Absorbing. Growing. Churning. Splitting.
Over and Over (*Subscript* 1)

The phrase "What delicious risks" appears in the first chapter, and its gesture of welcoming risk and movement, although later balanced by homing and burrowing instincts, drives the narrative. Evolution is treated as a grand, albeit dangerous, adventure, a master narrative that is played from the inside out, with a "zing" of excitement rather than the portentousness of a creation story. In my "Discussion with Christine Brooke-Rose" (following chapter 10), Brooke-Rose expresses her lack of interest in the form of the *bildungsroman*, which charts the education of the protagonist over time and experience. One can think of *Subscript* as a strange and creative alternative to the genre of the novel of education and development *and* one of the most ambitious diasporic novels ever written. It is a "clan tale," or "Journey from the Setting Sun," as Aka refers to it (*Subscript* 153). In addition to the regulation of pronouns according to the evolving consciousness, other disciplined refusals of the traditional comforts of fiction are striking. Stripping fiction of its normal technologies, the novel begins at the beginning *before* consciousness, character, and language, indeed, in imitation of a point before the beginning of time. If *Thru* begins in metaterritory, warning the reader to beware of danger zones, *Subscript* constrains us to begin in a place and time before the comforts of story and storytelling. We witness the emergence of story from description, event from summary, a transition from the participial continuous present to a present out of which drama emerges.

Indeed, although evolution is the master narrative, emergence itself could be said to be the most significant subscript or understory in the narrative. For during the course of the story, we get to witness the emergence of life, language, time, and story. The text has us consider the following: How does life emerge from "stuff," genes from "junk," complexity and variety from "foreverness" as mere replication (*Subscript* 1); denotation from noise, reference from index, personal pronouns from impersonal pronouns, community from individual entities and, conversely, subjectivity from tribal identity; two genders from the masculine, and desire from need? Each of these transitions is marked and traced in Brooke-Rose's narrative, as we follow the tracks of material processes—accidental, involuntary, murderous, fortuitous, adaptive, and resistant. Chance, risk, error, loss, all become part of the story, beginning with the "zingy" joy in mudville. The novel subscribes to the scientific theory that evolution is not purposeful, but adaptive; it deliberately eschews a teleological narrative with a desired end. The narratorless present tense tracing the organism's perceptions of the body and the world conveys how it might feel to be in the midst of bewildering, fascinating change without secure purpose or continuity.

Beyond the evolution in pronouns, Brooke-Rose captures this sense of experiment and accident in her diction. Both in the chart of *Subscript* and her interview with Lorna Sage, she described her semantic as well as grammatical constraints: in fictionalizing the sensations of her increasingly complex "creatures," she deliberately confined herself to "what they can know" (*Invisible Author* 171), "never using a word for to-them-non-existent concepts" (see Figure A, pages 172–173). Although this constraint might sound pedantic, it generates considerable play in the language right from the beginning of the novel, a kind of guessing game for the reader that mimics the uncertain hermeneutic gropings of the creatures. The semantic constraints are often more noticeable than the grammatical, so that we become aware of being subjected to limitations of naming. It is as if we had one hand tied behind our backs as we search for clues to the words that describe but do not name. The novel begins within a cartoonish, comic, lyric, and exclamatory style. Pleasure of a very rudimentary kind is conveyed in the joyful exclamatory "zing." This joyful exclamation is then refined further into an adverb describing a certain exuberant feeling (the creature is "feeling zingy" [*Subscript* 13]). (The onomatopoetic language has a faint resemblance to the lyrics of Judy Garland's Trolley Song: "Zing, zing, zing went my heartstrings.") Compound, Anglo-Saxonate words like "earthfarts," "glowsalties," "warmturns" and "foodrot" capture both the evolution of language and the volatile, eruptive and compounding actions and reactions of the earth's beginnings during the millions of years that marked the transition from prebiotic to biotic life. Words agglutinate like particles. Energetic constructions are formed. Concepts, such as power, are described pages before the word itself appears (*Subscript* 8): "And the sweety acids become very active and mingle, pushing others around a bit, changing stuffs into other stuffs around the scattered acid strands" (*Subscript* 1–2). The concept of family is evoked before its emergence; it is described as "a new inside group feeling, not just a pack feeling" (*Subscript* 63). Instead of naming each new entity, we get descriptions of dynamic actions:

> Until suddenly, one stick of stuff, or maybe many more, gets enclosed by one other.

> Plonk.
> Gobbled up.
> It becomes two. One inside the other. (*Subscript* 3–4)

A nucleus is born when bacteria and host cell connect; the transition from prokaryote cell to eukaryote cell occurs in onomatopoetic language that might accompany comic book action.[6] The term "animation" seems more appropriate to this vivid and exuberant language than "anthropomorphism." The narrative offers a primitive reenactment rather than anachronistic comparison between the life of a eukaryote cell and that of a human being.

The scene above in which a nucleus forms is also the first record of a singular event; "plonk," records a specific action that presumably happened once after millions of years of (participial) churning, waiting, absorbing. Not only does the nucleus emerge from the prokaryote cell, but event emerges from summary. The iterative, simmering "soup" gives way to the singularity of a depicted scene as a nucleus forms. Something happens. We watch as the narrative rises above the threshold at which plot is born. Brooke-Rose's challenge is to translate the master narrative of evolution fictionally both accurately, according to scientific evidence, and dramatically in such scenic moments.

The disparity between the two time sequences of geologic and human time is a source of Brooke-Rose's humor in the text, her title page, and her chart. Chapters with the titles "Twenty-five million years later" emphasize the ludicrousness of writing a novel, accustomed at best to the span of family generations. The joke behind the "dating" derives from how bizarre it is to calculate so roughly over such a huge span of time. Two "time" sequences govern Brooke-Rose's chart, two types of dating: one sequence that moves forward from the beginning (the organism's trajectory) and one sequence that dates from the present back to the past (the paleontologist's perspective). The chart shows two columns of dates—the first, the "Titles" dating forward (4Kmyl) and the second, the "Time" dating from the "present" (4500 mya). In zigzag formation it is possible to derive a time for one chapter, such as chapter 4 (305–290 mya) by taking the latest "time" of chapter 3 (405–370 mya) and subtracting the "title" of chapter 4 (65 myl). Brooke-Rose once pointed out in conversation the "joke" of the back-dating, the way the "present" continually moves but so insignificantly in comparison with geologic time that it does not affect the scientific back-dating at all.[7]

The more serious side of the disparity between geologic and novelistic time emerges with the thematic of witness and memory. What does it mean to picture, to fictionalize, to imagine an event that took place millions of years ago before anyone was there to witness it? How is the trace of a moment recorded—materially in the earth and in the genes, fictionally in a novel about evolution? What is the bond between novel and archive? In "Typewriter Ribbon," Derrida speculates on a recent archeological discovery in France of the "intact cadaver" of an insect "surprised by death, in an instant, by a geological or geothermal catastrophe, at the moment at which it was sucking the blood of another insect, 54 million years before humans appeared on Earth." Another "report" captures the moment of "jouissance" in which two midges "made love," the trace of which is captured in amber. Derrida goes on to say:

> It is one thing to know the sediments, rocks, plants that can be dated to a period when nothing human or even living signaled its presence on Earth. It is another thing to refer to a singular event, to what took place one time, one time only, in a nonrepeatable instant, like that animal surprised by catastrophe at the moment, at some instant, at some stigmatic point of time in which it was in the process of taking its pleasure sucking the blood of another animal, just as it could have taken it in some other way, moreover. . . . There are many things on Earth that have been there since 54 million years before humans. We can identify them and analyze them, but rarely in the form of the archive of a singular event and, what is more, of an event that happened to some living being, affecting an organized living being, already endowed with a kind of memory, with project, need, desire, pleasure, *jouissance,* and aptitude to retain traces. (Derrida 331)

It is this kind of dramatization of event, perception, choice, and accident that Brooke-Rose fictionalizes when she translates evolutionary theory into a narrative of evolution, prehistory into novelization. The challenge she sets for herself is how to capture the project, need, pleasure, and aptitude that predates mankind, how to localize desire in a living instrument of perception and information before mammalian consciousness exists. The tension between what Genette calls the iterative and the singular is exaggerated in a plot that extends over almost 4500 million years. In this kind of text, the words "until" and "suddenly" work overtime:

> until suddenly, one stick of stuff, or maybe many more, gets enclosed by one other. (*Subscript* 3)

Until at last, after many unwelcoming bays and more egg scatterings and losses, the exhausted creatures enter a quieter, a warmer sea. (*Subscript* 18)

Until the offspring, suddenly as soon as adult, disappear. (*Subscript* 28)

Suddenly, before any answers can possibly be given, if meant to be given, the lake disappears. Well, perhaps it's still there underneath, if waters can flow on top of each other without mixing. (*Subscript* 54)

Perceptions are increasingly localized in the consciousness of the organism, but we are unsure if the "event" summarizes a million-year process or represents an *exemplary* moment in time. We cannot always distinguish between a sudden perception of an action that occurred thousands of years ago (such as the disappearance of the lake) and a potentially mistaken perception (the lake might not have disappeared but may remain underneath the land). Although deictics (here, there, now, then) increasingly represent a located consciousness perceiving the world, what do these words actually represent on such a vast historical and geographical scale?

As Richard Fortey writes in *Life: An Unauthorised Biography: A Natural History of the First Four Thousand Million Years of Life on Earth* (a book Brooke-Rose consulted in writing *Subscript*), there are enormous difficulties in writing the "story" of evolution, specifically, in relating one discovery to another over so many millions of years. How can a story of life be told that depends upon some causal connections, when the novel covers such a huge swath of time and space? Fortey refers to a putative description by Isaac Newton in which Newton "described his sampling of phenomena from the physical universe as a kind of beachcombing, where by he could pick up only the brightest shells that caught his eye from an infinite litter on the strand."[8] ("And as to monster predators," the narrative tells us in *Subscript*, "that's another story or part of the same story, about huge scaly animals as tall as trees that ruled everywhere, destroying every forest and all smaller animals as they went" (Brooke-Rose, *Subscript* 74). What does the locution, "that's another story," mean in the narrative of evolution? Fortey goes on to say that "all stories need a chronology. Geological time is paradoxical and difficult. The further back in time we go the more obscure are the events, the less certain the narrative" (Fortey 27). If we go back 3500 million years ago, "the possibility for aligning an event in one part of his world with that in another might be askew by some millions of years. . . . The past is continually erased, and the record of the most distant time survives only by a chain of minor miracles" (Fortey 27–28). How can discoveries of life-forms millions of years and thousands of miles apart be knitted into a continuous narrative? Brooke-Rose follows current evolutionary theory in refusing to view evolution as progress toward the creation and development of man. Indeed, she deliberately works against the pressure toward "development," exerted by both the genre of the novel and an androcentric understanding of evolution.

In her attempted fidelity to scientific theory, Brooke-Rose tries to capture the nonprogressive and discontinuous elements as part of the archive. In later sections of the novel, she represents both the simultaneity of development of life-forms in different places and the disappearance of species not in the direct line of descent of man. Hominids encounter each other in tribes and possess a rudimentary historical consciousness of concurrent development that has occurred in different places over long periods. Indeed, the explicit emergence of storytelling as an activity in chapter 14 allows for acknowledgment of other tribes and clans, predecessors whose lives continue in language. The role of storytelling accelerates with the European migration in chapter 16. Stories of how various clans arrived in Europe and encountered one another circulate throughout the narrative, providing conjectures about the movements of the Paleolithic populations of Europe.

In a new rhetoric of the unreal, storytelling transmits stories of the extinct as well as the dead. Near the end of the novel, storytelling brings with it a whiff of the future, as the traveler brings stores of astonishing cultural developments from afar (a displacement from time to space). However, in the early sections of the novel the code allows for recognition of the gaps, accidents, errors, and unsuccessful adaptations that mark the story of evolution. It serves as the book of forgetting as well as memory: "The code may be a present memorial to ancient memory but never explains anything at the time. Or very little. . . . The code is much too busy replicating and recombining, forecasting or at least ordering, to record absolutely everything, let alone communicate. But some remains in the body, for the body also remembers, even if it forgets that it can remember. The body knows that it has landgear, like others. Even those mottled monsters with vast long bodies and tiny legs had that. Of a sort. But they didn't survive. Or else went elsewhere" (*Subscript* 30). The code serves as an explanatory fiction for the creatures who project intention, carelessness, and neglect onto the code, as each creature tries to understand its place in the chain of biologic development: "A huge deep envy of erectness, carried in some ancient memory lost by the careless code, ripples through the entire group of smaller kin scattered all over the landmass" (*Subscript* 36). "The frail memory of erectness hovers and is gone" (*Subscript* 48). Erectness envy, so to speak (the double entendre occasionally surfaces) is one of the persistent, if fragile, memories retained in the body, a remnant saved for future use. In this way, Brooke-Rose represents chance and adaptation. The acknowledgment is sometimes explicit, as when we come across the line "something unassimilable has occurred" (*Subscript* 23). Or it appears in the thoughts of the creatures: "Why are these changes never explained?" one of the creatures thinks. "They just happen, and the body somehow adapts to them" (*Subscript* 46). In *Amalgamemnon*, modal possibilities are proposed and entertained; in *Subscript*, the speculation of roads not taken are called "intimations of other versions" (*Subscript* 73). The theme of traces found throughout Brooke-Rose's fiction meshes with evolutionary theory, as disappearance requires detective work by creature and reader alike: "Impossible to know for sure now exactly where the sea was or wasn't, unless the plants still taste too salty" (*Subscript* 41). "Some movement in the code intimates that they've [the huge ones] vanished from everywhere, for good" (*Subscript* 72). "[L]iterature is full of loose ends," Brooke-Rose points out, comparing it to evolution ("Interview" *Invisible Author* 170). Like the characters who disappear suddenly from the narrative of *Textermination*, we gain and lose organisms throughout *Subscipt*.

In the evolutionary context of *Subscript*, the threat of obsolescence found in Brooke-Rose's novels takes on added meaning. From the sick white man in *Out*, "out" of a job after the color reversal, to Mira Enketei, the soon to be out of work classicist, to the out of work characters in the texts of *Textermination*, Brooke-Rose concerns herself fictionally with redundancy, obsolescence, and use. In *Subscript*, the theory of adaptive use is often fictionalized in terms of the labor required by the organism. Sentences describing chimps becoming bipedal echo other examples in her fiction of the perceived need to be useful: "Using the backlegs for long, however, is very painful, and tiring. The legs ache, especially in the ankles and behind the knees, and even all the way up the back of the neck. Because the head shoots forward. It hurts less if we force the head and shoulders backwards, but then that hurts too, in the back. Why do we try so hard if it hurts so? Something must be driving us. The desire to be different perhaps. Or the need to see about the high thin shag, what animals are lurking there" (*Subscript* 93). These detailed descriptions of the difficulty of ordinary physical labor reappear in Brooke-Rose's final memoir, *Life, End Of*, with the poignancy and irascibility of old age.

Although teleology is eschewed, the narrative at various points considers the relationship between chance and labor in the phenomena of emergence, when something changes into something else, either gradually or in a sudden "plonk." In these often contradictory instances, alternative explanations are entertained dialogically, without resolution; a single occurrence suggests the possibility of a drive toward increasing complexity and the counterforce of chance and lack of purpose:

> As if the code, or some superior mastercode of the code, were directing everything towards more and more interlocking dependencies.
> That's impossible. There's too much slapdash workmanship and sloppiness in the acid strings to see any kind of purpose in it all, or why all these living creatures couldn't just have remained sticksful of stuff. Which no living animal can do without. Says the code. (*Subscript* 46)

Evolutionary debates surface in the interior musings of the creatures as well as in the representation of successive life species. Stafania Cassar writes in "Science as Post-Theory? Discourses of Evolution in Christine Brooke-Rose's *Subscript*," that Brooke-Rose studied both neo-Darwinian theories of evolution (that it is nonteleological and mechanical) and vitalist theories that suggests the organism's inner drive toward increasing complexity.[9] Despite the fact that Brooke-Rose does not list Bergson's *Creative Evolution* as one of her twenty-seven sources for the novel, Cassar applies Bergson's theories in *Creative Evolution* to the sense of the increasing development of consciousness in *Subscript*. Although Cassar is more interested in the specifics of the evolutionary debate than is relevant to the present discussion, the vitalism in Bergson, like the idea of some kind of life force in Freud, is indeed apposite to Brooke-Rose's novelistic representations. Uninterrupted progress and design are contradicted in the novelization of evolutionary theory; however, the evolving consciousness of Brooke-Rose's creatures does suggest the organism's deliberate and deliberative internal quest to thrive. Cassar sees this as evidence that Brooke-Rose "resurrects and represents this suppressed 'other' of evolutionary discourse [directionality and purpose], thus contesting the assumptions and structures of thought underlying the neo-Darwinian theory of evolution" (Cassar 203). Rather than viewing the representation of both chance and interior consciousness as an intervention in evolutionary debate, however, I believe Brooke-Rose was more interested in the way theoretical debates can "translate" creatively into fiction. *Subscript* represents what a theory of chance and adaptation would feel like on the inside if the organism increased its awareness of its own sensations. Would there not be an inner need to believe that one's labor effected change? What would it feel like, Brooke-Rose seems to ask, if a creature were to experience emergences on its very pulses, in its perceived sensations and increasing abilities to interpret these changes?

The pathways of the pronouns play a significant role in the writing of evolutionary theory charting the increasingly sophisticated cultural intimations of like and unlike creatures, including gender formation. The pronoun "we" measures the development of a sense of community based on identity and difference. A choral feeling emerges, particularly apparent in apostrophic questions like "Shall we have to move?" (*Subscript* 79). Brooke-Rose notes two "exceptions" to the refusal of the pronouns "you" and "me" (I found three, on pages 76, 77, 81).

> Yes, we can look into each other's eyes, and exchange meanings and deep appreciation of each other's beauty and being. You, me, the eyes say. (*Subscript* 76)

> Sometimes we stare at each other from different trees, as if to start up play, but they seem both friendly and unfriendly. We know you, they seem to say, we're like you but you've grown away, for your own good reasons, so we'll keep our distance. (*Subscript* 77)

> We know you, they signal with their tails. And we have to signal the same back, not with our tails since we have none, but with heads shaking side to side. (*Subscript* 81)

Issues of identity frighten the tribe of presimian chimps as they confront "a large, stout kin animal, still with tail and more fur":

> We're all left oddly upset. Us. Not us. Shall we turn into anything like that? Or were we like that before? Or is it one of us, gone beserkly wrong? Vulgar even. Or beserkly right. It was very alluring. (*Subscript* 81)

The few uses of the first-person singular ("I" and "me") develop the scene of interpersonal recognition and confirm the speech mode. The greater refinement of identity and identification intensifies with the emphasis on sex and gender that begins in chapter 10. The consciousness represented is clearly gendered female (as opposed to earlier descriptions of the female sex): "But many feel completely settled here, especially the females. Each of us belongs to one male who willingly goes off seeking fleshfood while we collect sweet fat roots and stalks and berries to go with it or feed our young under the few trees, or just sit and break stones" (*Subscript* 99).[10] From this point on, the narrative is "inside one female per chapter," as Brooke-Rose has said (*Invisible Author* 170), although Aka is not named until chapter 13. Again, the development of pronouns plays an important role in the representation of cultural evolution, with possessive pronouns (male only—"he/his/him" in chapter 11), entering into the narrative. The sudden appearance of these possessive pronouns signals the more monogamous culture in which the female belongs to one male, part of a tribe with one male chief: "The owner male stays behind, with his young supporters and their females, who treat him as the new chief" (*Subscript* 117).

The invention of language is attributed to the females of the species, demonstrated first implicitly by the increasing interest the female consciousness takes in the practice of naming. It begins with the female's sense of the need to communicate while working together: "But there's a great need to exchange pictures and feelings behind our eyes. About the shape of stones" (*Subscript* 108). The practicality governing the development of language, however, is clearly superseded by the sheer joy the female takes in making and exchanging noises:

> But there's more to it than just a different kind of noise. The real fun is to attach a noise to a doing, and then to remember it. And have everyone else remember it. So we break a stone and utter E from the depth of the throat as we break. . . . And we soon discover that if the mouth closes suddenly it stops the voice, and if it opens again at once the breath continues but without the voice, P, P, P. . . . Some get discouraged. There are so many bits of any doing and so many doings and not enough noises. (*Subscript* 108-9)

Increasingly, the females recognize their own superiority with language and they regard speech as the province of women. The women keep their secret pleasure (and skill) from the males. Sometimes these communication skills are buried for millennia as cultural reversion occurs. Later, there is a distant memory among the females of a past that included more sophisticated language: "Yet here, with some of the females from the old tribe, in our eyes, when we sometimes try to utter as we work and look at each other, there is a strangely anguished story exchanged, of how some of our ancestors invented something very exciting and somehow it came to nothing. How can that be?" (*Subscript* 120). Without the more highly developed language of the past, the sense of time has diminished ("Most of them can't follow, can't even distinguish now from always" (*Subscript* 122). The chief does offer speech ("So the other thing the chief has to say comes out soon after, in more noises and gestures. Tribe up" (*Subscript* 125), but the female creature, now a member of the species *Homo erectus*, realizes inchoately that the group has "long forgotten how to link noises to so many things, and we've never learnt to link noises to each other" (*Subscript* 125).

By chapter 13 (seven hundred thousand years later), males have learned to appropriate speech, as in *Amalgamemenon*: "The meeting has gone on almost since lightrise. But then, males do so enjoy hearing males make speech" (*Subscript* 127). The female story has it that females "invented language," and then "the males discovered it and took it over and thoroughly improved and complicated it" (*Subscript* 127). Comically, Brooke-Rose describes, without naming, the competitive masculine behavior of interrupting one another:

> And they do this to each other too, never letting one male finish but barging in with a louder voice so that both are making noises at the same time and no one can hear either of them till one of them stops, always the one with the softer voice. Unless the chief speaks, then all are silent.
> Perhaps it's our fault, because we teach them to talk in the first place, when they're very young, and maybe we don't do it well enough. (*Subscript* 128–29)

Females become the storytellers, the ones who sing the young to sleep with myths and stories ("But also because we tell stories. And sing our very young to sleep. In songs that tell stories" [*Subscript* 129]). Even so, it is Gedem, the male master of stonework, who becomes a wordmaster, inventing "small link noises" and with them, plot itself: "IF one thing or doing, THEN another. Or WHEN one thing or doing, THEN another. After all that's what we do all the time, whether preparing to mate or skinning an animal or, surely, hunting and foraging. What's hard is to remember the noises for it. But even the slow ones grasp this link and learn to use it. In fact this kind of linking seems easier than learning to link noises to things and doings" (*Subscript* 135).

As in her other novels, in *Subscript* Brooke-Rose explicitly attends to questions of grammar. Tenses, possessives, pronouns, plurals—the increasing conceptual sophistication of the *Homo erectus*—is tracked in descriptions of grammar without benefit of grammatical terms. Take, for example, the description of tenses and iterative versus singular verbs: "he adds noises to the noises for the doings, when single or several, or when done, or being done, or still to be done, or not done at all. But that's very hard to grasp" (*Subscript* 136). As always in Brooke-Rose, the concept of absence is both fruitful and elusive. Despite the importance of Gedem, women are the Wordwomen (*Subscript* 176) and language teachers (*Subscript* 191) (as they are the prophets in *Amalgamemnon* and translators in *Between*). In chapter 16, the history of modern man detours into the story of Neanderthal culture, the species once thought to be a stage in human development, only to have been exposed as a detour from, not a point on, the adaptive path. A captivity narrative, the chapter charts the capture and rape of the female ancestor of modern humans by the Neanderthals (a variant of the history as told by Herodotus). In chapter 17, the disappearance of the Neanderthal is the subject of a "clan congress" on the European landmass. Baludin, the male host of the meeting, explains the disappearance in proto-Darwinian terms, speaking of the better organization and better instincts for survival in the humans. Aka protests the cold and calculating description of the extinction of the Neanderthals (as their forced captive in chapter 16, "she" senses something close to humanity in them). Brooke-Rose has fun ending the chapter on a note of protoimperialism, the will to live fast becoming, in the rhetoric of the leader, "the will to better ourselves. The will to conquer the world" (*Subscript* 187).[11]

In the two final chapters of the novel, art and travel, also male activities, provide a counterpart to this imperialism. In both, Aka longs to have the freedom available to the male of the species, particularly the freedom to imagine and represent what does not exist in the small world she inhabits. Again, the attraction is to something not yet there; speculation and alternative possibilities are theorized. In various permutations, the female longs to consider what is beyond experience, what does not yet exist, in the form of art, fantasy, dreams, and the future (a proto-Brooke-Rose!). In the penultimate chapter, which takes place 20,000 years ago, the woman follows Bitarzute, the artist, into his cave to watch him paint. Discovered at the entrance of the "sacred cave," she is forbidden to enter it; Bitarzute, "the magic imager" assumes that she has followed him because she is seeking sex. After having sex with her, he abandons her to return to his work and expects her to leave. Instead, she secretly watches him paint. And what she sees is the delight in creation that has stalked Brooke-Rose's women protagonists throughout her novels: "He wails and yells to the hammering rhythm like a woman at peak. It's breathtaking. It's godmade. It's alive" (*Subscript* 194). Somehow, Aka understands the immortality of art, its quickness, the way it continues to live. She steals back into the cave and paints on the wall, a woman's hand: "leaving its other self on the wall as a pale hand on a red wall. It lives! It stares out, fascinated. It's much better than the fish" (*Subscript* 196). The artists reach for something expressive, something imperfectly understood, something not already there.

In the final chapter, an Odysseus-like foreign traveler comes from the East to tell of distant places and more advanced societies, a time-traveler of sorts who predicts the future for the clan because he has seen it. He tells of homesteading "a plot by the women to keep us from moving" (*Subscript* 202), and presents a verbal picture of agriculture and domesticity, with all that attends these developments—territoriality and nationalism, animals as beasts of burden, labor-saving devices, diseases, medicine. The traveler leaves the clan but his words haunt them, "The mind can only feel and hear his vibrant but now absent presence" (*Subscript* 210). A new Aka longs to see the inside of the Sacred Cave and plumb the mysteries of art generated by the male image makers. She tries to pump the male artist, Izuri, for information on the images he has created on the walls of the Sacred Cave. The Basque name locates the final scene in a region of Europe dotted with ancient caves that shelter painted records of these ancient civilizations. Ironically, the novel ends with Aka in the Sacred Cave only by virtue of a life-threatening fall into its darkness. She loses, and then briefly regains, consciousness. With broken bones and in great pain, she hovers at the edge of consciousness, so that the concept of time, so hard-won over millions of years of hominid development, slips back, through the intrusion of bodily agony, into the "foreverness" with which the book began. Aka can momentarily see the cave paintings with the help of an impromptu lamp she creates. She feels some disappointment in the lack of imagination she perceives in the paintings. She thinks, "From the way Itzuri talked we all imagined flaming red bulls charging and orange horses galloping and fish flying and birds swimming, well, rock can be air or water or anything" (*Subscript* 214). The novel ends with what seem like feverish hallucinations that transform the art into another rhetoric of the unreal, the marvelous. On the wall, monsters appear with "two heads, a woman's head and a bison's head," and then she fades out of consciousness imagining the future of her clan fulfilling the terrifying vision of the traveler, with "hordes and hordes of wheat-rearers and animal-tamers invading the huge forestless plain, the entire landmass, growing grains and greens and fruits and lambs and pigs and horses and having endless offspring and living happily ever after" (*Subscript* 215). In pain ("Every move means pressing on the left leg"), the woman presumably dies alone in the Sacred Cave, ironically able to view what she has longed to see, only on the eve of her death. In this grand hallucination domesticity as well as domestic fiction ("reader, I married him") are predicted.

Aka's hallucinatory vision at the end of the novel is only one form in which Brooke-Rose yet again expands her rhetoric of the unreal, giving fictional life to the categories of the nonexistent. The grand narrative of evolution provides her with the opportunity to represent the unreal in different forms (with an eye to potentially different genres, from the fantastic to the detective story to the horror story). *Subscript* is the archive of the dead, the extinct, the vestigial (forms that continue but have lost their function); the disappeared (forms whose sudden disappearance is experienced as loss but whose fate is unknown); the monstrous (earlier forms preserved in storytelling as horror stories ("They have mouths like crevices between huge rocks and teeth as tall as small fish. Still, that too may be the code indulging in frightening stories, rather than regretful ones, to justify that long journey" [*Subscript* 34]). Traces haunt the living, in the material archive of anthropology and genetics and in Brooke-Rose's novel of evolution. As Henri Bergson wrote in *Creative Evolution*, "The act by which we declare an object unreal therefore posits the existence of the real in general. In other words, to represent an object as unreal cannot consist in depriving it of every kind of existence, since the representation of an object is necessarily that of the object existing."[12] In representing the unreal, Brooke-Rose breathes life into evolutionary theory, representing the unbearable lightness of being on the massive scale of the history of life itself. Suffering and survival, life and death, are part of the same archive. If *Xorandor* focuses on the unreality of the real in the nuclear politics of the twentieth century, *Subscript* catalogues the reality of the unreal. In her interview with Lorna Sage, Brooke-Rose says, "I believe experimenters like me are doomed to die and be forgotten, but that something of the technique survives, or seeps through, without later users even knowing it. . . . It's true that experimenters often get ignored or forgotten for the mainstream. I'm a duck-billed platypus, and hope my beak will somehow develop in new birds" (*Invisible Author* 178). The "Invisible Author" of *Subscript* experiences her own lightness of being and potential extinction, a possible fate her novel is intended to prevent.

FIGURE A

CH	TITLE	TIME	PERIOD	CREATURE	CONSTRAINT
1	Euka	4,500mya	Precambrian (prebiotic to biotic)	Prokaryote cell to eukaryote to multicellular	No pronouns, even <u>it/its</u>, or impers. <u>it/there</u>
2	4Kmyl	500mya	Cambrian	Prechordates/Chordates	ditto (+ **group/shoal**)
3	25myl	405-370mya	Devonian	Tds Tetrapods, 1st sight land	ditto
4	65myl	305-290mya	Carboniferous	Tetrap. reptile	1st <u>it</u> for code or body only, <u>they/them</u> for code-sequences, or "others" (few) + **group**. No reflexives (ever)
5	25myl	265-240mya	Permian	synapsid tds therapsids (mammal like reptiles)	<u>it</u> for more things/ <u>they</u> + **pack**
6	15myl	225-220mya	Triassic	therapsid tds small mammals	<u>it/they</u>, 1st time <u>its</u> (pack) impers. <u>it</u> + **pack**
7	75myl	145-65mya	Cretaceous	Presimian (tarsiers)	<u>it/its/they/them</u>, no <u>their</u> + **pack**
8	45myl	20mya	Miocene	Presimian (chimps)	We/us/our + their. Two exceptions to no <u>you/me</u> (eye-recog.) + **tribe**
9	13myl	7mya	Miocene	Chimps: Australopithecus	All pros except <u>I/me/my</u>, he/him/his, she/her/hers reflexives
10	One myl	6-4mya	late Miocene	Australopithecus	ditto. + **tribe**
11	2m100Kyl	1.9mya	Quatern/Pleistocene	Homo habilis (early attempt speech)	he/his/him (no she etc.)

#				
12	900Kyl	1mya	Homo erectus + Other Species (H. ergaster, robustus, etc.)	ditto + **tribe**
13	700Kyl	300Kya	(Pleisto.) Lower Paleolithic (Archeulean)	he/him/his but no she/her/hers, I/me/you etc + **clan**
14	120Kyl	180Kya	Lower Paleo. (Acheul.)	All except I/you/she and cases, + **clan**
			H. erectus (speech)	
15	130Kyl	50Kya	Lower Paleo. (Mousterian)	All except I/you/she and cases **(clan)**
			Archaic H. sapiens	
16	10Kyl	40Kya	Mid Paleo. (Moust./Levallois)	1st <u>she</u> (old woman) & 3p (the guest etc.) for I/you **(clan)**
			Anat. Modern Man	
17	10Kyl	30Kya	Upper Paleo./Early Aurignacian	all pronouns except no I/me/my for Aka
			AMM + Neanderth.	
18	10Kyl	20Kya	Upper Paleo./Aurignacian	ditto
			AMM (end of N)	
19	9Kyl	11Kya	Upper Paleo./Gravettian	ditto
			AMM	
			Upper Paleo./end of Magdalenian	
			AMM	

myl = million years later
mya = million years ago
K = thousand
+ the collective noun changes, e.g., shoal to group to pack, tribe, clan

CHAPTER 9

The Art of Losing

REMAKE, INVISIBLE AUTHOR, AND LIFE, END OF

SINCE 1996, BROOKE-ROSE has produced three "remakes" of her own life, turning and returning to the theme of the archive of her life and work. Although her previous novels fictionalized aspects of her own autobiography, three valedictory addresses, *Remake,* a fictional autobiography (1996), *Invisible Author: Last Essays* (2002), and *Life, End Of* (2006) engage her "techniques for living" in the project of looking back at life. All three texts make the invisible author visible: *Remake,* a work of "memesis" that mixes memory and invention; *Invisible Author,* a series of critical essays on her writing practices and the state of narrative criticism (which I have cited throughout); and *Life, End Of,* which Brooke-Rose describes as "a therapeutic memoir."[1] Realizing she is on the verge of extinction, the duck-billed platypus attempts to theorize and fictionalize her life and life's work.

Invisible Author begins, "Have you ever tried to do something very difficult as well as you can, over a long period, and found that nobody notices? That's what I've been doing for over thirty years" (*Invisible Author* 1). In these three autobiographical texts, Brooke-Rose takes herself as experimental subject, expanding and explaining her archive simultaneously. Yet in attempting to make visible what has gone unnoticed and set the record straight, these three texts come to terms with the fragility of the archive. "Official" memory reflected in literary tradition, the "Dow Jones Index of Authors" (*Remake* 13) is mercurial, with the authors' stocks rising and falling. Indeed, for an experimental novelist like Brooke-Rose, age, sex, and nationality conspire to ensure her invisibility ("Ending up as a harmonious Houyhnhnm, invisible as old, as woman, as English to the French and vice versa, as offbeat novelist barking up the wrong tree . . ." (*Remake* 169). Likewise, personal retrospection is subject to chance. Adumbrating her evolutionary subject in *Subscript*, she writes in *Remake*: "Chance, evaded by the human sciences imposing pseudo-systems, is at the heart of biology, of life. Memory is unique, random and fragile, like life, and like life dies for ever" (*Remake* 171).

Exploring the similarities and differences between the storage of memories in a computer and the human brain in *Remake*, Brooke-Rose plays on the anagram of "file" and "life," with each of the eleven chapters labeled a "file." Who and what survive the cut, which "files" are saved and which are lost—these are questions that continue to absorb her. Characteristically unsentimental and impersonal even in her most autobiographical writing, Brooke-Rose nonetheless attempts to ensure her own survival. As always in her writing, technique combats textermination, as "something of the technique survives, or seeps through" (*Invisible Author* 178). The author of *A Grammar of Metaphor*, the narratologist who loves to grapple with the formation of narrative sentences, applies grammatical analysis to her own life; self-confrontation is the encounter of subject and object, passive and active.

In *Remake* and *Life, End Of*, Brooke-Rose sets for herself the difficult and paradoxical task of looking back in the present tense. In both, she applies her signature narrative constraint, her impersonal present tense Narrative Sentence (NS), to her own life. Described elsewhere by Brooke-Rose as an "objectified narratorless mode" which "not only privileges the time of story over the time of discourse but, more concretely, never lets this central consciousness say 'I' except in dialogue" (*Invisible Author* 58), Brooke-Rose's signature impersonal narrative sentence is used to test the limits of what I would call her technique of "impersoning." *Remake* begins, "The black car limousines along the colonnade. . . . The viewer, an old lady of seventy-two, has professed literature, for twenty years as teacher in a Paris University but for forty years as writer, retired to Provence" (*Remake* 1). As she acknowledges in her chapter "Remaking" in *Invisible Author*, the genre of the fictional autobiography is not in itself unusual; "most autobiographical novels are written in the third person with a fictional name, or even with 'I' and a fictional name. Indeed, most novels use autobiographical material, far more so than I have ever done" (*Invisible Author* 57). What is different about *Remake* as a fictional autobiography, however, is the use of grammatical constraints to further distance the writing from the writer, the dancer from the dance. In *Remake* she ups the ante in the use of her constraint on the first person pronoun "I" in two ways. Except for one chapter that includes a diary entry about her mother's death, she eschews *all* personal pronouns and possessives in her text. Without possessives, the notion of self-belonging, of self-possession is called into question. Second, the self as object, as well as subject, is constrained because pronominalization of the self is disallowed. Without pronouns for the self, no secure substitution principle underwrites self-confrontation as it does with the reflexivization in a common phrase like "the girl saw herself." Bizarrely, in a novel about something as intimate as one's own life, in which the self confronts itself in writing, we are deprived of the familiarity of pronouns.

The title of the novel, "Remake," also reminds us of the distance between the self and its composition in writing, the writer and her writing. It emphasizes the image-making process in life-writing, the distance between the life lived and the making of an image of the self in which memory, desire, and invention are fused. The self-described genre of this writing exercise is "bifografy" (*Remake* 11). The author is fictionalized as a writer, "an old lady of seventy-two" (*Remake* 1), with multiple appellations signaling her different selves at different stages, including "the little girl" and the proper name Tess Blair-Hayley. The old lady peruses the "files" of her own life in order to write her life story at the suggestion of her publisher. The novel presents scenes from various stages: the protagonist first as a little girl shuttled between Geneva, London, and Brussels; Tess as a young woman during wartime, serving as an intelligence officer at Bletchley Park, then briefly married to an English officer named Ian, and still later, married to a Polish poet named Janek; Tess as a daughter experiencing her mother's entrance into a convent at age fifty and the mother's subsequent death; Tess as a doctoral student in her forties at the University of London, later offered a job to teach at a university in Paris. In fictional form, these elements of plot adhere to the events of Christine Brooke-Rose's life. The name "Tess" evokes the layered, textured, even tactile nature of the self remade: "only a name [Tess] and memory can tesselate and texture all those different beings . . ." (*Remake* 41).

But another author surrogate appears prominently in the narrative, a surrogate who, like the name "Tess," captures the multiplicity of selves that make up the subject and object of the writing. Brooke-Rose calls this author surrogate "John," after the classic, masculine proper noun that Noam Chomsky uses to illustrate the rules of transformational grammar. At the end of the novel, Tess explicit refers to Chomsky's "rule of reflexivization." In a final chapter in which the selves of the protagonist turn dialogic, Tess tells the old lady that she understands that "John began as a Chomsky rule about reflexivization" (*Remake* 165). This confirms the old lady's thoughts at the beginning of the novel about the techniques of fiction, specifically the grammar of most autobiographies: "Clearly grammar supports self-confrontation. John^1 confronts John^1. The rule of reflexivization requires a coreferentially repeated Noun Phrase in the deep structure to become pronominalized" (*Remake* 3). The problem confronting the old lady, however, is that "the entities are not of equal status and stature, the confronter is a speck in time compared to the army of confrontable selves." In other words, pronominalization is impossible because "[g]rammar doesn't say how many Johns or how many selves (and what colour), or whether some past Johns are confronting one present John or one present John is confronting one or all or a selection of past Johns" (*Remake* 3). Thus John doesn't confront "himself": he confronts a host of other "Johns." The different "Johns" are assigned subscripts: John^{13}, "the litcritter" (*Remake* 11); John, the "lighting engineer" (*Remake* 52); John^{21}, the "script-writer" (*Remake* 65); John^{45}, the "focus-puller" (*Remake* 52).

In an essay that anticipates the novelistic treatment of the writer in *Remake*, entitled "Self-Confrontation and the Writer," published in 1977, Brooke-Rose discusses Chomsky's transformational grammar and his illustrative uses of "John." John functions as the names for the split selves of the writer (habitually masculinized, as in many of theory's illustrative examples). It is in this essay that she links her own emergence as a writer with her discovery of the importance of grammar and grammatical constraint. She says she became a writer only after she "learned the rules" and after she wrote four ordinary novels."[2] The name "John" signals the crucial role that grammar plays in Brooke-Rose's texts. As in *A Grammar of Metaphor*, where grammatical analysis provides a new way to think about metaphor in English poetry, *Remake* finds in grammar the generative principle for enlivening the genre of autobiography. What is the grammar of the self?

First, in Brooke-Rose's hands, the self and the other are not clearly separable. Brooke-Rose dismantles autobiography's conventional split between the self and the world, its convention of tracing the self as either acting on the world or being acted upon by others. Instead, "John" stands for both the writing selves *and* the significant "mentors" and "tormentors" who helped form that self. Because all "others" are seen through the fog of memory in autobiography (or "bifografy") and "memory is necessarily self-centred" (172), "other people are fogs, alter ego et galore. . . . In memory all the parts are played by actors called John, in self-confrontation" (172). Because in the genres of biography and autobiography, others cannot be known from the inside (as they can in fiction), the name "John" stands for all the important actors in Tess's life who have played a role in constructing her. The usage is explained in the text: "Bifografy's like that. Can't invent, can't be free to go inside. All the main characters male or female, the mentors, are called John, for that reason" (165). All the "mentors" and "tormentors" in her life share some form of the name John: her mother, Jeanne, her sister Joanne, her husbands Ian and Janek, her aunt Vanna (Giovanna), a cousin Jean-Luc.[3] In a play on the Academy Awards show or *This Is Your Life* (television's habitual remaking of images plays a central role in the novel), the old lady thinks, "There are so many others to confront . . . executive producer, director, and innumerable others contributing to the life remade alter ego et galore. . . ." (13).

Finally, the name "John" stands for the possibilities and constraints of language itself. Grammar, like a computer, is a system of opened and closed gates. Emphasizing the infinite possibilities for John before he is dispatched into grammar, the old lady thinks: "John is whole languages. John has as many selves as utterances, virtual or realized, as many selves as there are words in lexicons, each word an aetiology, a phoneyetic fragility, with semiantic seachanges, infinite contiguities and tall spokes of paradismatic possibilities. John is the excitement, the pursuit of knowledge, the donor with the magical auxiliary, an eagle, a flying horse, an invisibility ring" (3).[4] A life is a grammatical sentence, with paradigmatic and syntagmatic choices, seemingly infinite before the choices are actualized in a sentence, before the first word constrains what may follow. And there are rules about what can or cannot happen to grammatical subjects and objects, passive and active players: "John builds a house but cannot be built by a house, John can't be admired by sincerity, nor can John elapse" (4).

Yet, as always, Brooke-Rose is interested in the surprises of grammar, the way constraint, like the absence of "to be" or "to have," or the absence of past tense, generates something new. The old lady gets impatient with the normal grammatical rules that John is meant to illustrate, for example, the different roles assigned to "John" when he is active or passive, the difference in function between animate and inanimate actors. She thinks of writers who have revitalized the parts of speech— the way Donne created metaphor with pronouns by making them act as nouns, or the way e e cummings converted adverbs to adjectival use in his "pretty how town" (4). *Remake*'s grammar surprises us out of predictable patterns and expectations. During the course of the novel, the rules stand on their heads. We are told that John is built by a house, that is, by "the house of fiction" (172). As in *Amalgamemnon*, Brooke-Rose challenges us to evade our own predictable internal grammars as a weapon against "the smart empty talk of the quidnappers, orbiting round the world like a dead language with an internal grammar generating only dead sentences" (*Remake* 49). Generative grammar's ability to generate structures systematically is also grammar's generative ability to surprise us. Out of the parade of grammatical examples of deep structures that run the risk of endlessly repeating only their own predictable patterns, a kind of poignant self-knowledge emerges. According to Chomsky's rule, "John cannot elapse"; yet, we discover that "John is not easy to please . . . and seems to have elapsed after all" (6), as many of the loved ones, including husbands, exit from the life being told. The dry, bureaucratic word, "elapse," more commonly attached to licenses than to lives, suggests the poignancy of loss. Without self-pity, this elapsing is extended to the disappearance and death of the author. Seemingly casually, the old lady mentions that the name "Blair-Harley" itself will disappear because the old lady has no children. Names do elapse. Fiction is one way to preserve the survival of the writer's name.

Elsewhere Brooke-Rose admits that *Remake* itself was a remake of sorts. In *Invisible Author,* she tells the story of the book's composition. She first wrote her autobiography in conventional form (past tense) and then deliberately remade it along experimental lines, the constraints against personal pronouns freeing her to confront herself in the genre of autobiography.[5] As in most of the stories Brooke-Rose tells about her fictions, the story of *Remake* is a story of hitting on the right grammatical constraint, as if fiction were generated from a formal challenge, in this case, one of Chomsky's weird illustrative examples sprung to new life, like Minerva from the head of Zeus. Brooke-Rose's "John" is the residue of the shadow of transformational grammar that spawns a new kind of autobiography. As critic, as well as writer, Brooke-Rose was attracted to the idea of materializing fiction out of illustrative grammatical example. Among her papers is a letter to Joseph McElroy in which she ventures a fanciful theory about the origin of his novel *Plus*, the story of a brain who receives impulses from Earth. *Plus,* Brooke-Rose conjectured, might have been generated by Chomsky's famous "Colourless ideas."[6]

In its embargo on the grammatical rule of reflexivization and constraint on personal and possessive pronouns, Brooke-Rose's technique resembles the Oulipean emphasis on generative or transformational grammar. In *Literary Memory, Consciousness, and the Group Oulipo,* Peter Consenstein speaks of the "Oulipean remake" of literary genres through the use of constraints: "As a practice, the members of the group publicly discuss the constraints they employ and if we look upon the landscape of literature, there are no genres, periods, or forms that are not susceptible to an Oulipian remake."[7] In "announcing" her constraint in the mock dialogue between the old lady and Tess that ends the novel, Brooke-Rose departs from her habitual practice of burying the constraint without explicit critical comment in the text.

Unlike the finished autobiography, however, the life continued, and in a kind of sequel, Brooke-Rose has returned to the old lady, now as an "invalid" in *Life, End Of.* The book is a memoir that Brooke-Rose did not intend to publish, part therapy and part experiment. It reflects her declining personal situation; through her increasing disabilities, her life has narrowed to the confines of two rooms in a house in the south of France. Characters are fictionalized, including the protagonist, who is sometimes called Tess. In painstaking detail, the narrative captures Brooke-Rose's experiences as her contact with the world diminishes with the deterioration of her health. The book is explicitly a final confrontation of the self in writing, the final valediction. Predicted in *Remake,* the decline has arrived, the pain only partly deflected by the use of a pun "Heredotage" (62).

If the title "remake" suggests not only the remaking of the life but also the prepackaged images that pass for "news" on the television that the old lady watches, ironically, poignantly, in her memoir television images serve increasingly as her technological pipeline to the world. The word "love" enters only through the scores of the tennis matches which the old lady watches on the screen ("Globalisation. Ah, the globe. Or is it the lobe of the universe? The lob of a tennis star? Neuronic games, games to exercise the neurons" [116]. *Life, End Of* presents the old lady's further lapses and losses and deprivations, the decomposition of the self occurring bit by bit, piece by piece.

In *Remake* we are told that "the old lady's publisher" had provided the impetus for her autobiography: "Why is the old lady trying to intercept all those interseptic messages? Old-age self-indulgence? No. The old lady's publisher has asked for an autobiography. But the resistance is huge. The absorbing present creates interference, as well as the old lady's lifelong prejudice against biographical criticism, called laundry-lists by Pound. Only the text matters, if the text survives at all" (*Remake* 6). The invitation, recorded in the fiction itself, seems aimed at countering the charge of vanity by a writer who has repeatedly gone on record renouncing the self-absorption of the autobiographical. In *Life, End Of,* there is no invitation from the world. Indeed, the trope of self-confrontation that underwrites *Remake* becomes increasingly urgent as the invalid's contact with the world progressively closes off. "The immediate environment always shrinks, from house to flat to room to bed to coffin to earthworm-tums then grows again to compost to earth to planet to universe" (*Life, End Of* 12). This is Stephen Dedalus at eighty, the movement outward from the self to the universe ironically refigured.[8] The opposite of the "bildung," the process of decline in Brooke-Rose's "memoir" catalogues the losing of body parts and memory files. The invalid, progressively loses "pieces of herself" (balance, eyesight, feeling in her extremities, memory), virtually imprisoned in her two rooms. "Earth-bound but abandoned by the galaxy the universe" (95), her feeling of being severed from the world return us to the amputated landscape of "The Foot."

If not an invitation from the world, what occasions this further remaking? It is a question asked explicitly early on in *Remake*: "but then can stimulus for confrontation of all those fogs come out of mere serenity, for undoubtedly the old lady is serene rather than out of ruthless hurt thru and thru" (*Remake* 18). In *Life, End Of,* the invalid addresses the issue and again comes out on the side of serenity: "the small activities left become trebly precious. And astonishingly those ailments are not accompanied by clinical depression. Serenity remains" (*Life, End Of* 11). "Nuns Fret Not at Their Convent's Narrow Room" is the title of a Wordsworth poem—the invalid reassures us that she is coming to terms with her narrowed straits.[9] As the manuscript progresses and further bits are lost, it is clear that if writing issues from serenity, it is also the last stay against oblivion: "This bit of life is made a bit more of life by writing" (76). She calls the memoir she is writing "a dying diary, undated except indirectly because the sense of time is lost" (*Life, End Of* 87). Near the end of the memoir, the invalid writes, "Montaigne says life's purpose is to teach us to die. However, the standard of teaching is now so low that the task is getting tougher and tougher as more and more people among the six to nine billion rightly have access to it" (*Life,*

End Of 93). Wryly, as the bits of her life disappear—body parts, friends, husbands, lovers—the writing remains, giving poignancy to the idea of "techniques for living."

Pathos, however, is unwelcomed in a Brooke-Rose narrative, and *Life, End Of* is no exception. As in her other texts, Brook-Rose refuses to sentimentalize, to personalize her experience in first-person representation. Loyal to the end to her invention, she makes use of the impersonal Narrative Sentence (NS) that has been the hallmark of her fiction, only this time, imagining *herself* as the other, a twist on the thematic of seeing the other's point of view. The important ability to "imagine the other" continues as a theme in *Life, End Of*. The invalid identifies "Other People" (O.P.), as opposed to "True Friends" (T.F.), as those with a "disability of the imagination" (26). The most interesting 'othering' in the narrative is the process of self-estrangement that comes with disability, the representation of the body as intimate stranger. The splits between subject and object, mind and body that absorbed the old lady in grammatical self-confrontation and subscript (John[1], John[2], Tess, the old lady, the little girl) are now *embodied*. Although Yeats's line, "How can we know the dancer from the dance?" from "Among School Children" plays an emblematic role in the memoir (a friend quotes it to suggest the author may be too close to her subject in parts of her memoir), it is a line from "Sailing to Byzantium" that seems to capture the invalid's sense of closing off from her own body. The heart of Yeats's poet is "fastened to a dying animal" and "knows not what it is."

With a play on words that is also an enactment of self-division, Brooke-Rose parses the way the body "feels." The body experiences the world through physical contact; hence, the body's relation to "feeling" (pun intended) is explored. The body is both subject (it touches and feels things) and object (it is touched and felt). Yeats's line from "Sailing to Byzantium" is disconcertingly apt. As in "The Foot," in *Life, End Of*, Brooke-Rose explores the extremity of losing the extremities in their role as grounding one in the world. Oddly, the loss of feeling in the feet leads alternately to a sense of absence and a sensation of pain. The invalid's neuropathy leads to a condition in which her body loses its sensitivity to contact on the one hand, since her feet do not feel themselves touching the floor. On the other hand, her legs feel like twin burning poles, experiencing intense pain. "The legs now burn permanently, hot charcoal in the feet creeping up the shins and knees and growing tall, two burning bushes, two pillars of fire for frail support. At every step they flinch wince jerk shirk lapse collapse give way stagger like language when it can't present the exact word needed, the exact spot where to put the foot" (*Life, End Of* 9). The analogy to language is both telling and misleading—whereas the writer is in perfect control of the verbs of quasi-synonyms she ticks off, the legs (unlike language) misbehave.

To compensate for the legs as anchor, a curious, even comic, reversal takes place. The head becomes the point of ballast. The book begins with a characteristic narratorless sentence reminiscent of the careful, inertial description in *Out*:

> The head top leans against the bathroom mirror so that the looking glass becomes a feeling glass. But what does it feel? This position is for body-balance during the brushing of teeth and the washing of face neck arms and torso. Below is for the biddy, and the feet, if sitting on a stool. But especially the torso. For in fact the teeth can also be brushed if the loins touch the washbasin however cold, or the hand grips the edge, on condition neither is wet. (*Life, End Of* 7)

Less ironically, although perhaps more poignantly, the invalid recognizes that as the body fails, the head must compensate as the portal of discovery for the world. "Heredotage. The quest for brain activity to compensate for the body. For constant intake as opposed to output" (*Life, End Of* 62). Yeats understood that for the old, the mind-body problem takes on a new dimension. Brooke-Rose explores these implications. "The floor the ground the earth are for walking on feet, the world the universe for walking in the head. A walking illness keeps the universe for the head but leaves, for the feet, only the floor. How long will the head last? The few remaining pleasures are not the sex-drive, nor body-temperature hunger thirst or blood pressure but pleasures in the head so rich and devious, and, also, pain as the dubious pleasure of a constant companion" (*Life, End Of* 10).

In tending to this wounded body, Brooke-Rose returns to the themes of her early fiction. Like the perceivers in Robbe-Grillet's novels, consciousness in "The Foot," *Out*, and *Life, End Of*, operates most in isolation, the world a series of objects to be experienced but not fully engaged. Physical inertia prevails. But if "The Foot" explores the erotic dimension of pain as constant companion, a lover's discourse in which narrative issues from desire for the missing body, in *Life, End Of*, the relationship to pain is played in a much different register, that of an old and true friend. Paradoxically, as memory, feeling, friends, contacts, all fall away, pain reliably remains.

However, as the narratorless narrative catalogues its own losses, the absences threaten to become all absorbing. That which is missing becomes formative and formidable. "The old have to think so hard and continuously of every physical detail, physical movement, it's not surprising they develop a senile self-centredness" (*Life, End Of* 62). The invalid ponders the question, "What is central and what peripheral? The peripheral polyneuritis feels totally central, responsible for all the burning flinching stumbling falling and for the half bent walk when picking up the cordless phone or Black holes, says a tele-scientist, can, in this case, now forgotten, become creative. Can a black hole become an ivory tower?" (62).

The question of "self-centeredness" is embedded in a chapter in which the ban on first-person narrative threatens to be broken. Or IS broken cannily, in two ways: through the use of speech mode in which the invalid begins to question herself, and so splits into an "I" and a "you" dialogically; and through the self-conscious topic of the dialogue, which is narrative technique, specifically, the use of the first-person in narrative. Thus, the first-person enters not only IN dialogue but as the topic of discourse, as the author and the literary critic have it out in the midst of the memoir. Brooke-Rose reprises her earlier explanations of her "techniques for living" in *Stories, Theories and Things,* interviews, and in *Invisible Author*. In the seventh chapter of *Life, End Of,* Brooke-Rose risks breaking the fictional frame she has constructed. The persona of Tess slips away as author, critic, and character merge. The persona of the invalid pertains to all three roles. As in chapter 7 of *Invisible Author,* called "The Author is Dead, Long Live the Author," in this chapter 7, Brooke-Rose returns to a description of her signature technique. Reprising her historical overview of the use of narrative vs. speech mode through the twentieth century, she says:

> Oh hell, I'm doing it again. The details of narrative art, which interest no-one, are my Ariadne threads. I can't create, but I absorbed them and analysed them with enthusiasm all the way through. Enthusiasm is life. End of, please forgive me. (*Life, End Of* 66)

She goes on to describe the effect of using the present tense without the first person, which is to drop "subjectivity" but retain "immediacy and distance" (67): "A few authors succeed in renewing the tired narrative sentence in this way, with the present tense and no 'I,' but it hasn't really caught on for the novel. It creates characters who must be constructed by the reader entirely out of what they see hear feel think or say, that is, without any help from the author" (67). Later she returns to this aspect of the consciousness tracking its surroundings, this time in self-reference to the present text being read: "Here, moreover, the character is disabled. Is he old as well? Is he a he or a she? To know these and many other things, if the Author doesn't tell, the Dear Reader (the costly reader) must patiently construct the character from what he sees and thinks, bits and pieces, the way we do in life. . . . " (68).

In this seventh chapter, the author/character/narrator flirts with the collapse of the boundaries of her normally three-personed god. The interrogative mode that has been used, without pronouns, earlier in the memoir, now turns into an act of ventriloquy in (at least) three parts, all the while with the authoritative voice, paradoxically, lecturing on their necessary narratological separation. "Who speaks?" one "person" asks and the other answers, "Ah, the twentieth-century question. In fact, since you ask, nobody speaks" (64). We have returned to the metalandscape of *Thru*, with its insistent refrain of "chi parla?" The technology of the television and the radio, the voices from the world entering the invalid's room, blend ("Who's talking? To whom? The telly?" [31]). The narratorless narrative begins to question its own home invasions. "The question about on-going business home-grown is clearly author-interference. Breaking in to the I-less narrative sentence with the self more than implied" (92). Breaking and entering, the personal seems to intrude on the code of impersoning that is Brooke-Rose's terrain: "Could the infirm character be slowly merging with hisher author? A mere mirror? And if so why the devil or wolf doesn't heshe use the freer and self-comforting first person, as everyone else does now?" (92).

Self-interrogation is part of the stance of self-derision, a way of distancing the writing self from its own worst impulses to spill into something personal. This intervention is likened to "resuscitation" (76). Paradoxically, "[a]s soon as the author recovers his I-less and speakerless grammar, or uses it properly for the details of disability and death, it'll all spring to life again. Because disability and death cannot be borne by any of the participants without that double distancing of self-derision" (77).

The relation between the survival of the author and the survival of the text are intertwined, too close for comfort. This is precisely the meaning of a line from Yeats's "Among School Children" that plays an emblematic role in the text: "How can you know the dancer from the dance" (paraphrased as "So, how can you tell the dancer from the dance?" [70])[10] It is a line alluded to by Tim, married to one of the invalid's "true friends" (T.F.s). He reads the invalid's unfinished manuscript (the one that becomes *Life, End Of*) and refuses to give her the critical advice she seeks. Instead, in a card that follows his and his wife's visit, he offers the line from Yeats as an excuse for his nonresponsiveness. Hurt and angry, the invalid suddenly understands what he means: the author and her character, the author and her text are not clearly distinguishable despite the "othering" that occurs. Moreover, as the invalid ponders the line, she thinks, "The one doing the writing, the other the end-living and dying? No, that's not right either. Can one die before the other? Still, Tim does penpoint the punpoint" (70). As in all of Brooke-Rose's fiction and criticism, the death of the author takes on new valences, as a new form of textermination is considered. We are told that the final two sections of the text, "the self-leering text" have been written in bed after a painful fall and hospital stay, whereas previously the manuscript has been reviewed in the armchair and written on the computer, a device no longer accessible. Although the author says that "survival is hardly the point," she also admits that "Whatever the bit of life has become, it is clung to. Or is itself doing the clinging. This bit of life is made a bit more of life by writing. . . . The desire to continue the self-sorting, slotting, stripping is so strong that the attempt is made" (76). Here is technique for living. Speaking of the term "post-human" that she heard recently, the invalid puns darkly, "But that will at once be confused with posthumous, as of course it should be, human becoming humus" (64).

The "art of losing," to borrow the title of Elizabeth Bishop's moving sonnet, is all too appropriate to this almost desperate act of writing in the face of the bit-by-bit loss of the self. The self-consciousness of the writing heightens, rather than mitigates, the pathos. Friends, husbands, abilities, even words are lost; near the end of the narrative, which began in "serenity," deprivation seems more the rule: "Now that the hands cause ten errors and two spaceless phrases per line, now that writing itself is more and more exhausting and confused, and eyes more and more glaucomish, and legs more and more furious, the three most precious gifts have become deprivations, soon to be reached: reading, writing, and independence" (113). In earlier chapters, she describes her feeling of self-annulment in the lack of consideration shown by O.P.s (Other People)—"Existence, which seems to concern only agendas and arrangements, is constantly annulled long before life is. All the time and automatically when disabled, automatically when old, automatically when female though less so than before. The three together means being placed in a different category of humans" (57–58). However, near the end of the manuscript, the self-annulment is an internal affair. Always more than a purely theoretical subject for Brooke-Rose, grammatical "personing" becomes more urgent. The first person feels impersonal, the way public concern and kindness become busy routine, and the personal wholly private, even when there's no-one there to be private from. As with that waking absorption of the bi-local bi-temporal, in hospital stripped of all such hauntings. Perhaps that is what occurs in death, the first person suddenly regained at the very moment of its effacement. (104)

"The first person suddenly regained at the very moment of its effacement"—the death sentence, the one that can never really be written in first person (as opposed to dying, death cannot be spoken in the first person), is the one that the invalid imagines here to be the moment of the personal regained. In *Remake,* the one chapter that departs from the constraint against the first person is a simulated diary, "full of pronouns," which is "a meditative account of a dying and a death, written between the acts" (27). Based on a diary Brooke-Rose kept about her mother's death in a Benedictine convent in 1984, the chapter retains the fictionalization of names and the present tense (rather than retrospective narration), but it does allow itself the immediacy of the first-person report. The fluid "I" in the diary section feels particularly moving after the third-personing of "the old lady," the emotion somehow earned after such discipline of self-report. In the chapter, "File: Pro-nouns," which include this diary entry, the old lady describes her mother's convent surroundings as "Serenity everywhere. But she is isolated in her god-Routine" (28). The diary in *Remake* is a rehearsal of sorts for *Life, End Of,* an intimate glimpse of the death sentence, but from the outside (as the early ghost stories are rehearsals of sorts, since only the ghost can speak of death in the first person). In *Life, End Of,* the actual appearance of the first person is not the closest fictional successor to the diary of the old lady's mother's death. As I have said, it is used to distance rather than to peer over the edge into the abyss at the moment of self-annihilation. Instead, it is in the more paradoxical yoking of the loss of the self and a sense of self-nearness (almost Hopkinsonian in the extremity of its self-touching) that being in the first person and nonbeing fuse in the archive of the self.

Near the end of *Remake,* the old lady thinks of the relationship of Tess and Janek in terms of their contrapuntal loss of organs; first Tess loses a kidney (a life-transforming event taken from a page of Brooke-Rose's own story), then Janek must have his gall-bladder removed (161).[11] Tess's subsequent new life in Paris is described as a remaking of the self, a recomposition "bit by bit." We are accustomed to such talk in autobiographical fiction—Janek "embarks on a slow yet thorough demolition job, piece by piece, upon Tess's idea of Tess, no longer the helpmeet but the castratrix . . . a self Tess will have to reconstruct in Paris, piece by piece" (*Remake* 162). This image of the self's reconstruction, even piece by piece, is a dead metaphor, a fundamental language for the way we think about the self. Veering uncomfortably close to the raw nerves of the dying animal, precisely through the danger zones of metafiction, *Life, End Of,* attempts to literalize the loss by charting the decomposition of the body. Picking up on the themes of Brooke-Rose's earlier fiction, particularly *Subscript, Life, End Of* gives us de-evolution. "The hands, the legs, the shoulders, the body. Super-valued by early man in eras long gone by. Yet evolution stops for all those bits and pieces, continuing only behind the control-board" (*Life, End Of* 101). As in *Subscript*, the record and the body are inextricable. *Remake* and *Life, End Of* join *Textermination, Xorandor,* and *Subscript* in focusing on the fragility of the human archive. This is the unbearable lightness of being replayed in different keys and on different scales, phylogeny and ontogeny. Ecological dangers of the kind that threaten extinction in *Xorandor* and *Subscript* invade the archive of the self in *Remake*: "The old lady's head is now a nuclear processing plant of lost knowledges, acquired with immense efforts, sometimes leaking or exploding and polluting, but now reduced to small clean nuggets buried in deep salt caverns of the mind" (*Remake* 153). If it is consciously hyperbolic to equate the loss of memory with threats of nuclear disaster and archeological oblivion, it is also another way in which Brooke-Rose shows her mastery of the grammar of being and nonbeing. Contrary to the Chomskyan rule, John elapses.

In *Remake* the "terminal blues" are, for the most part, kept at bay. Losses, while catalogued, are still represented under the sign of Thoth, the guide of writing: "Thoth as alternative god, writing as ringwit, to outwit the inwit" (158). The twin adventures of consciousness and language sustain a play on the relationship between the life and the file ("Isn't life a story? No. A story is arranged. Life is a file. A lot of files, mostly erased" [*Remake* 65]). The characteristic Brooke-Roseian pleasure in language is preserved in this link between character and language. The story of the writer is the story of language and the acquisition of a deep love of the sea changes wrought by the evolution of language:

> Philology is dry bones, but fillology slowly communicates magical seachanges, la mer la terre et l'air of a writer's material, the skeleton filling in with flesh and blood and sinews, molecules of desire, of creativity, vowels softening consonants, consonants breaking vowels, disappearing, changing places, becoming mute, still there as dried up fetuses in

the spelling but unuttered. . . . Language is like Tess, absorbing alien elements and yet somehow always elsewhere. (*Remake* 148–49)

In *Life, End Of*, we are reminded of just how much the craft of writing depends on manual labor, of just how much technique is a physical making. If Tess stands for language *absorbing* the alien, writing complex, self-distant, and full, the invalid is the writer disabled, alien of the species. If the lipogram in her early fiction relies on the belief that potential emerges from discipline and eschewal, *Life, End Of* invents death sentences out of the necessity of self-decline. Here, the need for fiction and fiction-making seems almost anthropological, the human necessity to continue to construct the "as if" of fiction, not only in the face of constraint, but *out of* constraint itself.

CHAPTER 10

Conclusion

THE BRITISH NOVELIST B. S. JOHNSON once wrote, "So many novelists still write as though the revolution that was *Ulysses* had never happened.... Nathalie Sarraute once described literature as a relay race, the baton of innovation passing from one generation to another. The vast majority of British novelists has dropped the baton, stood still, turned back, or not even realized that there is a race" (quoted in Randall Stevenson, "Postmodernism and Contemporary Fiction in Britain" 19).

In this book, I argue that the fifty-year career of Christine Brooke-Rose is a notable counterexample to Johnson's assertion. Brooke-Rose has continued the radical evolution of narrative in modernism's wake. Her strenuous and vital fiction offers survival strategies for the genre of the novel, new forms of telling the human story within the "unreality" of the twentieth century.

As critic and journalist in the fifties in England, Brooke-Rose wrote about contemporary novelists who were dismantling and reinventing fiction. In the *London Magazine,* she described Beckett's "anti-novel" novels (1958) and reviewed Robbe-Grillet's new narrative sentence in *Jealousy* (1961). Writing for the *Observer* (1961), she highlighted the phenomenon of "The Vanishing Author" in contemporary fiction and in 1966 spoke of "Making It New" in her review of Robert Pinget's experimental novels. Like her central consciousness in *Between* who facilitates cross-cultural conversations through translation, Brooke-Rose served as cultural go-between, trying to alert the English that the French were coming. After she moved to Paris in 1968, her efforts took the form of letters "home" from the cultural front. In her "Letters from Paris" in the *Spectator,* she conveyed the excitement of the French revolution occurring in fiction, drama, anthropology, and theory. In longer essay form in journals like *NLH, Poetics and the Theory of Literature,* and *Contemporary Literature,* she dissected the genre of the fantastic in Todorov and Henry James. In exploratory yet rigorous analyses in essays with titles such as "Transgressions: An Essay-say on the Novel Novel Novel" and "The Squirm of the True: An Essay in Non-Methodology," she restored the essay form to its roots as a series of theoretical "attempts."

The title of Brooke-Rose's 1980 essay "Where Do We Go From Here?" epitomizes her restless intelligence as a critic and author insistently impelled to take up the question of the future. This is a question not only of fiction's future, but of the future of the human archive itself. Thus, the "syntax-error" programmed into Xor 7 in *Xorandor,* an error that threatens to obliterate the human race if not for Xorandor's sacrifice, captures the stakes involved in paying vigilant attention to grammar and other elements of technique. In this context, and in other Brooke-Rose textual landscapes, to speak of her "techniques for living" is not hyperbolic. With the chiasmic crossing of the real and unreal in the twentieth century she has felt that new forms of representation were necessary, but rather than resisting the waves of scientific, technological, and broader cultural changes, she has deployed them as novelistic premises. Each of Brooke-Rose's narratives inscribes and transmits a cultural predicament. In these narratives, both the textual body of the novel *and* the bodies represented bear the trace of pain and loss that transcend the personal. Throughout her oeuvre, lipograms encode particular deprivations and defamiliarize the story from the point of view of the always threatened organism. If, as in "The Foot," "pain is a constant companion" in her texts, a reader's adventure in watching these texts unfold lies in the discovery of what endures, or what emerges anew, in response to originary losses. In her stories, theories, and things, Brooke-Rose's letters and languages "fraternize" in ways that "make it new." Trusting the novel form to capture the "corpus cryses" of her time, she produced a strikingly original body of work.

A Discussion with Christine Brooke-Rose

JUNE 2004, CABRIÈRE D'AVIGNON

I.

KL: As I have read your work over the years, I have been struck by a continuous element in both the fiction and criticism—an interest in the phantom and a certain kind of loss, beginning with the short story, "The Foot" and continuing in your complex and brilliant essay on *The Turn of the Screw* in *A Rhetoric of the Unreal*. This interest continues as a broad theme throughout *Textermination*, with the disappearing or missing persons, and into *Subscript* as well.

CBR: Everyone is dead there. Every chapter is called something like "Five hundred million years later."

KL: That's true. And the collection of short stories in which "The Foot" appears, *Go When You See the Green Man Walking*, seems posthumous. The stories are ghost stories. So you started with a ghost story and this phantom quality is carried forward in your work. What I would call "the unbearable lightness of being" is a thematic, from this ghost story on. It is found as well in your idea of the "dissolution of character." You deal with so many deaths in your fiction—the death of the author, the death of the novel, the death of the narrator—and some of them intentionally are part of the constraints, which can be regarded as grammatical absences.

CBR: Thank you, that's wise. I haven't been all that conscious of this as a continuous theme but I enjoy your insight.

KL: In your work there's a continuity that bespeaks life and survival and living on. But there are a lot of disappearances as well.

CBR: The death of the author is on a different level. I try to tackle this problem in "The Author is Dead, Long Live the Author."

KL: *Subscript* is the last novel. Are you writing anything else? You had told me you weren't writing any more novels.

CBR: Well, I have been hesitating the whole of this visit whether to tell you or not.

KL: You have another?

CBR: Not really. During the earlier parts of my illnesses, last autumn, I wrote a kind of therapeutic text. First of all I couldn't write, but discovered a writing-board for an armchair position. And I felt the need to write and something came into my mind, and I found myself being funny about the movements I couldn't make and things like that. There's an article I read, by a friend, on the handicapped, one of them said it wasn't the handicap that caused problems—one learns to cope and adapt—it was other people. So I called them O.P.s. And that's sort of nasty of me, because I don't come out very well either. I fuss too much because they are being thoughtless, you know as you saw in my e-mails. Losing one's physical abilities is like learning to belong to another human species. That's why real friends become so precious; you can keep on the same thought process. But there are very few, they have their own problems, after all. I used to know hundreds of people and now just a handful. But there are advantages in that too. But I'd rather not talk about this text. It's very short. It's called *Life, End Of.* Or LEO. The process was interesting and quite funny.

KL: Have you completed it?

CBR: Yes, and if you want an offprint, I can do one.

KL: You have it on the computer?

CBR: I have it on the computer. But I have trouble getting diskettes.

KL: I don't even use diskettes anymore. But if you send it as an attachment to someone, then it's there.

CBR: What a lovely ambiguous sentence.

KL: Let me look at your computer. Your executor should have a copy of your manuscript.

CBR: I want Jean-Michel [Rabaté] to have it, so that he can decide posthumously whether to publish it or not, for instance there's no point if I'm forgotten.

KL: If you send it to him as an attachment a copy would exist and you could work on it. On the computer it could get lost any time. I'll show you. As I told you I'm a technological illiterate, but I know how to create an attachment.

CBR: And I'm a technodunce. I mean the *techno* from Greek *techné*, skill. They often merge, art and science. Today they're split again. All writers can press a button but not always understand what goes on inside the machine.

KL: Of course.

CBR: I think there's an age when one can take in with pleasure but not retain. Twenty years ago I wrote a novel about a computer. But he is a rock, even if he had an internet. So I loved him like a child, but then went on with other experiments. Seven books later I tried to catch up, in vain. It'll be funny to change from being neglected as a difficult experimental writer to being dismissed as an old has-been. Nathalie Sarraute has written well of this.

KL: As I read and reread each of your books, I was struck by how much learning was involved in each one, how many different sets of concepts and vocabularies you used—astrophysics, structuralist and poststructuralist theory, computer technology, evolution. It has taken me so long to write this book partly because I needed to bone up on all these areas of knowledge!

CBR: Everything I've learnt in addition—psychoanalysis, philosophy and such—are the first to drift off. And technical linguistics, well, generative grammar is a bit as maths must be, you've got to do it, not just learn it passively, you've got to climb up and down those trees. I went to seminars on it because I was interested. But I never really practiced it in this way. I learnt tons of stuff, well, that's all gone.

KL: My father has Alzheimer's and almost everything is gone. But it's strange—he can remember every lyric of every song, so there's something about that kind of memory that's intact. Something Proustian.

CBR: Yes it's all together, you're right. The long-term memory—the childhood and all that—remains. What goes is remembering what you went into the other room to get.

KL: He'll ask something and then forget what he asked. My parents are afraid because I'm here for three weeks even though I talk to them everyday. My mother just said, "I don't know why you're not coming home."

CBR: That's something that happens. The self-centeredness of age which I'm fighting against. My favorite aunt was like that. She died at 94. She was my mother's sister. My mother a Benedictine nun, my aunt a Protestant, but I went to see them regularly.

KL: I'm traveling with my children but she still expected me to return home. And Andy is staying in Paris to study French until he begins his job.

CBR: Is he the one who likes tennis?

KL: No, that's Jeff, our youngest son. He is playing tennis at Amherst. Jeff is working for Michael Wood at the Breadloaf School in Guadalajara. You know him, I think.

CBR: From Princeton. I sat next to him at lunchtime during that conference in Utah. Is he the same Michael Wood who does those television shows?

KL: No, he isn't. He writes about Latin American fiction . . . the movies. Nabokov. He writes for the *London Review of Books*. I chaired a panel at the recent Joyce conference and he participated. He gave a paper on Coetzee. Have you read *Elizabeth Costello*?

CBR: No, not yet.

KL: In the book there's a fictional novelist named Elizabeth Costello who writes a book called *The Lives of Animals*. Michael gave a talk on that. Coetzee gets into imagining the other through fiction, which is something that you talked about in your experience during the war as a young girl, dealing with German codes—not decoding, as has been said, but reading decoded German messages. As an Intelligence Officer.

CBR: I quietly left the panel he was directing in Utah because there was a student doing a paper on Christine Brooke-Rose and Pynchon. The theme was the outsider and he took *Out* as example, versus *V* and *Gravity's Rainbow*, it seems. Way above me. That's what I'm always so aware of. People take on a themelet—which is all the two writers have in common. It's already content criticism. It's the same with that fashion publishers had for a while, and maybe still do, of lumping three authors together simply to save money. There are one or two on me like that.

KL: Are you thinking of Judy Little, who wrote on Virginia Woolf and you and Barbara Pym.

CBR: No, that was real criticism. I'm sorry, I've gone astray. What about *Penelope Voyages?*

KL: Yes. In *Penelope Voyages,* I wrote a chapter on *Between* and Brigid Brophy's *In Transit.* It discussed your "postmodern" travel, and is more about narrative than travel.

CBR: Yes, I remember that, it was very unusual. I must reread it. Of course I remember now. I was very pleased.

KL: Did you think that I "lumped" you with her when I discussed you both?

CBR: No, of course not. In fact, there's a logic you have on the two novels. They came out together, and many years later, after her death, I wrote a Preface for the Dalkey Archives. They asked me for an Introduction two years ago. I even asked their permission to compare *In Transit* with *Between.* They gave it.

KL: I didn't realize that.

CBR: They were pleased with the result.

KL: My new book—should I ever finish it, which I'm planning to do—is about you but not in comparison . . .

CBR: I wasn't asking that.

KL: No no, no, I know. But the panel I served on in Texas, when I e-mailed you about your papers in the Ransom, was held at a modernism conference. The topic of the panel was "the fate of the single author." And they asked me to be on the panel because they discovered that in soliciting panel topics, they realized that there were no panels on single authors.

CBR: Well, that was a conference, that's understandable. I'm talking about publishing. You've got to think of the buyer.

KL: But this was about publishing too. It was called "the fate of the single author" because the publishing business has changed even at university presses and there are fewer monographs than there used to be. This is partly a function of economic necessity and partly a change in critical fashion. So the conference organizers invited a few people to be panelists who had written books on single authors, in my case Joyce, and one of the organizers knew I was writing a book on your work. I discussed you and your work as well as the demise of the monograph on one author. It's even rarer to have dissertations on one author. Not "marketable."

But, Christine, I would like to return to discussing the trajectory of your own work. I'd like to talk about your development of the female consciousness in *Between*, after using mostly male narrative consciousnesses up until then. In fact, in my book, I am playing off the idea of the "dead white male" who comes back from the dead in *Such*. You might say the male narrative consciousness dead-ends in that book. You read the chapter on *Such* and took issue with some of it.

CBR: No, I've said all I feel about that chapter. It's very impressive. But I'm wondering whether the "dead white male" applies to all of my novels. I mean, Xorandor isn't a dead white male. Still, you're right, he does disappear, as computer-rock, to Mars.

KL: *Such* is about a dead white male, so to speak, but in much of your work, as I said before, loss and phantom existence is a consistent theme. The early fiction is told from a male point of view—"The Foot," and *Out*, as well as *Such*. In "The Foot," the narrator is the phantom limb, a male consciousness severed from the female body of a woman who has lost its leg.

CBR: I've just realized that this phantom of a female leg gives a weird bisexuality to the phantom.

KL: Well, I think of it more in terms of abjection, but I see what you mean. And *Out* is about a dying white male, and is about race and other things

CBR: The color reversal.

KL: The color reversal. So, *Such* is the death and resurrection, one more time, of the dead white male, or how to die laughing. There is a kind of joke behind the seriousness. And then in *Between* the central consciousness becomes female. And that's true in *Amalgamemnon* and in *Textermination* although that female consciousness wanders in both. It doesn't apply to *Xorandor*, which is wholly in dialogue.

CBR: Between two whiz kids.

KL: Let me go back to "The Foot," which generates narrative out of loss. Even the constraints are in some way about losing things, about doing without certain things. The constraints cross discipline with loss. But in "The Foot," the conceit is that the narrative is generated from this discarded, abject phantom limb . . .

CBR: I'm so glad. What is interesting about such texts is that I was a slow developer. In my twenties, I would write a poem every day. What happened to me as a writer is that I just realized I wasn't a poet, and I stopped writing poems, just like that. And I found myself in the novel, but even that took me time, and I had to write four traditional novels to find out what I really wanted. And, you know, when I tried to turn to short stories, I wasn't very good at it. I was a very self-critical writer, so in fact I tackled the novel as a result.

But do tell me more about "The Foot." No one else has ever talked of it so well, or will, so might as well feast.

KL: Well, I do like it very much. I think the genre of the novel is the genre you discovered most suited to you—not because it usually encodes change, but because it is such an arena for experimentation. But your collection of short stories, in which "The Foot" appears, seems to me to test out a number of things in shorter form. A narrative told, as it were, from the other side. You have a number of such stories in the collection, "George and the Seraph," and other stories of hauntings. And actually "The Foot" I think is the best of the group.

CBR: It's over forty years ago. But you're right. I think there's a strong link with *Such*. I was quite unaware that an early story could so pre-echo later ones. They must have been written close together and both when I was close to death from my serious illness. I was quite astonished to recover. No, that's true of *Out*, but affecting what came later.

KL: Did anyone single out "The Foot"?

CBR: Not at the time. I was very much out of things. But not anyone later either, except, oddly, Derrida, who asked his wife Marguerite to translate it, but that didn't come off. It was translated some twenty years later by a professional French translator. But I just thought of something that connects "The Foot" and *Such*—a sort of treble voice.

It's the closeness yet deep difference of the two texts. They both have three levels. Not levels but a sort of tress. After all the beautiful things you said about "The Foot" and *Such*, I feel they must be closely linked, even though it happened some forty years ago, and it was astute of you to see it. And it's in the style, a sort of treble language, idiom, or discourse, as the French would call it.

KL: How do you mean treble?

CBR: Well, sometimes double. But the feel of it is often treble.

KL: Example?

CBR: I'm just thinking aloud. This has to do with a treble discourse idiom I was inventing without being all that conscious of it. Two of these idioms are, first, the presence and tone of a death idiom, the second, scientific—and not necessarily true—all correct, in fact wrapped up in the third.

KL: Which is?

CBR: Poetry, opens up the first two into a magically unreal world, which isn't real. I'm trying to remember. In both those texts but especially in *Such,* to recall a straightforward example, a law of astrophysics is turned into a metaphor. Oh I know science fiction writers have been doing this kind of thing for some time but very differently. Why? Because their science is "true." I think that is the essential difference. And this description may not be "true." But it's the difference between science fiction and what I'm trying to do. You've been very patient, but if you allow me two little anecdotes you'll feel what I mean. Okay?

My husband was Polish so we had many Polish friends. I showed "The Foot" to a Polish doctor friend we knew whose wife was our dentist. He ran the amputee department at Roehampton Hospital. He loved to talk about his speciality, phantom pain, familiar to patients and doctors. Excited, I found out more about it. The result was "The Foot," which I gave him to read. He loved it. "Extraordinary," he said, "there's nothing wrong in it." Enthusiastic, he tried to get it published in a medical journal.

KL: Really? And they didn't? But you had captured the sense of sensation, sensation through absence.

CBR: That's very well put. Though I don't remember doing it.

I was delighted with his approval, but the way I see it now is that he didn't feel the "poetic" part of the tress, let alone the death one. His idea of approval was "there was nothing wrong." Of course, I'm being harsh. He was being very kind. That's my point.

The other anecdote is at Jodrell Bank, the British astrophysical center, much in the news then. I sent a typescript of *Such* to the director, asking if someone could help me. He gently passed me on to his assistant director, who was very charming, took me round, and said I was at the second level in astrophysics, but he was glad I hadn't asked him to be a literary critic. Joke probably. So nonscientists are very well treated as honorable visitors but not, of course, given a tutorial, naturally enough. It meant, however, as in the first anecdote, getting no help at all except for the general introduction as it were to all friends and visitors. That's no doubt how it should be.

KL: You mentioned Jacques and Marguerite Derrida. Did you read Derrida in the '60s, when his work was published in France? Three of his works were published in the same year.

CBR: Nineteen sixty-seven. A year before my arrival in Paris. But I had very little time then, though my attention was irresistibly drawn. *Speech and Phenomena, Of Grammatology, Writing and Difference.* People forget all those who were sort of antistructuralism before poststructuralism, they are treated as though it happened consecutively—George II, George III, George IV, and such. In fact they ran concurrently, like those three works. But Americans wouldn't feel that, since translation came later I think, at different dates. I immediately tackled one, I can't remember which, and they speedily influenced Barthes out of pure structuralism into *S/Z*. I was teaching structuralism to first-year students and poststructuralism to graduates. And learning it all myself. At least at the beginning of this new university at Vincennes, it was difficult. I also learnt that a good teacher is someone who can reimagine his own ignorance. I didn't have to, it was there.

KL: And Derrida's *pharmakon* discussion that you talk about in your notes on Pound was published in *Tel Quel*, so you must have been reading it at that time. You wrote in your Pound book about this idea of literature as a cure and a poison.

CBR: I was cheating a bit. The book was actually finished. I had written it in the Pound castle, and I was revising it and plunged into Derrida later. I said, oh, this is exciting. So I put it in there, but it didn't really fit so well.

KL: Was Derrida an important . . .

CBR: To me?

KL: Yes.

CBR: Very important at the beginning. But I became ultra-busy at first, and went on reading voraciously, Foucault and all the rest. In fact later I became rather disappointed in him.

KL: You did?

CBR: Maybe it's me turning against my masters, or against French philosophy, or simply too interested in other, linked aspects. And whenever I tried him again I feel a new distance. He did these weird interviews with that Romanian woman, for instance.
    I think he's had a little bit of head-turning from his star situation. But I don't know. Not as much as Lacan, who once said "je cogite, éperdument"(funnier in French, where cogiter is more restricted to philosophy, and éperdument a wild contrast). Derrida had great charm. But I don't really know.

KL: There have been two films about him. The first, by an Egyptian woman, was actually quite good.

CBR: In fact I later used his deconstruction in several essays. It was great fun. Anyway I stopped reading philosophy, sociology, linguistics (only about them) when I began my retirement in '88 and I was just concerned with my own books, which seemed to have nothing to do with such disciplines. Seemed, I don't know, you'll have to tell me. I wrote five novels since retiring and two critical books. It was rather nice to read just for pleasure. Not for a seminar or panel. The way children read.

KL: I know.

CBR: Of course, I forget all the reading I did, after retiring, for *Textermination* and the reading I did for *Subscript*. Pleasure or work? I'm still fascinated with prehistory and ordered a book that's just come out. But I'm not reading for anything except my novel, and this is lovely. And I'm glad I gave up theory, because, yes it was important to me, but once it had ceased to be important, I didn't want to get mixed up with all those quarrels, you know?

KL: But when one looks at your notebooks for the novel, each one is almost a tutorial on another science—you took on huge subjects—just look at the notes for *Subscript*.

CBR: Yes, they're not really notes contributing to a science. They're just notes of my reading. To learn.

KL: But most people don't go into the depth. There are notebooks, even for "The Foot." You know, what you did about the brain and the autonomic nervous system.

CBR: That's just books, not treatises. That's hardly depth.

KL: That's great. I look at this and my head swims because it's not my area. But to look at . . .

CBR: I kind of swept into one particular thing. That's when you know what you're looking for. That's what I call cheating. So the realist novel—and I'm not a realist novelist—cheats just like anyone else.

KL: But realism as a kind of cheating. Meaning what?

CBR: George Eliot says somewhere that the author need not be in the workshop, the door ajar is enough. After all, look at the fuss we make about identity. Identity is formed in a child very young, repeated blindly by his parents, his teachers, his religious guides, and is a dead loss when something goes differently.

KL: You're generalizing again.

CBR: From highly personal but more or less free experience. I've always hated belonging to a particular party or religion or whatever. Like a club. Which reminds me—Peter had a lovely joke yesterday. We were talking about the early part of *Subscript*, the prokaryote cells—no nucleus—and the eukaryote ones—with a nucleus. I asked him what he felt about how they evolved from one to the other and he said: "They form clubs."

Every single person seems to be having trouble with this word identity.

A fairly recent concept—eighteenth century I think. It was from Locke and Hume, it was called the self. I have always loved the etymology of identity as *id + entity* (the wholeness of the *id*).

KL: I never thought of that.

CBR: Well you were right, because it was wrong. Incorrect. The *OED* says identity is "peculiarly derived" from *idem* [same] + *atis* [ness] in Low Latin, in other words, far too early to acquire my invention, my modern *id + entity*, which I prefer. My modern *id + entity*, with id as not necessarily Freudian. The word *"id"* for me is a way of concentrating on specific cases. Here *"it"* may be a black hole producing sudden violence in those who go out and die for identity.

KL: But identity now often refers to social, group identity.

CBR: Clubs again. It always has been. In the class system it was very very strict. Perhaps it was less so in America. I think they had a class system too, one feels in James.

KL: Yes, it is not always talked about in America, but it's true.

CBR: I didn't think that a society can exist without these groupings. They are essential. But not as used.

KL: I think many discussions are about those kinds of identity groups, as opposed to Freud or Erikson who stress the individual stages of identity formation.

CBR: So in that sense, I am a Freudian.

KL: It's in terms of group identity that the concept of identity has become a part of contemporary political discussion. It's a real issue. Also sometimes about language.

CBR: Yes. Someone even came to interview me about bilingualism.

KL: Oh, who?

CBR: No, no namings. It was very strange. The questions seemed so naïve that I assumed they were way above my head. Still, I think Freud has been really overrated. Of course he's important. But he also comes out with bizarre primitive ideas. I mean as if the id and the ego were physically there. With a map. Lacan used this too.

KL: Which reminds me of the way you play with the idea of drives in *Such*.

Someone and Something are in vehicles. There is almost a pun on drives. It struck me that the drive—the Freudian drive—was part of what was being played with there.

Of course, people are also remembering that Freud was a Victorian, that his "mappings" were not separate from his time.

CBR: It was a sexist period and men have taken a long long time. Lean to the left and live to the right.

KL: I was invited to give a talk about administration and I asked my fellow deans whether they thought gender made any difference, whether it was a marked sign in terms of administration. And all the men, except one, said, "no," and all the women said, "yes." The men thought women might have a tougher time, but they didn't see themselves as part of a system that privileges them. They just saw women as potentially thinking about it. I think that's still true.

In that vein, I wanted to ask you about your novels—"The Foot," *Out*, and *Such* all have male narrators, not narrators, but central consciousnesses. Without the sign of third-person narration, but central consciousness. And it does seem to me with everything you've said about starting *Between* with an androgynous consciousness, writing *Such* instead, which has a male physicist and psychiatrist in the first person but as a central consciousness. You were working through these things . . .

CBR: It took me a long time to realize that translation is in a sense a female activity, the idea that you have no ideas of your own, you're translating others. And this realization began to surge in Oslo, where I gave a short speech on something semantic—I forgot what. I showed the English text to the French translator in his cabin and that gave me ideas. He translated it well. My husband didn't want to go up to the fjords as I wanted to, so we ended up in Portugal. And then I started writing from a translator's viewpoint, but it didn't work out.

KL: With *Between*? You mean with that novel?

CBR: Yes.

KL: Okay.

CBR: And I don't remember how long all this took. But I wrote *Such* instead, which starts "Silence says the notice on the stairs"

KL: Which is in Portugal, right?

CBR: And this went off in a completely different direction, not translation as a theme anymore. And then I realized . . . the following year we went off on a long, long journey. He had a sabbatical term at last from the Slavonic

School and added the Easter plus the summer vacation to make six months. We went all round Eastern Europe, still communist, by car. Hardly any tourists. I started collecting those mineral water labels.

KL: Wasn't Vichy one of them? I noticed that one in particular in *Between* because of its historical resonance.

CBR: I'd collected lots, Bulgarian, Turkish and so on. I had all these labels and also notices in the hotel rooms, also in odd languages, about this and that and the other. And then I realized that the central consciousness had to be a woman. But it took me a long time. Why? It seems to me a very obvious idea, at least as an accompaniment. And picked up the pronounless narration of *Out*.

KL: But you went on in all of the subsequent books.

CBR: Yes once I'd hit on it. But with variation. It's closer to my own life. I've never been an interpreter, but I have always been bilingual, partly tri—so I could understand the feelings and the problems. I was in a way dealing with that, so she *had* to be a woman.

KL: But we're localizing this more around the problem of translation, which I think was part of the discovery, of course

CBR: Hence the planes, the constant travel.

KL: But what I'm getting at is that once that happened in *Between*, all of a sudden, there was a sense of discovering the centrality of the woman as the main consciousness.

CBR: Absolutely, and I wrote *Between* in flowing sentences. We ended up at the Pound castle, which we visited before in the Italian Tyrol.

KL: We? Who's we?

CBR: My husband. Plus me. Our last complete year, 1967.

KL: And that was Mary de Rachewiltz, Pound's daughter?

CBR: We became deep friends and still are. Anyway, that summer I finished *Between*. Even had a photograph of me in Milan or somewhere writing in a café. That was where we did all our writing, cafés. And I knew it was okay. It's one of the few novels I felt certain about. Usually I would keep it back and look at it the following summer. Then all the wrong things leap out at you. But this I never needed to. And it did me a lot of good. It was best of all so far, and I knew it was a very original idea, so there we are.

KL: It seems to me very important that *Amalgamemnon*, too, has a woman consciousness.

CBR: Yes. Once I was on to this female thing it was all I'd hoped. I was out of the third person narrator and the squeamish wriggling first. I think a woman writer should be able to be a man and vice versa. But it's true, I feel more at ease with the woman in *Amalgamemnon*, in fact, so much so, it's more personal that I go into the first person again. I slide back into the first person, still nameless and subjectless, because I do other things, difficult things with grammar. I don't stick to my experiment but discover other ones.

KL: Your constraint.

CBR: Is a very different one. Tenses.

KL: First person plus future.

CBR: The first sentence is . . .

KL: "Soon I will be obsolete."

CBR: Yes. I think the word is "redundant." Anyhow, it's about her obsolescence.

KL: Right, as a humanities professor. But the constraint is the future.

CBR: If you look at the use of the future as a constraint, yes. You can't do too many things at once. One has to keep in control with the constraints. And some constraints, one doesn't really see the point. I've never understood the point of writing a novel without the letter *e*.

KL: And Perec did that around the same year you published *Between* without the verb "to be"? But you wrote this a bit before.

CBR: Perec. Yes. That's right. His other important book, *La Vie, mode d'emploi*, experiments with narrative structure, much more interesting.

KL: Well it is a challenge to think of French without an *e*.

CBR: Yes, but English has a lot of *e*'s too. To me, a constraint must be a grammatical or a syntactical constraint, part of the syntax, not a letter. But that may be a prejudice, about form. Because that becomes going through dictionaries and looking for words. I mean, I like him. But I don't see the point.

KL: Do you think that when they read *La Disparition* . . . is that the title in French? It was translated as *A Void*.

CBR: Yes, that's very good. I couldn't have found such a title myself.

KL: Is it "disparition"?

CBR: *La Disparition.* And you see there's a kind of semi-plot about a person disappearing.

KL: I read it. Can you tell as you read it that in French there are no *e*'s? I thought you might be able to . . .

CBR: He announced it loud and long, so it was known. I didn't say anything about no verb "to be" until much later. And then it did get repeated, but without further comment and once it was attributed to the wrong book, *Such,* I think. But I forgive them all. Because I used to be a reviewer, with deadlines, space limitations. In fact the only serious article about this aspect of my work is Jean Jacques Lecercle's, on *Amalgamemnon.*

KL: That's a great article.

CBR: He analyzes my use of future. As with you, he taught me things I didn't fully understand about what I was doing.

KL: He analyzes the use of the future in *Amalgamemnon.*

CBR: A long introduction.

KL: About Heidegger.

CBR: Yes, which seemed alien to me. At least that's how I felt. But once he gets into the text he does some very interesting things, which I was unaware of at least as to their effect and meaning. And that's amazing, that a critic should know more about the technique than the writer. He showed me that I was, as I knew, indeed using the future, but that was not a constraint. The real constraint I had chosen was all the other tenses.

KL: And *Amalgamemnon,* you saw as a constraint of not using the present and the past?

CBR: Yes, but not so clearly. I thought of it as using the future and other nonrealizing verbs, but I must in practice not have used the other ones, and he analyzes that twist in the use of the future in terms of illocutions. Very well.

KL: It is a great essay. Do you know him?

CBR: I used to know him quite well, and his English wife, in Paris. He taught at Nanterre, and did that paper on me in a seminar there. I saw his name connected with Bristol but it may be temporary. Or not. It's amazing how many French academics are leaving for America.

KL: Are they?

CBR: Well, Jean-Michel finally chose Philadelphia. The Americans don't take away money and staff and so on. Perhaps I'm prejudiced.

II.

KL: In my manuscript, I don't discuss your early novels. Can we talk a bit about them? Although you have described them as conventional.

CBR: I was very much dissatisfied with *The Sycamore Tree* after my delicious first novel, *The Languages of Love*. These are conventionally written. Then I got involved with what I discovered, in the fifties, about my father's shame and prison in 1898. Twenty years before he even met my mother. I decided to do research and wrote about it in *The Dear Deceit*. Quite funny in fact, people still like it. And I began thinking about experiment around then because I wrote it backwards, the first time to my knowledge anyone had done this. In each chapter you want to know what happens next but no, you go back in time. That's not always very clever. There have been two novels written backwards since.

KL: Martin Amis's *Time's Arrow*.

CBR: Very interesting. In this experiment, though, you can't go beyond a certain point. He included dialogue, when all you have to do is to read the words backwards. If you pursue that and do it with letters it merely becomes unreadable. Of course the unreadable is also part of some experiments. I don't think he went that far. I can't remember. I'm looking at it theoretically. Sorry, none of this is relevant for you.

KL: It's all interesting.

CBR: Okay, then I wrote *The Middlemen*, back to satire. And that was the real change. I had slowly realized, after my backward writing, that I couldn't write that sort of novel any more, either easy satire or joke direction, and I started writing *Out*.

KL: But you became ill, didn't you?

CBR: Yes, in the South of France, at my favorite aunt's. My husband had gone to Italy to write. Kidney trouble, as usual, and I lost one. Complications and it all lasted longer than it should have. Slowly I wrote one sentence and fell back on the pillow. And it was completely different. And that was the one that owed most to Robbe-Grillet.

KL: Right. And that was around the time you were translating *Dans le labyrinthe?*

CBR: Well, I don't remember. But I wanted to get away from those obsessive detectives and such. His topics didn't interest me. So I tried to go beyond him, using his startling syntax to do something more original, or interesting for me. I mean my plot—well there wasn't one really. But the ideas I explore are quite original. What do you think?

KL: Very original, and taking his method for something that seems to me to be quite different. Robbe-Grillet's experiment was fascinating, but very claustrophobic, very individual.

CBR: Funnily enough, the method I'm talking about is fully used (I think) only in one novel, *Jealousy*. No first person, of course, we're inside the unknown consciousness and we have to reconstruct him solely from what he sees, hears, thinks. Anyway, I think I got out of this direct influence but still going on with the method. The real freedom was *Such*, as you happily suggest. And then there was *Between*. But you're right, I was always suppressing something. People don't notice, why should they?

KL: I was looking back through your papers in the Ransom library—all the reviews. Don't you feel most of the novels did receive attention? Lorna Sage was a particularly good reviewer.

CBR: Yes, she was. But don't get me wrong on this, I'm not complaining. The only plaintiveness I ever felt (if I did) was early on, during my beginnings in experiment, that men experimenters seemed to attract more attention. But I soon got used to that, familiar still in many domains, the university, for instance.

KL: Who, for instance?

CBR: No, I won't name anyone. Some of them vanished anyway. But don't forget I was also a critic, of myself as well as others. As well as a professor judging theses, and it's easy to don the don's robe.
And when I was a reviewer for instance we had eight hundred words for four or five novels out of ten sent. And now fewer and fewer get reviewed, but get a longer, later, and more individual space. That's good, I think. *The Sunday Times* review of *Amalgamemnon* came a year later. One loses the immediate expectation.

KL: You talk about that in *Invisible Author*.

CBR: I can't remember.

KL: I'd like to go back to *Such*. I wanted to return to our discussion of Freud.

CBR: The Freud fraud.

KL: I know that Canepari-Labib calls it an attack on psychoanalysis or on psychological theory.

CBR: I was glad of that book on me, but barely remember it . . . I was already detached.

KL: That's just a way for me to introduce some questions about *Such* and psychoanalysis—because I disagree with Canepari-Labib's way of characterizing your relation to Freud and psychoanalysis. In *Such*, there is certainly criticism of any ironclad system for codifying the human psyche. That a system could specify, for example, *five* of anything to explain the psyche, is satirized.

CBR: But these are the character's ideas, his reborn phases as kids, not the author's.

KL: Yes, nevertheless, it seems to me that despite the satire of systemization and the way Freud has been misused, the work of language in *Such* owes much to Freud's analysis of the language of dreams and jokes. And this kind of language was important to you.

CBR: Yes, it's a question of how it's used. I'm sure excellently in your case. There's quite a lot of Freud in my work, but it's not sort of exclusive. I float on phantoms.

KL: In *Such*, in particular, I found it very fruitful to think about the work of condensation and displacement in terms of verbal play—a joking quality that includes the motif of dying laughing. The protagonist is both a physicist and a psychiatrist, right?

CBR: Yes. I was involved in psychoanalysis but more Jungian than Freudian at the time.

KL: At that time? I'm very interested because this seems like confirmation of my hunches about the language.

CBR: No, you're right. I did have a brief analysis by an Austrian lady. Someone, a friend of mine, who was a psychoanalyst, sent me to a Jungian analyst living in Hampstead, and it was all very difficult. But it didn't last more than a few months. Resistance, they call it. She blocked me with her heavy accent and grammatical errors.

KL: So when was that?

CBR: The late fifties it must have been, because out of it came the book about my father. So she obviously did help. But *Such* was not written until 1963, published in '64. I must have got more interested in Freud than I thought. But found Jung uselessly fanciful.

KL: Actually, me too. But Freud remains still fruitful for literature.

CBR: Yes, of course. The important thing for me is not to get caught up in them, however deeply I may have studied them—or not. That's the trouble with everyone. I fear being labeled as Freudian merely because I use him. Not by you in your book but by others using you. After ten years of my life working on Pound, nobody has called me Poundian. I might as easily be called Hopkinsonian or Mallarmian. Reminds me of an old sad funny Turkish story about most Armenian names ending in ian. An American lady-tourist mistakenly wrote her profession where the name should be. The profession was librarian. She was swiftly taken away.

KL: But I thought Canepari-Labib took your satire of Freud as a wholesale attack on psychoanalysis. I think it ignores the relevance of the language you use that draws on Freud. Did you read *Jokes and the Unconscious*?

CBR: Yes, of course. And the dreams book.

KL: There are dreams, but the connection between the way language works in dreams and jokes seems to me important for *Such*, because part of it is like a stand-up comedy routine. There are some "one-liners."

CBR: Yes!

KL: Even in the beginning . . .

CBR: I'll tell you what I suddenly remember now. I went through a period of several years when I had learned how to jot down my dreams and to remember them—literally in the dark. I would wake up from a dream, and I had a two-page notebook: a dream on the left page, leaving the right for the next day's interpretation, well, my free association. And I think that helped me very much. I think I must have thought that after going to this woman that this is something I can do on my own.

KL: So she became obsolete, and you continued.

CBR: She did release me in some way. And there came a point where I stopped remembering dreams, so I took it that my unconscious said *"basta,* you know, I don't want to tell you anymore."

KL: Or it'll come into your conscious . . .

CBR: Not that it effaced my faults. I just recognize them better. All this is very Freudian of course.

KL: And was this contemporary with working on *Such?*

CBR: It started earlier, before the publication of that book about my father, written in '59. But published in sixty I think. It was all very intermittent. Then I went to Paris, end of '68, and plunged into Structuralism, but also Derrida and Lacan, who brought Freud more alive to me. I went on jotting dreams but ceased when I became far too busy. I can't remember whether I was doing it during the writing of *Out* and *Such* and *Between.*

I know it's very much part of me. But so are other things. You're pinpointing my id, but it doesn't mind.

When you wrote to tell me about some of your thoughts on the "children" in *Such,* I was simply frightened that you would take these . . . what I remembered about these planetary children that represented psychological states of the psychoanalyst. And I thought you were perhaps inventing a whole biography.

KL: No, no, no, but it's not so easy to see. I actually *had* figured out that they doubled in age, but wasn't sure what to do with that. So I didn't do very much with it, but it was clear that these children were parts of his psyche. . . . I appreciated getting your letter about that, especially since it confirmed what I had deduced about the relationship in their ages.

There's a line in *Such* about "energy passing through matter" that I thought might almost be an epigraph for what I want to talk about in your books. My project is not just one of looking at theory separate from its fictional working out. The theory materializes in language and linguistic experiment. What I am interested in is how much the fiction is an embodiment and wrestling, both intellectual and material, with a particular problematic.

CBR: Oh, lovely. I just wanted to make it clear that all the adventures in *Such* and its sequels—well except *Remake* obviously—are not consciously out of my dreams, but invented. I realize this makes no difference in psychoanalysis.

KL: Well, of course. But for me to say "theory" sounds very abstract, and what I'm interested in is the concrete as well. These are *novels,* so it's concrete in *different* ways that each novel works out a particular problem, and not necessarily the same one. In the process, there are some important issues that get taken up that form a kind of intellectual history. In each fiction, the constraint helps you work out that problem linguistically. For example, reversing the color bar in *Out* is connected to the way you use the narrator-less narrative. Unlike Robbe-Grillet, you use the technique to deal with what are also social problems.

CBR: That's good to hear. Indirectly you mean. I never sort of look back biographically at my novels as I've been doing here. But once I start talking to someone who's interested it's true, things do come back and seem relevant. My early war experience for one. General reports on me say I was a Decoder. No, of course not, I'm not clever enough. But all day I read the German messages that were decoded, masses of it, and the experience, slowly, or fast for my youth was seeing the whole war from the enemy's viewpoint. *Der Feind*, was us. That does something to one's imagination. Like inventing characters in weird situations for example.

And the second thing is how, before I started writing novels, I was a medievalist for some eight years. A visitor once commented that the characters in my novels don't seem satisfied with whatever they happen to know and they don't *learn*, you know. Well, I've never been interested in the *bildungsroman* and it seems to me that the novel was rather badly influenced by this idea. But I think there are other reasons, and they do involve my own experiences as a medievalist. Poetry mostly anonymous, and when a name is attached biography is more or less impossible, and even irrelevant. And so my interest in literature was much more through allegory, and it's a very static literature. But I obviously didn't learn, or wasn't interested in change. I don't really get that until the picaresque, you know. That is change; I mean, for instance, in one thirteenth-century French manuscript on the Grail, you follow all the knights looking for this Grail, and at one point Lancelot is found as a hermit in a hermitage. He is full of repentance of his adultery. I was so surprised; it's not like medieval literature at all. Even in Chaucer, people are fairly static. The idea of *learning* something . . . of course I think my characters *do* learn something, but I don't announce it. So these things that one does that in themselves have nothing to do with what one intends to write do influence one. I must stop saying it has nothing to do with what I am. Of course it has, but not in the way most people ask.

KL: Let me ask you about the role of grammar in your work. Both in the work you did on the importance of verbs in the use of metaphor in English poetry (in *A Grammar of Metaphor*), and also your work on Pound, there seems to be a point when semantics becomes less important and you shift the discussion to grammar.

CBR: Absolutely. That's really my upbringing. In a trilingual family, you get really grammar conscious very early. And you get all those bilingual puns . . . which I went on doing automatically and come up in *Between*. There's one I remember there: *lecheria* (milk shop in Spanish). But of course, in English means lechery. French keeps the latin, *luxuria*.

KL: So there are wonderful puns that have to do with nouns, but then it seems to me that there's also an increasing interest in relationships—prepositions—and syntax and verbs. In other words, how you get from one thing to the other. Increasingly in your novels . . . "out," "between," "through" are words that are not nominative, and that are about direction or interstices, moving away from a state of something, or a noun. Structuralism puts less emphasis on the *actual* nouns involved than it does on the relationships, the links.

CBR: In fact in that book, *A Grammar of Metaphor,* which I worked on through the fifties, I go wild about verbs, which create this movement. And as Latin verbs slowly lost or weakened their declensions, prepositions grew stronger and stronger. They're functional, not independent, and three of my first experimental books use one as title. Except *Such,* which is pretty near but more static than a preposition. In old-fashioned grammar, I think it's called an indefinite adjective. I've forgotten its status in modern grammar.

KL: I was thinking of the meaning of *Tel Quel?* It means "as such"?

CBR: As such, yes.

KL: So I was wondering actually . . .

CBR: It's *Tel Quel* that gave me the title.

KL: Very good! I'm glad to hear it.

CBR: I got it from *Tel Quel,* which I was reading. And it's not easy because I say once or twice, "interested in things as such." There's a character who is "not interested in things as such." But otherwise, it's not underlined.

KL: No, I'm so glad. I was also trying to think about what to make of my conjecture that *Tel Quel* was a source for the title.

CBR: It must have influenced me strongly because I was determined to go to the prepositions and "such" wasn't a preposition.

KL: But the reversible "as such" and "such as" are so interesting as locutions. Because if you say "such as," then it creates a simile or comparison, right? In one part of the novel it says something like, "define presence such as a banister," where you take something abstract and create an analogy. So "such" can also be "such as," as in looking forward to a new analogy. Or it can be "as such," which has more to do with a kind of etcetera or predictable path.

CBR: Things as such.

KL: What does that mean?

CBR: "Such as" would be *tels que*.

KL: I would like to ask you about your autobiography without pronouns, *Remake*. You have said that you wrote a first version of it, didn't you, that was close to your life, and perhaps, more standard, but then you rewrote it with a constraint on pronouns. Is that accurate?

CBR: More or less. Most of my books were written in one summer. But I would put them away, not satisfied, and I'd pick them up the following summer. Or usually in the Pound castle. And everything wrong sort of leaps out at you. So it's much easier to rewrite. But *Amalgamemnon* took four such summers, so I never know what to say when they ask me how long does it take to write. Is it eight months or is it four years?

But of course it keeps working in you. Because I could never write during the academic year. Too much is going on at different levels. So I have to have this concentration. People have such little understanding about concentration. They can interrupt you at any time, and so on. You find that . . . as a Dean. But that's your job, you know. But with writing a book, I need to be in it morning, afternoon, evening and for no pay. And I don't want to be interrupted. Here, for instance, when I have any job to do and I have a physiotherapist who comes anytime in the morning between nine and twelve, I won't sit around for any kind of writing, or even a letter or anything that needs concentration, because I know I'm going to be interrupted. So one gets quite absurd and neurotic about that.

KL: I think that is the essence of administration. You put yourself out there to be interrupted. When I had small children and was doing administration, the two activities seemed very similar in some ways. A little child has no compunction about claiming your attention.

CBR: They all want attention.

KL: It was such a great pleasure to go to Texas for the modernism conference. And then I stayed two extra days, and I just worked from nine in the morning until five, and looked at your papers and read all the materials. And it was such a treat to be back in the library and to be doing work on the project that I wanted to be working on.

CBR: That's why I isolated myself here. A mistake, I guess, with some advantages.

KL: Do you still have students who are writing to you who are reading you?

CBR: No, I've stopped. I've really lost touch. Partly my fault, can't be theirs, you know. I'm too ill to cope with this kind of perpetual thoughtlessness. I really can't. That's why I dealt with this problem. But I usually drop them myself. I can't explain to people why you can't take this kind of behavior anymore. So they drop you and feel good about it and that's fine.

KL: What are you reading now? I take it you get the *New York Review of Books*.

CBR: Yes, I subscribe to that. And the *TLS*. And the *London Review of Books*. I've spent all my week reading that, no time for other things. I'm reading the *TLS* on Shakespeare. You get that when you subscribe. The early ones were anonymous. And I've had lots of books I ordered even the Potter, the Harry Potter books.

KL: I haven't read those yet.

CBR: I wanted to see what the success is about. Curious, not jealous—just curious.

KL: Have you read it?

CBR: I have read it, and I must say. It was a book you didn't put down, you wanted to know what happens next. But from the point of view of structure, she uses all sorts of subgenres, repetitively mixes them up. The vampire or the monster. Substory, etc. . . . that thing in the first book. The villain is discovered so you forget the actual adventures. Turns out to be someone that was never even introduced before you got to that. And that's not a good story. You've got to introduce everyone. In the end the readability is spurious.

So it's kind of strange and patterned always. Every book starts with his horrible family. And then he manages to get back to his school, so it's also a boy's adventure story, which she does very well, oddly enough. But it's always some danger or adventure, or something goes wrong, and then solution, and then another . . . all the time. You get bored with that structure. But that's obviously what people want. But I'm still very puzzled. I think the only original thing is that wizards are usually old men. To make the boy a wizard, that was quite original.

NOTES

PREFACE

1. I will return to the issue of the gender of the source.
2. In *Body Story: The Ethics and Practice of Theoretical Conflict,* Richard Terdiman discusses this vexed relationship between "language and bodies" in twentieth-century fiction, noting its antecedents in Enlightenment texts such as Diderot's. Brooke-Rose dramatizes this heritage and, like Terdiman, disputes claims of postmodern exceptionalism by including Diderot's Jacques, the fatalist, as one of her characters in her metacritical novel, *Thru.* See Richard Terdiman, *Body and Story: The Ethics and Practice of Theoretical Conflict* (Baltimore: The Johns Hopkins University Press, 2005).

CHAPTER ONE

1. Brooke-Rose's notebooks for the story read like the compulsive note-taking of a medical student studying for an exam on the nervous system, replete with diagrams of brain function. As in her later fiction, she is scrupulous in employing scientific terminology to create the operative metaphors of the text. She takes pains to ensure that her sadistic phantom limb "haunts" his victim in scientifically

reputable ways. It is a tragic irony constantly apparent to Brooke-Rose that in her eighties she has suffered from polyneuritis of the extremities and a permanent burning feeling in her feet. As she says in a private correspondence, "Pain is a companion" (e-mail to author, 1 November 2001).

2. Quoted in Sharon Cameron, *Lyric Time: Dickinson and the Limits of Genre* (Baltimore: John Hopkins University Press, 1979) 28. Cameron describes the experience of pain in Dickinson's poems as an experience of self-severing: "The self perceived as other" (28). She sees this as an explanation for the personification of body parts in Dickinson's poems: "They are, in the telling, isolated from the rest of the body and hence, metaphorically at any rate, severed from it." Cameron describes this experience as "survival."

3. Christine Brooke-Rose, *Thru*, in *The Christine Brooke-Rose Omnibus: Four Novels* (Manchester: Carcanet, 1986) 723.

4. See Christine Brooke-Rose, "The Squirm of the True II: The Long Glasses—A Structural Analysis," *Poetics and the Theory of Literature* 1.3 (1976). Felman's essay was published in *Yale French Studies*, nos. 55–6 (Summer 1977).

5. Roland Barthes's own 'fulcrum' text between structuralism and poststructuralism, *S/Z*, can be fruitfully contrasted to Brooke-Rose's essay. In the latter, the structuralist methodology produces the poststructuralist reading. In *S/Z* the systematicity of the codes coexists, but is never quite reconciled, with the starred sections of analysis. Barthes's fascinating riffs on interpretation seem to undo the system itself.

6. On the subject of formal constraint and invention, see Wordsworth's sonnet "Nuns Fret Not at Their Convent's Narrow Room," a poem about the sonnet form:

> Nuns fret not at their convent's narrow room;
> And hermits are contented with their cells;
> And students with their pensive citadels;
> Maids at the wheel, the weaver at his loom,
> Sit blithe and happy; bees that soar for bloom,
> High as the highest Peak of Furness-fells,
> Will murmur by the hour in foxglove bells:
> In truth the prison, unto which we doom
> Ourselves, no prison is: and hence for me,
> In sundry moods, 't was pastime to be bound
> Within the Sonnet's scanty plot of ground;
> Pleased if some Souls (for such there needs must be)
> Who have felt the weight of too much liberty,
> Should find brief solace there, as I have found.

William Wordsworth, "Nuns Fret Not at Their Convent's Narrow Room," *The Poetical Works of Wordsworth* (Boston: Houghton Mifflin Company, 1982) 346.

7. See Raymond Queneau, "'Potential Literature,'" trans. Warren F. Motte, Jr., *Oulipo: A Primer of Potential Literature*, ed. Warren F. Motte, Jr. (Lincoln: University of Nebraska Press, 1986) 51.

8. Motte's collection, which includes biographical and bibliographical material on the Oulipean group, cites only one woman, poet Michèle Métail, who joined the group in 1974. Among the best known Oulipeans beside Queneau are Georges

Perec, Italo Calvino, Marcel Duchamp, François Le Lionnais, Harry Matthews, Jacques Roubaud, and Albert-Marie Schmidt. See Warren F. Motte, Jr., ed., *Oulipo: A Primer of Potential Literature* 175.

9. See a discussion of Oulipo's advertisements of constraints in Peter Consenstein, *Literary Memory, Consciousness, and the Group Oulipo* (Amsterdam: Rodopi, 2002) 41.

10. An interesting side note is that Gilbert Adair, the translator, also published a novel called *The Death of the Author*.

11. I am reminded of an anecdote a close musician friend told me. Several years ago, Jim Hill, a very talented jazz guitarist, played a solo at the memorial service held for Bill Evans, one of the greatest jazz pianists and a musician with whom Hill had made a series of recordings. Hill played a tune that struck my friend as particularly odd, although she could not identify the reason for her discomfort. Many hours after the service ended, she realized what it was. Without announcing it, Hill had been playing the notes that he had played with Evans in one of their duos. What was missing was Evans's part. Some time later, my friend saw Hill and mentioned her intuition. He told her she was the only one at the service who seemed to understand that Hill had expressed Evans's absence *technically* through omission.

12. Francesco Orlando, *Obsolete Objects in the Literary Imagination: Ruins, Relics, Rarities, Rubbish, Uninhabited Places, and Hidden Treasures,* trans. Gabriel Pihas and Daniel Seidel (New Haven: Yale University Press, 2006) 64. Orlando sees literature's obsession with the nonfunctional as the return of the repressed, a negating of society's emphasis on functionality and productivity.

13. In my decision to exclude *Next* and *Verbivore* from my reading of Brooke-Rose, I have taken my lead from her own assessment of the novels. In her summary of her novels in *Invisible Author* and in her critical discussions of her work in general, Brooke-Rose gives only cursory attention to *Next* and to *Verbivore*, her sequel to *Xorandor*. Calling *Next* her "least original in terms of subject matter (streetsleepers)" (19), she further admits that its reliance on dialect imposed a disconcerting visual screen between the reader and the text. Thus her assessment is that the "what" of the novel was less interesting and its "how" obstructive. It should be clear that the category of difficulty intrigues rather than daunts me; however, I do find *Next* both more predictable in its content (and politics) and less fruitful in its narrative experiments. For different reasons, Brooke-Rose dismisses *Verbivore* as the less successful of her two science fiction novels. Faulting herself for sending the manuscript too quickly to the publisher after its completion, Brooke-Rose opines that she missed an opportunity to develop a "splendid idea" further "(creatures feeding on our broadcast words and getting so overloaded they demolish all our systems)" (18). In this case, I am in sympathy with my writer's criticism at the expense of her fiction. I, too, find the dialogic *Xorandor*, with its amalgamations of hardware, software, and wetware, a much more fascinating example than *Verbivore* of technology's potential threat and possibilities.

CHAPTER TWO

1. Christine Brooke-Rose, *Out*, in *The Christine Brooke-Rose Omnibus: Four Novels* (Manchester: Carcanet, 1986) 11.

2. Christine Brooke-Rose, "Samuel Beckett and the Anti-Novel," *The London Magazine* 5 (1958): 46.

3. Brooke-Rose has linked the almost trance-like state of *Out* to her own experience with serious illness in 1962, when she lost a kidney and almost died. "I was very much thinking of death as the meaning of life. And I began to write *Out*, which is a very 'sick' novel. I think one can feel that." See Ellen G. Friedman and Miriam Fuchs, "A Conversation with Christine Brooke-Rose," *Utterly Other Discourse: The Texts of Christine Brooke-Rose*, eds. Ellen G. Friedman and Richard Martin (Normal, IL: Dalkey Archive Press, 1995) 30.

4. In an earlier essay entitled "Dynamic Gradients" (1965), Brooke-Rose describes the way the subjective and objective converge in Sarraute's writing: "The intensely subjective is treated, not just with 'ironic detachment'—that critical cliché bestowed on most lady-novelists—but with total scientific objectivity and humility, qualities not found in Virginia Woolf with whom Nathalie Sarraute is so often compared. These half-conscious movements and murderous impulses are viewed like organisms caught and enlarged in an electron microscope." Christine Brooke-Rose, "Dynamic Gradients," *The London Magazine* March 1965: 93.

5. In *Christine Brooke-Rose and Contemporary Fiction*, Sarah Birch views the "new epistemology," or what I am calling the "yoking" together of disparate realms, as a negative example of the "coercive use of metaphor" in *Out* (56). However, she does acknowledge another use of metaphor, which she links to the mind of the central consciousness who produces "creative metaphors which distort, subvert, and 'mobilize' the language of authority" (Birch 62–63). But the narratorless narrative is more labile than this parsing into good and bad uses would suggest. The coldness, what I am describing as the "flattening" effect of this yoking resembles the intellectual conceits of the Metaphysical poets. Brooke-Rose herself says that this kind of conceit "resolv[es] the contradictory aspects of emotional experience in relation to the changing validities of time and the physical world" (Christine Brooke-Rose, "The Baroque Imagination of Robbe-Grillet," *Modern Fiction Studies* 11.4 [1965–66]: 410). In an excellent discussion of the novel, Ursula Heise says, "The peculiar disjunctiveness of perceptions in *Out* does not seem due to illness so much as to a world whose basic functional parameters have changed so radically that conventional reasoning cannot account for them anymore" (229).

6. In "'Look into the Dark': On Dystopia and the *Novum*," Tom Moylan refers to Darko Suvin's dictum that "a significant SF [science fiction] text must be based on 'new configurations of reality in both inner and outer space'" (64).

7. The doctor tells the man, "We're not only able to telescope a dependence that used to take years to build up, we telescope the let-down as well. You'll see, the wrench will be fairly painless" (141).

8. In my reading of *Disgrace*, I am indebted to two excellent lectures on the novel: Gayatri Spivak's discussion of the desublimation and counter-focalization in the novel , (UC Irvine, 5/24/02); and Derek Attridge on the new fluidity of human relations in the South Africa of the novel (rev. and published in Attridge, *J. M. Coetzee and the Ethics of Reading: Literature in the Event* [Chicago: The University of Chicago Press, 2004]).

9. Christine Brooke-Rose, *Such*, in *The Christine Brooke-Rose Omnibus: Four Novels* (Manchester: Carcanet, 1986) 295.

10. See Birch, 64–69; Canepari-Labib, 71–75 and 185–204; and Brooke-Rose, *Invisible Author*, 17.

11. It is the parsing of parts of the self (as in the case of the orbital "children") that may account for this uncharacteristic reliance on speech mode and, along with it, the first person pronoun. In an exchange with Brooke-Rose, she balked at the description of her narrative sentence as "first-person," surprised that she had somehow broken from the "narratorless" sentence she developed in *Out*: "When I read your description '1st person narrative' I jumped (mentally). For years I have thought, and probably said, that the first three 'experimental' books from OUT develop 'my' Narrative Sentence (NS), in fact Robbe-Grillet's in JALOUSIE but he doesn't develop it further and returns to the 1st person, whereas I have played around with it throughout, with only a few sidesteps, for specific reasons each time (AMAL, XORANDOR, VERBIVORE ... then back to the NS from REMAKE on, with experiments like NS in changing multiviewpoint." Brooke-Rose acknowledges the presence of the personal pronoun in *Such*, but maintains that at the end of the novel, NS reappears and Larry's 'I' vanishes (Brooke-Rose e-mail, 22 July 2004).

12. Brooke-Rose, who aggressively resists the label "Freudian," read Jung, Freud, and Lacan in Paris. She has admitted reluctantly that for a brief time even before the Paris period, she was treated by a Jungian analyst who told her to record her dreams every morning (see "A Discussion with Christine Brooke-Rose"). Along with the essay "Id is, is id?," Brooke-Rose's analysis of James's *The Turn of the Screw* in *A Rhetoric of the Unreal* draws most explicitly on Freud, including, in the latter essay, *Jokes and their Relation to the Unconscious*. In this reading, Brooke-Rose mentions the Freud text in detail, along with Jeffrey Mehlman's fine interpretation in "How to Read Freud on Jokes: The Critic as Schadchen."

In an e-mail to me about Freud, dated October 11, 2004, she writes that she "must have read Dreams and Jokes since everyone had. But there was no specific or personal F. influence till SUCH, and there it's always Larry thinking or speaking, not me."

13. See Hanssen on Derrida 208 and Eating Well.

14. Christine Brooke-Rose, *Between*, in *The Christine Brooke-Rose Omnibus: Four Novels* (Manchester: Carcanet, 1986) 395.

CHAPTER THREE

1. For an earlier version of this chapter and comparison with another postmodern "vessel of conception," see Karen R. Lawrence, "Postmodern 'Vessels of Conception': Brooke-Rose and Brophy," *Penelope Voyages: Women and Travel in the British Literary Tradition* (Ithaca: Cornell University Press, 1994) 207–36.

2. This is not the place for airing my reservations about Barthes's basic binary schema, which seems to characterize types of reading rather than to offer a typology of texts. For a helpful discussion of Barthes's model, see Kaja Silverman, *The Subject of Semiotics* (New York: Oxford University Press, 1983).

3. See chapter 4 for a more detailed discussion of *Thru*, Brooke-Rose's most explicit fictional engagement with French theory.

4. In an excellent article on Brooke-Rose's fiction, Robert Caserio discusses the burdens this kind of free play places on the reader, who has to run to keep up with the hectic and unexpected trajectory of the narrative: "The xorandoric text needs a reader who is critically hyperactive. He who runs may not read any longer,

unless he runs and reads with an unparalleled quickness to catch up with and catch hold of meanings that are rigorous and self-contradictory, determinate and indeterminate, at crucial points" (293). In speaking of the "hectic mobility" of this type of contemporary fiction, Caserio uses Brooke-Rose's own term, "xorandoric," which refers to semantic disjunctions and incoherences more than to the kind of syntactic displacements described in Brooke-Rose's statement above. *Between* relies on both syntactic errancies and semantic gaps of the sort Barthes describes to create a dizzying dislocation in the reader. See Robert L. Caserio, "Mobility and Masochism: Christine Brooke-Rose and J. G. Ballard," *Novel* 21 (Winter–Spring 1988): 292–310.

5. For a discussion of anomie, see Christopher Herbert, *Culture and Anomie: Ethnographic Imagination in the Nineteenth Century* (Chicago: University of Chicago Press, 1991).

6. In Brigid Brophy's *In Transit: An Heroi-Cyclic Novel* (New York: G. P. Putnam's Sons, 1969) Brophy also uses air travel as the quintessential metaphor for twentieth-century culture: "I adopt the international airport idiom for my native. Come, be my world-oyster" (28). The narrator accepts the way the pure products of postmodern jet-age culture collapse the foreign into the familiar: "This airport was the happy ape of all other airports. Its display case cased and displayed the perfumes of Arabia and of Paris, packaged in the style to which they have become acCustomed [*sic*] through the universal Excise of capital letters and full stops in the typography. Every artifact in sight excited me, raised me towards tip-toe. None was everyday. All were exotic. Yet nothing chilled or alienated me, since nothing was unfamiliar. The whole setting belonged to *my* century" (26). Brophy and Brooke-Rose were friends for many years.

7. In a letter to me, Brooke-Rose specified that this false start consisted of about twenty pages (Letter to author, August 5, 1992).

8. See Nancy Armstrong, *Desire and Domestic Fiction: A Political History of the Novel* (New York: Oxford University Press, 1987).

9. Dean MacCannell, *The Tourist: A New Theory of the Leisure Class* (New York: Schocken, 1976).

10. For a good statement of this change in tone and attitude between modernism and postmodernism, see Alan Wilde, *Horizons of Assent: Modernism, Postmodernism, and the Ironic Imagination* (Baltimore: Johns Hopkins University Press, 1981). For my critique of this approach, see my review of Wilde's book in *Novel* (Karen Lawrence, *Novel* 16 [1983]).

11. See Leo Bersani and Ulysse Dutoit, *Forms of Violence: Narrative in Assyrian Art and Modern Culture* (New York: Schocken Books, 1985) for an antinarrative theory that privileges art that represents the "pleasurable movement" of desire and meaning (105) and Caserio's critique of Bersani in his excellent discussion of Brooke-Rose in Caserio, "Mobility and Masochism: Christine Brooke-Rose and J. G. Ballard" 295–98.

12. In a critique of Ihab Hassan's definitional distinctions between modernism and postmodernism, Brooke-Rose objects to the oppositional structure of his paradigm as much as to the overly broad and simplified categories she discovers in much theorizing of the postmodern: "I find both terms peculiarly unimaginative for a criticism that purports to deal with phenomena of which the most striking feature is imagination, and I shall use them only when discussing critics who use them. For one thing, they are purely historical, period words, and in that

sense, traditional" ("Eximplosions" 344). In recent years Brooke-Rose has come to identify her own experimentalism with postmodernism and does make use of the term. Still, her novels, including *Between*, explore the continuity between modernist and postmodernist literature, destroying the neat divisions hypothesized by many theorists. In *Constructing Postmodernism* (which I read after this chapter was written) Brian McHale categorizes *Between* as a modernist novel with a "postmodernist undertow" (215).

13. Reed Way Dasenbrock's Modern Language Association (MLA) paper "Anatomies of Internationalism in *Tarr* and *Howards End*" (unpublished paper presented at the 108th MLA Convention, 28 December 1992) offers a lively and important discussion of nationalism and internationalism in the related contexts of 1932 and 1912.

14. See Brooke-Rose's more recent essay on Pound in Christine Brooke-Rose, *Make It New: The Rise of Modernism*, ed. Kurt Heinzelman (Austin, TX: Harry Ransom Humanities Research Center, 2003).

15. Brooke-Rose's novel often echoes Eliot's poetry of the twenties, such as *The Waste Land* and *The Hollow Men*, particularly in its insistent litany of "betweens" ("Between doing and not doing the body floats" [395], or as one character says, "We live between ideas, nicht wahr?" [413]. This cadence of the "between" conveys an Eliotic feeling of interstitiality, a sense of waiting for *chronos*, or "ordinary time," to be transformed into *kairos*, or "time redeemed." How to discover the sacred in the detritus of culture—this, the question of both Eliot and Pound—recurs in *Between*. "The gods have left this land says Siegfried now the boss" (431), the jaded former German soldier and past lover of the translator. Near the end of the novel, the anonymous translator and Bertrand, an aging French suitor who writes love letters to her, discuss Eliot's poetry. He asks if she has ever read Eliot's poem "la figlia che piange," which reminds him of her, and he quotes some of its lines. She has only heard of Eliot: "He wrote something called The Waste Land didn't he?" (548–49). "Tired of your still point?" Siegfried taunts the translator when she announces her plans to sell her domestic refuge in Wiltshire.

16. See Brooke-Rose's discussion of Susan Suleiman's "close reading and imaginative criticism" as opposed to a rigid, more flat-footed "biographical criticism," against which Brooke-Rose has inveighed many times in print ("Splitlitcrit," in *Invisible Author* 32–35).

17. I am indebted to Robert Caserio for this notion.

18. See also Blanchot's exploration of passivity: 14–18.

19. The importance of prepositions in general can be seen in the titles of Brooke-Rose's other novels as well—*Out* and *Thru*, included with *Between* in the four-novel collection *Omnibus*. For a meditation on the sexuality of grammar, see Shari Benstock, *Textualizing the Feminine: On the Limits of Genre* (Norman: University of Oklahoma Press, 1991).

20. All sorts of puns on the idea of height circulate in the novel: "I have conducted my higher education by transmitting other people's ideas," says Siegfried (*Between* 426).

21. Even the "myths" of deconstruction are caught in this euphemizing, this gendering. In his essay "Des Tours de Babel," Derrida tropes the translator as the male in hot pursuit of the virgin translation: "The always intact, the intangible, the untouchable *(unberührbar)* is what fascinates and orients the work of the translator. He wants to touch the untouchable, that which remains of the text when one has

extracted from it the communicable meaning. . . . If one can risk a proposition in appearance so absurd, the text will be even more virgin after the passage of the translator, and the hymen, sign of virginity, more jealous of itself after the other hymen, the contract signed and the marriage consummated" (191–92).

22. For the most thorough description of Brooke-Rose's development of her "narratorless present tense" narrative sentence (153), her main narrative "constraint" in her novels since *Out*, see "The Author is Dead: Long Live the Author" in Brooke-Rose, *Invisible Author*.

23. The "distant brain" in *Between* is technologically updated in Brooke-Rose's novel *Textermination* by the "aerobrain"—both a vehicle of transportation on which characters travel (and thus a "vehicle" of plot) and a computer-like memory containing a host of fictional characters from various literary traditions and periods.

CHAPTER FOUR

1. See Patrick Ffrench, *The Time of Theory: A History of Tel Quel (1960–1983)* (Oxford: Clarendon Press, 1995).

2. See Paul de Man, *The Resistance to Theory* (Minneapolis: University of Minnesota Press, 1986).

3. See Christine Brooke-Rose, "Letter from Paris: Ganging Up," *Spectator*, 27 March 1976: 26.

4. Christine Brooke-Rose, "Viewpoint," *Times Literary Supplement* 1 June 1973, 614.

5. In "SplitlitCrit," she comments on "the great innovation of Structuralism," which signaled a "new attention to narrative structure—new, I mean, in the West" (*Invisible Author* 24).

6. See de Man, *The Resistance to Theory*. "Nothing can overcome the resistance to theory since theory *is* itself this resistance. . . . Yet literary theory is not in danger of going under; it cannot but flourish, and the more it is resisted, the more it flourishes, since the language it speaks is the language of self-resistance" (19–20).

7. See, for example, her discussion of the structure of the imaginary, in "The Turn of the Screw," Christine Brooke-Rose, *A Rhetoric of the Unreal* 47.

8. Hanjo Berressem, "Thru the Looking Glass: A Journey into the Universe of Discourse," *Review of Contemporary Fiction* 9.3 (1995): 129–33. Berressem is particularly good at explaining Brooke-Rose's subversion of the subject in relation to the Lacanian mirror, in which the subject's self-recognition (and misrecognition) loops through the domain of the "Other." See also Sarah Birch's excellent discussion of the mirror in *Thru* in chapter 3 of *Brooke-Rose and Contemporary Fiction* (Oxford: Clarendon Press, 1994), 76–112.

9. See Glyn White, "'You Are Here': Reading and Representation in Christine Brooke-Rose's *Thru*," *Poetics Today* 23.4 (2002): 611–31.

10. "Subversion of the Subject and Dialectic of Desire in the Freudian Unconscious," in Jacques Lacan, *Écrits*, trans. Alan Sheridan (New York: Norton, 1977) 316.

11. In representing the contents of the girl's dream, Brooke-Rose joins Lacan in linking the problem of "Who speaks" with the perception that the problem is

related to the operations of the unconscious. "'I am merely referring obliquely to . . . the right way to reply to the question, 'Who is speaking?,' when it is the subject of the unconscious that is at issue. For this reply cannot come from that subject if he does not know what he is saying, or even if he is speaking, as the entire experience of analysis has taught us" (See "The Subversion of the Subject and the Dialectic of Desire in the Freudian Unconscious" [Lacan, *Écrits* 299]). The self-reflexivity of the narrative in *Thru*, however, exceeds any single "key," including psychoanalysis as a reading practice.

12. See Birch's fine discussion of Greimas's paradigm (91–92).

13. Derrida mentions Democritus in his fascinating discussion of blindness and self-portraiture in Jacques Derrida, *Memoirs of the Blind: The Self-Portrait and Other Ruins*, trans. Pascale-Anne Brault and Michael Naas (Chicago: University of Chicago Press, 1993).

14. Martin Jay notes that in Sartre's work, as in Bataille's, "the eye is identified . . . with liquid images of the fetus or womb, which links it to the mother in repellent ways" (281).

15. Glossing this section, Brooke-Rose refers to "the wax tablets or early writing (stone and parchment written horizontally), as well as Freud's mystic writing pad as discussed by Derrida (1978)" (*Invisible Author* 76).

16. Charles Bernheimer and Claire Kahane, eds., *In Dora's Case: Freud-Hysteria-Feminism* (New York: Columbia University Press, 1985) 2. In "Woman as Semiotic Object," Brooke-Rose alludes to Hélène Cixous and Catherine Clément's discussion of hysteria in *The Newly Born Woman* and observes that the very word "*hysteria*, from *ustera*, uterus, womb, is misogynous." See Hélène Cixous and Catherine Cléments, *The Newly Born Woman*, trans. Betsy Wing (Minneapolis: University of Minnesota Press, 1986).

17. A number of reviews of the novel confirm the risk involved in the writing strategy.

18. Cristopher Nash, *World Postmodern Fiction: A Guide* (London and New York: Longman, 1987) 157.

19. Foreword to Monique David-Ménard, *Hysteria from Freud to Lacan: Body and Language in Psychoanalysis*, trans. Catherine Porter (Ithaca and London: Cornell University Press, 1989) xii.

20. See Brad Buchanan, "'A Blind Spot in Your Own Youdipeon Discourse': Christine Brooke-Rose, Oedipus, and the Synecdochic Narrative," *Hungarian Journal of English and American Studies* 5.2 (1999): 195–208. Brooke-Rose acknowledges the richness and staying power of the myth of Oedipus that underwrites cultural narratives so durably, and displays no nostalgia for the narrative. Contrast Steven Spielberg's treatment of the Freudian Oedipal narrative in *AI*. Although the film is highly imaginative technically and technologically (according to the norms of science fiction), it is surprisingly traditional in envisioning the radical future. The film ends with an Oedipal wish—to sleep in the bed of the mother. For all the technical adventurousness and dark apocalyptic resonance, resolution seems to lie in the body of the mother.

21. In "Mobility and Masochism: Christine Brooke-Rose and J. G. Ballard," *Novel* (1988): 292–310.

22. Christine Brooke-Rose, "Woman as Semiotic Object," *Stories, Theories and Things* (Cambridge: Cambridge University Press, 1991) 238.

CHAPTER FIVE

1. See Brooke-Rose, *Stories, Theories and Things* 10.

2. Mira has an intertextual presence in both *Verbivore* and *Textermination*. Indeed, there is speculation within *Textermination* that Mira is the author of the text, and in *Verbivore* she creates one of the other characters on her computer. This "transfer" between texts might be one playful meaning of the term "Intercom" in Brooke-Rose's phrase for the grouping of her four novels.

3. See Ellen G. Friedman and Miriam Fuchs, "A Conversation with Christine Brooke-Rose," *Utterly Other Discourse: The Texts of Christine Brooke-Rose*, eds. Ellen J. Friedman and Richard Martin (Normal, IL: Dalkey Archive Press, 1995) 34.

4. "This century seems to us more and more fortuitous despite all our attempts at rational planning, scientific analysis, and system-building (including rhetoric). Never before have the meaning-making means at our disposal (linguistic, economic, political, scientific) appeared so inadequate, not only to cope with the enormity of the problems we continue to create (since every apparent solution creates new problems), but simply to explain the world." Brooke-Rose, *A Rhetoric of the Unreal* 6.

5. In *A Rhetoric of the Unreal*, Brooke-Rose comments on what she calls the "gnostic dream of the best of scientific, technological and artistic brainstuff enveloping the earth" in terms that provide a gloss to the neologism "Oblitopia" in *Amalgamemnon*. She compares this "dream" to "Wells's collective mind or worldwide information service . . . which presupposes an unprecedented harmony of minds: a mad and perhaps naïve fusion of oblivion and utopia one could call oblitopia" (388–89). She calls this fantasy "an elitist dream" (388).

6. See Michael Wood's discussion of this myth in Michael Wood, *The Road to Delphi: The Life and Afterlife of Oracles* (New York: Farrar, Straus and Giroux, 2003) 28.

7. Gertrude Stein, *Narration: Four Lectures by Gertrude Stein* (Westport: Greenwood, 1969) 37.

8. For a reading of prophecy and the writing of the future in Stein's *Mrs. Reynolds* and Brooke-Rose's *Amalgamemnon*, see Karen R. Lawrence, "Who Could Have Read the Signs? Politics and Prediction in Gertrude Stein's *Mrs. Reynolds* and Christine Brooke-Rose's *Amalgamemnon*," *Western Humanities Review* 59.2 (2005): 18–38.

9. In an undated letter commenting on an early version of *Amalgamemnon* entitled "Soon" that Brooke-Rose sent to him, Joseph McElroy shrewdly but gently assesses the tonal successes and weaknesses that result from the constraint of nonconstative verbs. He comments on the "worldweariness" of parts of the novel, which he says is "so much at odds with the bursting appetite that lives in the book's main voice." He contrasts this weary tone with those sections where "the future tense becomes a mad, rich sluice or pivot or music that lets us into good possibilities. So I wd say, go easy on the future's I've-seen-it-all resignation and use the ingneuities [sic] and poignance of speculation more." McElroy's letter can be found in the Brooke-Rose archive at the Ransom Center at the University of Texas at Austin.

10. Brooke-Rose also identifies Jean-Jacques Lecercle's excellent discussion of the omission of constative sentences as a help to her in clarifying her own technique (48). For Lecercle's essay, see Jean-Jacques Lecercle, "'Reading *Amalgamem-*

non,'" in *Utterly Other Discourse: The Texts of Christine Brooke-Rose* 153–69.

11. In Ernst Bloch and Theodor Adorno, *The Utopian Function of Art and Literature: Selected Essays,* trans. Jack Zipes and Frank Mecklenberg (Cambridge, MA: The MIT Press, 1988) 1–17.

12. *Xorandor* is an example that could qualify as alternative fiction, as is the dystopian novel, *Out.*

13. For critiques of Jameson's view of the ideology of modernism, see Karen R. Lawrence, "'Close Encounters,'" *James Joyce Quarterly* 41, nos. 1 and 2 (Fall 2003 and Winter 2004): 129–30 and Robert L. Caserio, "'Edwardians to Georgians,'" *The Cambridge History of English Literature,* eds. Laura Marcus and Peter Nicholls (Cambridge, England: Cambridge University Press, 2004) 281.

14. In "'I draw the line as a rule between one solar system and another': The Postmodernism(s) of Christine Brooke-Rose," Brian McHale refers to characters "ontologically enfeebled by their 'native' context" [in *Amalgamemnon*], and makes the intriguing suggestion that their reappearance in later novels of the Intercom Quartet helps them "somehow" acquire "a degree of ontological robustness 'between' texts, in the passage from their home text to its sequel" (202).

15. See Michela Canepari-Labib's detailed discussion of the shifting ontological levels in *Amalgamemnon* in *Word-Worlds* 83–94.

CHAPTER SIX

1. In *ET*, adult receptivity is gendered: the mother is child-like and incompetent, more on the wavelength of her children than the scientific/patriarchal continuum of either her husband or the scientists who invade her home. In *Xorandor*, the mother's irritability seems to be a symptom of her marginality and frustration. The twins report, but do not dwell on, her sometimes bizarre public behavior.

2. Brooke-Rose, an inveterate researcher who takes copious notes from scientific source material for some of her novels, has said that in writing *Xorandor*, she relied on Terrence W. Pratt's *Programming Languages: Design and Implementation,* 2nd ed. (Englewood Cliffs, NJ: Prentice-Hall, 1984). See Pratt 68.

3. See "The Dissolution of Character in the Novel," *Reconstructing Individualism: Autonomy, Individuality, and the Self in Western Thought,* ed. Morton Sosna, Thomas C. Heller, and David Wellerby (Stanford, CA: Stanford University Press, 1986) 193. See also Christine Brooke-Rose, "Where Do We Go from Here?" *Granta* 3 (1980): 161–88.

4. Bolter goes on to say that the design of the digital computer "is perfectly logical down to the scale of electrons; it has conquered the disorder of the natural world by the hierarchical principles of symbolic logic" (73–74).

5. See Ambrose Bierce, "Moxon's Master," *The Complete Short Stories of Ambrose Bierce* (Garden City, NY: Doubleday & Company, Inc., 1970) 89-97.

6. In "The Dissolution of Character in the Novel II," Brooke-Rose herself points to the limitations of the binary logic of the computer, though citing different failings, namely, a reification of the dominant binaries of Western civilization exposed in deconstruction, particularly the persistence of phallocentricism in the multiple semiological systems. She argues that Western society has been locked in such thinking for centuries, and computers, unless creatively used, could merely reify and confirm these coded clichés. She says, "[C]omputer science seems

to root our thought structures—either again (i.e., despite the apparent escape of deconstruction) or even more deeply—in the absolute limitation imposed by logical operations based on binary oppositions, whose positive and negative values, since they are mere electric impulses, are of course completely neutral and unprivileged" (194).

7. See Caserio, "Mobility and Masochism: Christine Brooke-Rose and J. G. Ballard," *Novel* (1988): 292–310.

8. Zab, in particular, refers to Plato often, including a Derridean reading of Plato's logocentric privileging of speech over writing. Her explanation to Jip is Brooke-Rose's playful citation of Derrida's "Plato's Pharmacy" and refers to reading notes she took on Derrida's 1968 essay, first published in French in *Tel Quel*. She took the notes when working on Pound, but used them later in *Xorandor* and in an allusion to Derrida's essay in *Thru:* " . . . what begins in banality has to go through the whole signifiying chain from idyll to catastrophe until it can be returned to banality, beneath contempt, amusing maybe and harmless, a poison and a pharmakon that immunises. And he is the temporary pharmakos or scrapegloat, but only for a time." Christine Brooke-Rose, *Thru* 711–12.

9. Jacques Derrida, "No Apocalypse, Not Now (Full Speed Ahead, Seven Missiles, Seven Missives)," *Diacritics* 14 (1984): 20–31.

10. In her essay, "Id is, is id?" published a year after *Xorandor* (and reprinted in *Stories, Theories and Things*), Brooke-Rose speculates on how Freud and Derrida would make use of the technological possibilities of computer memory to "update" Freud's analogy between the mystic writing pad and psychic memory. In mentioning Derrida's essay, Brooke-Rose emphasizes the link between death and memory explicit in the French term for computer memory, or Read-Only Memory (ROM), *mémoire morte*. In the same article, Brooke-Rose refers to Derrida's description of the machine as "a mechanism without its own energy. The machine is dead, it is death." Christine Brooke-Rose, "Id is, is id," *Stories, Theories and Things* 35–36.

11. The impulse to write beyond the ending of the story is one that Brooke-Rose pursues in the "sequel" to *Xorandor*, *Verbivore*, which takes place twenty-three years after the events of *Xorandor*. The sacrifice of Xorandor has not put an end to the nuclear threat, as interference from Xorandor's offspring wreak havoc on the world economy. Brooke-Rose has admitted her own dissatisfaction with the novel.

12. N. Katherine Hayles, *How We Became Posthuman: Virtual Bodies in Cybernetics, Literature, and Informatics* (Chicago and London: University of Chicago Press, 1999) 56.

13. Sarah Birch, *Christine Brooke-Rose and Contemporary Fiction* (Oxford: Clarendon Press, 1994) 126.

14. Tom Boncza-Tomaszewski, "Christine Brooke-Rose: The Texterminator," *The Independent Online Edition* March 27 2005.

CHAPTER SEVEN

1. See "The Ideology of Modernism." In *20th Century Literary Criticism: A Reader*, ed. David Lodge (London: Longman, 1972) 474–87.

2. However, as the narrative progresses, we discover the identities of some of its "authors."

3. See Brian McHale's discussion of the "ontological effects" of characters appearing in a text and its sequel. "These effects, familiar from realist (e.g., Balzac) and modernist (e.g., Faulkner) as well as postmodernist poetics (e.g., Barth, Pynchon), arise because characters who exist 'between' texts, intertextually, seem to approach the ontological status of beings who exist 'outside' texts, in the real world." McHale specifically mentions the transfer of characters, including Mira Enketei, from *Amalgamemnon* to *Verbivore*, which, he says, "has the effect of actualizing them retroactively. It is as if these characters, ontologically so enfeebled by their 'native' context [i.e., the lack of "realized" tenses], somehow acquired a degree of ontological robustness 'between' texts, in the passage from their home text to its sequel" (202). Brian McHale, "'I draw the line as a rule between one solar system and another': The Postmodernism(s) of Christine Brooke-Rose," *Utterly Other Discourse* 192–213. Brooke-Rose includes a joking allusion to the "non-realized" tenses of *Amalgamemnon* in a piece of dialogue in which Mansall Roberts comments on her speech: "That's a lot of conditionals, my dear Miss er-Inkytie . . . ." (*Textermination* 101)

4. One can see this kind of "speculation" as a fictional analogue to the critical conjecture of Virginia Woolf, who ponders what kind of novel Jane Austen would have produced had she written after *Persuasion*: "Her sense of security would have been shaken. Her comedy would have suffered. She would have trusted less (this is already perceptible in *Persuasion*) to dialogue and more to reflection to give us a knowledge of her characters" (231). See "Jane Austen," in *The Virginia Woolf Reader*, ed. Mitchell A. Leaska 220–32. Into the future, beyond Woolf's surmise, Brooke-Rose casts Emma, giving her a postmodern afterlife that is manifested in a split sense of identity.

5. See "Palimpsest History" in Christine Brooke-Rose, *Stories, Theories and Things* 189.

6. For a comparison between Brooke-Rose's use of fantasy to wage cultural critique and Sandra Gilbert and Susan Gubar's "academic" melodrama, *Masterpiece Theater*, see Karen R. Lawrence, "Saving the Text: Cultural Crisis in *Textermination* and *Masterpiece Theatre*," *Narrative* 5 January (1997): 108–16.

CHAPTER EIGHT

1. See John Maynard Smith and Eörs Szathmáry, *The Major Transitions in Evolution* (Oxford: W. H. Freeman, 1995).

2. Quoted in Laplanche and Pontalis, *The Language of Psycho-Analysis*, trans. Donald Nicholson-Smith (New York: W.W. Norton & Co., 1973) 153.

3. Lorna Sage, "Interview by Lorna Sage: Subscript," *Invisible Author: Last Essays* (2002) 170.

4. See Jacques Derrida, "Typewriter Ribbon: Limited Ink (2) ("within such limits")," *Material Events: Paul De Man and the Afterlife of Theory*, ed. Barbara Cohen, Tom Cohen, J. Hillis Miller, and Andrzej Warminski (Minneapolis: University of Minnesota Press, 2001) 345.

5. With the author's permission, I have reproduced this chart in Figure A (pages 172–173). The chart itself is mentioned in chapter 7 of *Invisible Author* in which Brooke-Rose discusses giving it to her publisher and literary executor "to help possible translators, if any, who could otherwise, especially in Romance languages, bring in an unwanted reflexive (pronominalized) verb, often equivalent

to an English intransitive; or fall into other traps in the Slavic languages, which can do without pronouns altogether except for emphasis." Brooke-Rose, *Invisible Author: Last Essays* 155.

6. Although Brooke-Rose is a master of creating poetic metaphors for altered states of being and consciousness, this impulse to represent the basic materials of life in such playfully material language seems to infect scientific journalism (and possibly even scientific writing) as well as her novels. Journalistic representations of the startling completion of the map of the human genome in 2001 include a surprising amount of such language, as found in a striking article in *The New York Times* Science section entitled "Genome Shows Evolution Has an Eye for Hyperbole" by Natalie Angier. In the article Angier describes scientists as having gathered "clues to the sticky, stringy, springy, dynamic, garrulous, gorgeous and preposterous molecule of life that resides in nearly every cell of every human being on earth" (D1), (*Science Times*, Tuesday, February 13, 2001, D1, D5). Eric Lander of the Whitehead Institute for Biomedical Research describes the parasite LINE (Long Interspersed Element) as "the ultimate selfish element that evolved at the beginning of eukaryotes.... It's been wildly successful. It's the perfect parasite" (D5). Some kind of pull toward metaphor as well as mimetic exuberance infects the language of science when it is called upon to convey such momentous discoveries in familiar terms.

7. Telephone conversation with the author, 25 September 2005.

8. Richard Fortey, *Life: An Unauthorised Biography: A Natural History of the First Four Thousand Million Years of Life on Earth* (London: Harper Collins, 1997) 26.

9. Stafania Cassar, "Science as Post-Theory? Discourses of Evolution in Christine Brooke-Rose's *Subscript*," *Post-Theory, Culture, Criticism,* ed. Ivan Callus and Stefan Herbrechter, vol. 23, Critical Studies (Amsterdam: Rodopi, 2004) 202.

10. Brooke-Rose's notes include references to theories of gender differentiation within "a masculine mode of signification." Brooke-Rose Archive, Harry Ransom Humanities Research Center, Austin, Texas.

11. An entire file of notes in Brooke-Rose's archive covers "The Neandertals and their Contemporaries."

12. Henri Bergson, *Creative Evolution* (New York: Random House, 1944) 310–11.

CHAPTER NINE

1. In a telephone conversation, 27 July 2005.

2. Christine Brooke-Rose, "Self-Confrontation and the Writer," *New Literary History* 9.1 (1977): 134.

3. In the chapter "Remaking" in *Invisible Author*, Brooke-Rose discusses her use of this device. See 164–65.

4. Here Brooke-Rose plays on the various geometries of narrative confrontation imagined in structuralist paradigms, a theme developed fictionally in *Between* and *Thru*. As we have seen, the gendered aspects of these paradigms, involving white knights rescuing damsels from evil dragons, is a continuing theme in Brooke-Rose's fiction, replayed in *Remake*. As Brooke-Rose has pointed out, there are constraints for women writers in these paradigms, constraints unacknowledged by male theorists and critics like Todorov, Benveniste, and Jakobson.

5. "So I wrote down my life as I remembered it, in a conventional order, and the result was dreadful. The general formula, to exaggerate a little, was "And then . . . I—this, and then . . . I—that." It was my own life, my own experience, but even I couldn't reread it. So I put it aside" (55). As Brooke-Rose recounts it, the sudden idea of the constraint against personal pronouns freed her to write her autobiography: "Now this was a real challenge: an autobiography without personal pronouns. Suddenly, I got interested again. I had the constraint I needed" (57).

6. Imp Plus, the protagonist, thinks of the word "vegetable" and thinks: "And a green thing like an idea. Imp Plus remembered words that he did not know." Joseph McElroy, *Plus* (New York: Alfred A. Knopf, 1977) 4. Brooke-Rose presented her "theory" to McElroy in a letter, but, apparently, he never addressed it. According to Brooke-Rose, her own novel *Such* began with a sign that she saw while traveling in Portugal: "Silence says the notice on the stairs and the stairs creak" (203, *Omnibus*).

7. Peter Consenstein, *Literary Memory, Consciousness, and the Group Oulipo* (Amsterdam: Rodopi, 2002) 39. Consenstein points out that Jacque Roubaud's *La Boucle* is a life-story that employs the constraint of using the present tense to narrate the life (48). *La Boucle* was published in 1993.

8. In chapter one of *A Portrait of the Artist as a Young Man*, Stephen reads what he has written on the flyleaf of his geography book: "Stephen Dedalus/Class of Elements/Clongowes Wood College/Sallins/County Kildare/Ireland/Europe/The World/The Universe." A different passage in *Ulysses*, capturing an older Stephen Dedalus's thoughts about death as he walks on the strand, more resembles the passage on decomposition in *Life, End Of*: "God becomes man becomes fish becomes barnacle goose becomes featherbed mountain." James Joyce, *Ulysses*, ed. Hans Walter Gabler, 3, 477–79.

9. In the chapter, "File: Pro-nouns" in *Remake*, which includes the diary entry on her mother's death, the old lady describes her mother's convent surroundings as "Serenity everywhere. But she is isolated in her god-Routine" (28).

10. Paraphrase replaces quotation in this last text because, in a further case of life and art intertwining, Brooke-Rose, the author, like the invalid, can no longer ascend the stairs of her own home. Her access to her library and her computer is therefore limited to the assistance of the few people she hires to assist her.

11. Brooke-Rose described the way the book records a "clinging to the world, a world completely filtered by one's own memory." It captures the way that old people "see the body bits going" (telephone conversation with author, July 29, 2005). One thinks back to "The Foot."

BIBLIOGRAPHY

Angier, Natalie. (2001). "Genome Shows Evolution Has an Eye for Hyperbole." *The New York Times*, February 13: D1, D5.
Armstrong, Nancy. (1987). *Desire and Domestic Fiction: A Political History of the Novel*. New York: Oxford University Press.
Attridge, Derek. (2004). *J. M. Coetzee and the Ethics of Reading: Literature in the Event*. Chicago: The University of Chicago Press.
Barthes, Roland. (1974). *S/Z: An Essay*. Trans. Richard Miller. New York: Hill and Wang.
———. (1975). *The Pleasure of the Text*. New York: Hill and Wang.
———. (1978). *A Lover's Discourse: Fragments*. Trans. Richard Howard. New York: Hill and Wang.
Barton, Celia. (1982). "Review." *Poetics Today* 3(3): 233–38.
Beer, Gillian. (1992). "The Island and the Aeroplane: The Case of Virginia Woolf." In *Virginia Woolf*. Ed. Rachel Bowlby. London: Longman: 132–61.
Benjamin, Walter. (1969). "The Storyteller: Reflections on the Works of Nikolai Leskov." In *Illuminations*. Trans. Harry Zohn. Ed. Hannah Arendt. New York: Schoecken Books: 83–109.
Benstock, Shari. (1991). *Textualizing the Feminine: On the Limits of Genre*. Norman: University of Oklahoma Press.
Benveniste, Émile. (1971). "Remarks on the Function of Language in Freudian

Theory." In *Problems in General Linguistics*. Trans. Mary Elizabeth Meek. Coral Gables: University of Miami Press: 65–75.
Bergonzi, Bernard. (1983). "A Strange Disturbing World." *Encounter* 58(142): 58–67.
Bergson, Henri. (1944). *Creative Evolution*. Trans. Arthur Mitchell. New York: Random House.
Bernheimer, Charles, and Claire Kahane, eds. (1985). *In Dora's Case: Freud-Hysteria-Feminism*. New York: Columbia University Press.
Berressem, Hanjo. (1995). "Thru the Looking Glass: A Journey into the Universe of Discourse." *Review of Contemporary Fiction* 9(3): 128–33.
Bersani, Leo, and Ulysse Dutoit. (1985). *The Forms of Violence: Narrative in Assyrian Art and Modern Culture*. New York: Schocken Books.
Bierce, Ambrose. (1970). "Moxon's Master." *The Complete Short Stories of Ambrose Bierce*. Garden City, NY: Doubleday & Company, Inc.: 89–97.
Birch, Sarah. (1994). *Christine Brooke-Rose and Contemporary Fiction*. Oxford: Clarendon Press.
Blain, Virginia, Patricia Clements, and Isobel Grundy, eds. (1990). *The Feminist Companion to Literature in English: Women Writers from the Middle Ages to the Present*. London: B. T. Batsford.
Blanchot, Maurice. (1986). *The Writing of the Disaster*. Trans. Ann Smock. Lincoln: University of Nebraska Press.
Bloch, Ernst, and Theodor W. Adorno. (1988). *The Utopian Function of Art and Literature: Selected Essays*. Trans. Jack Zipes and Fran Mecklenberg. Cambridge, MA: The MIT Press.
———. (1988). "Art and Utopia." In *The Utopian Function of Art and Literature* 78–155.
———. (1988). "Something's Missing: A Discussion between Ernst Bloch and Theodor W. Adorono on the Contradictions of Utopian Longing. In *The Utopian Function of Art and Literature* 1–17.
Bolter, J. David. (1984). *Turing's Man: Western Culture in the Computer Age*. Chapel Hill: The University of North Carolina Press.
Boncza-Tomaszewski, Tom. (2005). "Christine Brooke-Rose: The Texterminator." *The Independent Online Edition*. 27 March.
Brooke-Rose, Christine. (1947). "La syntax et le symbolisme dans la poesie de Hopkins." *Europe* 25: 17.
Brooke-Rose, Christine. (1955). "The Use of Metaphor in Some Old French and Middle English Lyrics and Romances." Ph.D. dissertation, London: University of London.
Brooke-Rose, Christine. (1955). "The Voice of Eternity." *Times Literary Supplement* (17 June): 325–26.
Brooke-Rose, Christine. (1955). "The Mickiewicz Centenary." *Tablet* (26 November): 527.
Brooke-Rose, Christine. (1957). *The Languages of Love*. London: Secker and Warburg.
Brooke-Rose, Christine. (1958). *The Sycamore Tree*. London: Secker and Warburg.
Brooke-Rose, Christine. (1958). *A Grammar of Metaphor*. London: Secker and Warburg.
Brooke-Rose, Christine. (1958). "Samuel Beckett and the Anti-Novel." *The London Magazine* 5: 38–46.

Brooke-Rose, Christine. (1959). "Mood of the Month." *The London Magazine* (September): 45–50.
Brooke-Rose, Christine. (1959). "The Critic's Eye." *Times Literary Supplement* (20 March): 160.
Brooke-Rose, Christine. (1959). "Return from Avilion." *Times Literary Supplement* (25 December): 755.
Brooke-Rose, Christine. (1960). *The Dear Deceit*. London: Secker and Warburg.
Brooke-Rose, Christine. (1960). "Southey Ends His Song." *Times Literary Supplement* (1 April): 208.
Brooke-Rose, Christine. (1960). "His Name in the Record." *Time Literary Supplement* (10 June): 368.
Brooke-Rose, Christine. (1960). "Feeding Mind." *Times Literary Supplement* (1 July): 417.
Brooke-Rose, Christine. (1961). *The Middlemen: A Satire*. London: Secker and Warburg.
Brooke-Rose, Christine. (1961). "Ezra Pound: Piers Plowman in the Modern Waste Land." *Review of English Literature* 2(2): 74–88.
Brooke-Rose, Christine. (1961). "The Vanishing Author." *Observer* (12 February): 26.
Brooke-Rose, Christine. (1961). "The American Literary Scene: Writers in Search of Community." *Observer* (30 April): 28.
Brooke-Rose, Christine. (1961). "Anatomy of Originophobia." *Times Literary Supplement* (19 May): 308.
Brooke-Rose, Christine. (1961). "Buzzards, Bloody Owls, and One Hawk." *The London Magazine* (September): 76–80.
Brooke-Rose, Christine. (1961). "Review of *Jealousy*." *The London Magazine* (February): 74.
Brooke-Rose, Christine. (1963). "Notes on the Metre of Auden's *The Age of Anxiety*." *Essays in Criticism* 3(3): 253–64.
Brooke-Rose, Christine. (1964). *Out*. London: Michael Joseph.
Brooke-Rose, Christine. (1964). "L'Imagination baroque de Robbe-Grillet." *Revue des Lettres Modernes* 94(5): 129–52.
Brooke-Rose, Christine. (1964). "Lady Precious Stream." *The London Magazine* (May): 93–96.
Brooke-Rose, Christine. (1964). "Where Have All the Lovers Gone?" *The London Magazine* (June): 80–86.
Brooke-Rose, Christine. (1964). "Out of the Past." *Spectator* (12 June): 802.
Brooke-Rose, Christine. (1965). "Dynamic Gradients." *The London Magazine* (March): 89–96.
Brooke-Rose, Christine. (1965). "Metaphor in *Paradise Lost*." In *Language and Style in Milton: A Symposium in Honour of the Tercentary of Paradise Lost*. Ed. R. Emma and J. T. Shawcross. New York: Ungar: 252–303.
Brooke-Rose, Christine. (1965–66). "The Baroque Imagination of Robbe-Grillet." *Modern Fiction Studies* 11(4): 405–23.
Brooke-Rose, Christine. (1966). *Such*. London: Michael Joseph.
Brooke-Rose, Christine. (1966). "Making It New." *Observer* (2 October): 26.
Brooke-Rose, Christine. (1967). "Lettres Angleterre." *Nouvelle Revue Française* (June): 124–29.
Brooke-Rose, Christine. (1967). "Lay By Me Aurelie." In *New Approaches to Ezra Pound*. Ed. Eva Hesse. London: Faber and Faber: 242–69.

Brooke-Rose, Christine. (1968). *Between*. London: Michael Joseph.
Brooke-Rose, Christine. (1968). "French Fiction: The Long Revolution." *The Times* (3 August): 18.
Brooke-Rose, Christine. (1968). "La Devaluation du livre." *Le Monde* (24 January, Supplement to no. 7): 163.
Brooke-Rose, Christine. (1968). "Claude Lévi-Strauss: A New Multi-Dimensional Way of Thinking." *The Times* (2 March): 20.
Brooke-Rose, Christine. (1970). *Go When You See The Green Man Walking*. London: Michael Joseph.
Brooke-Rose, Christine. (1970). "On Terms." In *Go When You See the Green Man Walking*. London: Michael Joseph: 17–31.
Brooke-Rose, Christine. (1970). "George and the Seraph." In *Go When You See the Green Man Walking*. London: Michael Joseph: 7–16.
Brooke-Rose, Christine. (1970). "The Foot." In *Go When You See the Green Man Walking*. London: Michael Joseph: 43–64.
Brooke-Rose, Christine. (1971). *A ZBC of Ezra Pound*. London: Faber and Faber.
Brooke-Rose, Christine. (1973). "Viewpoint." *Times Literary Supplement* (1 June): 614.
Brooke-Rose, Christine. (1976). "An Excerpt from the Novel *Thru*: Author's Note." *New Directions* 33: 144.
Brooke-Rose, Christine. (1976). "Historical Genres/Theoretical Genres: A Discussion of Todorov on the Fantastic." *New Literary History* 8(1): 145–58.
Brooke-Rose, Christine. (1976). "The Squirm of the True I: An Essay in Non-Methodology." *Poetics and the Theory of Literature* 1(2): 265–94.
Brooke-Rose, Christine. (1976). "The Squirm of the True II: The Long Glasses—A Structural Analysis." *Poetics and the Theory of Literature* 1(3): 513–46.
Brooke-Rose, Christine. (1976). "Paris Letter: Dramatics." *Spectator* (28 February): 25.
Brooke-Rose, Christine. (1976). "Letter from Paris: Ganging Up." *Spectator* (27 March): 26.
Brooke-Rose, Christine. (1976). "Letter from Paris: Tricolor Tape." *Spectator* (22 May): 26.
Brooke-Rose, Christine. (1976). "Letter from Paris: Le Pop." *Spectator* (12 June): 26.
Brooke-Rose, Christine. (1976). "Letter from Paris: All the City is a Stage." *Spectator* (24 July): 25.
Brooke-Rose, Christine. (1977). "Self-Confrontation and the Writer." *New Literary History* 9 (1): 129–36.
Brooke-Rose, Christine. (1977). "The Squirm of the True III: Surface Structure in Narrative." *Poetics and the Theory of Literature* 2(3): 517–62.
Brooke-Rose, Christine. (1977). "Imitations are Proof of New Writing's Power." *The Times* (31 May): vii.
Brooke-Rose, Christine. (1978). "Trangressions: An Essay-say on the Novel Novel Novel." *Contemporary Literature* 19(3): 378–407.
Brooke-Rose, Christine. (1980). "The Readerhood of Man." In *The Reader in the Text: Essays in Audience and Interpretation*. Ed. Susan R. Suleiman and Inge Crosman. Princeton, NJ: Princeton University Press: 120–48.
Brooke-Rose, Christine. (1980). "Round and Round the Jakobson Diagram: A Survey." *Hebrew Studies in Literature* 8(2): 153–82.
Brooke-Rose, Christine. (1980). "The Evil Ring: Realism and the Marvelous." *Poetics Today* 1(4): 67–90.

Brooke-Rose, Christine. (1980). "Where Do We Go From Here?" *Granta* 3: 161–88.
Brooke-Rose, Christine. (1981). "Eximplosions." In *A Rhetoric of the Unreal*. Cambridge: Cambridge University Press: 339–63.
Brooke-Rose, Christine. (1981). *A Rhetoric of the Unreal: Studies in Narrative and Structure, Especially of the Fantastic*. Cambridge: Cambridge University Press.
Brooke-Rose, Christine. (1982). "Eximplosions." *Genre* 14(11): 9–21.
Brooke-Rose, Christine. (1983). "Théorie des genres: la science-fiction." In *Poétique(s): Domaine anglais*. Ed. Alain Bony. Lyon, France: Presses Universitaires de Lyon: 251–62.
Brooke-Rose, Christine. (1984). *Amalgamemnon*. Manchester: Carcanet.
Brooke-Rose, Christine. (1984). "Fiction, Figment, Feindre." *Fabula* 3: 121–32.
Brooke-Rose, Christine. (1985). "Woman as a Semiotic Object." *Poetics Today* 6(1): 9–20.
Brooke-Rose, Christine. (1985). "Palimpsestes en paragrammes: une 'phrase narrative' bien cachée." *Caliban: L'Esthétique de la science-fiction* 22: 87–99.
Brooke-Rose, Christine. (1985). "Illusions of Parody." *Amerikanstudien/American Studies* 30(2): 225–33.
Brooke-Rose, Christine. (1986). *The Christine Brooke-Rose Omnibus: Four Novels*. New York: Carcanet. Contains *Out, Such, Between, Thru*.
Brooke-Rose, Christine. (1986). *Xorandor*. Manchester: Carcanet.
Brooke-Rose, Christine. (1986). "The Dissolution of Character in the Novel." In *Reconstructing Individualism: Autonomy, Individuality, and the Self in Western Thought*. Ed. Morton Sosna, Thomas Heller, and David E. Wellbery. Stanford, CA: Stanford University Press: 184–96.
Brooke-Rose, Christine. (1986). "Ill Logics of Irony." In *New Essays on The Red Badge of Courage*. Ed. Lee Clark Mitchell. Cambridge: Cambridge University Press: 129–46.
Brooke-Rose, Christine. (1986). "Un poème sur tout." *Quinzaine Littéraire* 16(31) (May): 5–6.
Brooke-Rose, Christine. (1986). "Problématique de la réception." *Revue française des études américaines* (November): 393–98.
Brooke-Rose, Christine. (1987). "A for But: 'The Custom House' in Hawthorne's *The Scarlet Letter*." *Word and Image* 3(2): 143–55.
Brooke-Rose, Christine. (1987). "Cheng Ming Child." *PN Review* 13(5): 29–37.
Brooke-Rose, Christine. (1987). "Id is, is id?" In *Discourse in Psychoanalysis and Literature*. Ed. Shlomith Rimmon-Kenan. London and New York: Methuen: 19–37.
Brooke-Rose, Christine. (1988). "Ill Locutions." *Review of Contemporary Fiction* 8(3): 67–81.
Brooke-Rose, Christine. (1988). "Ill Wit and Good Humor: Women's Comedy and the Canon." *Comparative Criticism* 10: 121–38.
Brooke-Rose, Christine. (1989). "Illiterations." In *Breaking the Sequence: Women's Experimental Fiction*. Ed. Ellen J. Friedman and Miriam Fuchs. Princeton, NJ: Princeton University Press.
Brooke-Rose, Christine. (1989). "Ill Wit and Sick Tragedy: *Jude the Obscure*." In *Alternative Hardy*. Ed. Lance St. John Butler. Basingstoke: Macmillan: 26–48.
Brooke-Rose, Christine. (1989). "Stories, Theories and Things." *New Literary History* 21(1): 121–31.
Brooke-Rose, Christine. (1989). "Illicitations." *Review of Contemporary Fiction* 9(3): 101–9.

Brooke-Rose, Christine. (1990). *Verbivore*. Manchester: Carcanet.
Brooke-Rose, Christine. (1990). "Diary." *London Review of Books* (10 May): 25.
Brooke-Rose, Christine. (1991). "Id is, is id?" In *Stories, Theories and Things*. Cambridge: Cambridge University Press: 28–44.
Brooke-Rose, Christine. (1991). *Stories, Theories and Things*. Cambridge: Cambridge University Press.
Brooke-Rose, Christine. (1991). *Textermination*. Manchester: Carcanet.
Brooke-Rose, Christine. (1991). "Whatever Happened to Narratology?" *Poetics Today* 11(2): 283–93.
Brooke-Rose, Christine. (1991). "A Womb of One's Own." In *Stories, Theories, and Things*. Cambridge: Cambridge University Press: 223–34.
Brooke-Rose, Christine. (1991). "Woman as Semiotic Object." In *Stories, Theories and Things*. Cambridge: Cambridge University Press: 237–49.
Brooke-Rose, Christine. (1992). "Letter to Author." 5 August.
Brooke-Rose, Christine. (1992). "Palimpsest History in Umberto Eco, Richard Rorty, Jonathan Culler, and Christine Brooke-Rose." In *Interpretation and Over-Interpretation*. Ed. Stefan Collini. Cambridge: Cambridge University Press: 125–38.
Brooke-Rose, Christine. (1996). *Remake*. Manchester: Carcanet.
Brooke-Rose, Christine. (1999). *Subscript*. Manchester: Carcanet.
Brooke-Rose, Christine. (2002). *Invisible Author: Last Essays*. Columbus: The Ohio State University Press.
Brooke-Rose, Christine. (2003). E-mail to author. 20 October.
Brooke-Rose, Christine. (2003). "Gifts Above Price: The Legacy of Ezra Pound." In *Make It New: The Rise of Modernism*. Ed. Kurt Heinzelman. Austin, TX: Harry Ransom Humanities Research Center: 11–13.
Brooke-Rose, Christine. (2004). E-mail to author. July 22.
Brooke-Rose, Christine. (2004). E-mail to author." October 11.
Brooke-Rose, Christine. (2005). Telephone conversation with author. 27 July.
Brooke-Rose, Christine. (2005). Telephone conversation with author. 29 July.
Brooke-Rose, Christine. (2005). Telephone conversation with author. 25 September.
Brooke-Rose, Christine. (2006). *Life, End Of*. Manchester: Carcanet.
Brooks, Peter. (1984). *Reading for the Plot: Design and Intention in Narrative*. New York: Vintage Books.
Brophy, Brigid. (1969). *In Transit: An Heroi-Cyclic Novel*. New York: G. P. Putnam's Sons.
Brown, Norman O. (1966). *Love's Body*. New York: Random House.
Buchanan, Brad. (1999). "'A Blind Spot in Your Own Youdipeon Discourse': Christine Brooke-Rose, Oedipus, and the Synecdochic Narrative." *Hungarian Journal of English and American Studies* 5(2): 195–208.
Byatt, A. S. (1987). Programme 6: The Yorkshire Ripper, Melvyn Bragg, Christine Brooke-Rose. *Bookmark*. London: BBC 2.
Cameron, Sharon. (1979). *Lyric Time: Dickinson and the Limits of Genre*. Baltimore: John Hopkins University Press.
Canepari-Labib, Michela. (2002). *Word-Worlds: Language, Identity and Reality in the Work of Christine Brooke-Rose*. Oxford: Peter Lang.
Caserio, Robert L. (1988). "Mobility and Masochism: Christine Brooke-Rose and J. G. Ballard." *Novel* 21 (Winter–Spring): 292–310.
———. (2004). "Edwardians to Georgians." In *The Cambridge History of English*

Literature. Ed. L. Marcus and P. Nicholls. Cambridge, England: Cambridge University Press.

Cassar, Stefania. (2004). "Science as Post-Theory? Discourses of Evolution in Christine Brooke-Rose's *Subscript.*" In *Post-Theory, Culture, Criticism.* Ed. Ivan Callus and Stefan Herbrechter. Amsterdam: Rodopi. 23 *Critical Studies:* 189–204.

Cixous, Hélène and Catherine Clément. (1986). *The Newly Born Woman.* Trans. Betsy Wing. Minneapolis: University of Minnesota Press.

Coetzee, J. M. (1999). *Disgrace.* London: Secker and Warburg.

Consenstein, Peter. (2002). *Literary Memory, Consciousness, and the Group Oulipo.* Amsterdam: Rodopi.

Dasenbrock, Reed Way. (1992). "Anatomies of Internationalism in *Tarr* and *Howards End.*" Unpublished paper presented at the 108th Annual Meeting of the Modern Language Association, New York. 28 December.

David-Ménard, Monique. (1989). *Hysteria From Freud to Lacan: Body and Language in Psychoanalysis.* Trans. Catherine Porter. Foreword by Ned Lukacher. Ithaca and London: Cornell University Press.

de Man, Paul. (1986). *The Resistance to Theory.* Minneapolis: University of Minnesota Press.

Derrida, Jacques. (1977). "Signature Event Context." *Glyph.* Baltimore: The Johns Hopkins University Press.

———. (1984). "No Apocalypse, Not Now (Full Speed Ahead, Seven Missiles, Seven Missives)." *Diacritics* 14: 20–31.

———. (1985). "Des Tours de Babel." *Differences in Translation.* Ithaca: Cornell University Press: 165–207.

———. (1991). *Cinders.* Translation and introduction Ned Lukacher. Lincoln: University of Nebraska Press.

———. (1993). *Memoirs of the Blind: The Self-Portrait and Other Ruins.* Trans. Pascale-Anne Brault and Michael Naas. University of Chicago Press.

———. (1994). *Specters of Marx: The State of the Debt, the Work of Mourning, and the New International.* London: Routledge.

———. (2001). "Typewriter Ribbon: Limited Ink (2) ('within such limits')." Trans. Peggy Kamuf. In *Material Events: Paul de Man and the Afterlife of Theory.* Ed. Barbara Cohen. Tom Cohen, J. Hillis Miller, and Andrzej Warminski. Minneapolis: University of Minnesota Press: 277–360.

Dick, Kay. (1973). "Christine Brooke-Rose." In *Littérature de notre temps.* Paris: Casterman.

Dimock, Wai Chee. (2006). *Through Other Continents: American Literature across Deep Time.* Princeton: Princeton University Press.

Drabble, Margaret, ed. (1985). *The Oxford Companion to English Literature.* Oxford: Oxford University Press.

Felman, Shoshana. (1977). "Turning the Screw of Interpretation." *Yale French Studies* (Summer 1977); 55–56.

Ffrench, Patrick. (1995). *The Time of Theory: A History of Tel Quel (1960–1983).* Oxford: Clarendon Press.

Fortey, Richard. (1997). *Life: An Unauthorised Biography: A Natural History of the First Four Thousand Million Years of Life on Earth.* London: HarperCollins.

Freud, Sigmund. (1960). *Jokes and Their Relation to the Unconscious.* In *The Standard Edition of the Complete Psychological Works of Sigmund Freud.* Vol. 8 (1905). Trans. James Strachey. London: The Hogarth Press.

Friedman, Ellen G. and Miriam Fuchs (1995). "A Conversation with Christine Brooke-Rose." In *Utterly Other Discourse: The Texts of Christine Brooke-Rose*. Ed. Ellen G. Friedman and Richard Martin. Normal, IL: Dalkey Archive Press: 29–37.

———, eds. (1995). *Utterly Other Discourse: The Texts of Christine Brooke-Rose*. Normal, IL: Dalkey Archive Press.

Fuchs, Miriam. (1989). "Contexts and Continuities: An Introduction to Women's Experimental Fiction in English." In *Breaking the Sequence: Women's Experimental Fiction*. Ed. Ellen G. Friedman and Miriam Fuchs. Princeton: Princeton University Press.

Gallop, Jane. (1982). *The Daughter's Seduction: Feminism and Psychoanalysis*. Ithaca: Cornell University Press.

Garlinski, Józeph. (1960). Review of Wladyslaw Kozaczuk, *W. Kregu Enigmy*. *New Scientist* (October 16): 73–74.

Gilbert, Sandra M., and Susan Gubar. (1995). *Masterpiece Theatre: An Academic Melodrama*. New Brunswick: Rutgers University Press.

Greimas, A. J. (1987). *On Meaning: Selected Writings in Semiotic Theory*. Trans. Paul J. Perron and Frank Collins. Foreword by Fredric Jameson. Minneapolis: University of Minnesota Press.

Hall, John. (1976). "Christine Brooke-Rose." In *Contemporary Novelists*. Ed. James Vinson. London and New York: St. James Press and St. Martins Press: 182–84.

Hanssen, Beatrice. "'The Correct/Just Point of Departure': Deconstruction, Humanism, and the Call to Responsibility." In *Enlightenments: Encounters between Critical Theory and Contemporary French Thought*. Eds. Harry Kunneman and Hent de Vries. Kampen, Netherlands: Kok Pharos, 1993: 194–210.

Hawkins, Susan E. (1989). "Memory and Discourse: Fictionalizing the Present in *Xorandor*." *Review of Contemporary Fiction* 9(3): 138–43.

Hayles, N. Katherine. (1999). *How We Became Posthuman: Virtual Bodies in Cybernetics, Literature, and Informatics*. Chicago and London: University of Chicago Press.

Hayman, David. (1977). "Some Writers in the Wake of the *Wake*." *TriQuarterly* 38: 3–38.

Heidegger, Martin. (1968). *The Question Concerning Technology*. New York: Harper & Row.

Heise, Ursula K. (1997). *Chronoschisms: Time, Narrative, and Postmodernism*. Cambridge: Cambridge University Press.

Herbert, Christopher. (1991). *Culture and Anomie: Ethnographic Imagination in the Nineteenth Century*. Chicago: University of Chicago Press.

Hutcheon, Linda. (1988). *A Poetics of Postmodernism: History, Theory, Fiction*. New York: Routledge.

Irigaray, Luce. (1985). *This Sex Which Is Not One*. Trans. Catherine Porter with Carolyn Burke. Ithaca: Cornell University Press.

Jameson, Fredric. (1981). *The Political Unconscious: Narrative as a Socially Symbolic Act*. Ithaca: Cornell University Press.

Jay, Martin. (1993). *Downcast Eyes: The Denigration of Vision in Twentieth-Century French Thought*. Berkeley: University of California Press.

Joyce, James. (1986). *Ulysses*. Ed. Hans Walter Gabler. New York: Random House.

Kafalenos, Emma. (1980). "Textasy: Christine Brooke-Rose's *Thru*." *The International Fiction Review* 7(1): 43–6.

Lacan, Jacques. (1977). "The Agency of the Letter in the Unconscious or Reason since Freud." In *Écrits: A Selection*. Trans. Alan Sheridan. New York: W. W. Norton: 146–78.

———. (1977). *Ecrits: A Selection*. Trans. Alen Sheridan. New York: Norton.

———. (1977). "Subversion of the Subject and Dialectic of Desire in the Freudian Unconscious." In *Écrits: A Selection*. Trans. Alen Sheridan. New York: Norton: 292–324.

Laplanche, Jean, and J. B. Pontalis. (1973). *The Language of Psycho-analysis*. Trans. Donald Nicholson-Smith. New York: W.W. Norton & Co.

Lawrence, Karen R. (1983). Review of Wilde's *Horizons of Assent*. *Novel* 16: 177–81.

———. (1994). "Postmodern 'Vessels of Conception': Brooke-Rose and Brophy." In *Penelope Voyages: Women and Travel in the British Literary Tradition*. Ithaca: Cornell University Press: 207–36.

———. (1997). "Saving the Text: Cultural Crisis in *Textermination* and Masterpiece Theatre." *Narrative* 5 (January): 108–16.

———. (2005). Discussion with the Author.

———. (2005). "Who Could Have Read the Signs? Politics and Prediction in Gertrude Stein's *Mrs. Reynolds* and Christine Brooke-Rose's *Amalgamemnon*." *Western Humanities Review* 59(2): 18–38.

———. (Fall 2003 and Winter 2004). "Close Encounters." *James Joyce Quarterly* 41(nos. 1 and 2): 127–42.

Lercercle, Jean-Jacques. (1991). "Une lecture d'*Amalgamemnon* de Christine Brooke-Rose." *Tropismes* 5: 263–90.

———. (1995). "Reading *Amalgamemnon*." In *Utterly Other Discourse: The Texts of Christine Brooke-Rose*. Ed. Ellen G. Friedman and Richard Martin. Normal, IL: Dalkey Archive Press: 153–69.

Levitt, Morton P. (1983). "Christine Brooke-Rose." *Dictionary of Literary Biography*. Ed. Jay L. Halio. Detroit: Bruccoli Clark. 14: 124–9.

Lewin, Ronald. (1980). *Ultra Goes to War: The First Account of World War II's Greatest Secret, Based on Official Documents*. New York: Pocket Books.

Little, Judy. (1989). "*Amalgamemnon* and the Politics of Narrative." *Review of Contemporary Fiction* 9(3): 134–7.

MacCannell, Dean. (1976). *The Tourist: A New Theory of the Leisure Class*. New York: Schocken.

Martin, Richard. (1989). "Just Words on a Page: The Novels of Christine Brooke-Rose." *Review of Contemporary Fiction* 9(3): 110–23.

———. (1989). "Stepping Stones into the Dark: Redundancy and Generation in Christine Brooke-Rose's *Amalgamemnon*." In *Breaking the Sequence: Women's Experimental Fiction*. Ed. Ellen G. Friedman and Miriam Fuchs. Princeton: Princeton University Press: 177–87.

McElroy, Joseph. (1977). *Plus*. New York: Alfred A. Knopf.

———. (undated). Letter to Christine Brooke-Rose.

McHale, Brian. (1982). *Poetics Today* 3(2): 186.

———. (1982). "Writing about Postmodern Writing." *Poetics Today* 3(3): 211–27.

———. (1992). *Constructing Postmodernism*. London: Routledge.

———. (1995). "'I draw the line as a rule between one solar system and another': The Postmodernism(s) of Christine Brooke-Rose. In *Utterly Other Discourse: The Texts of Christine Brooke-Rose*. Ed. Ellen G. Friedman and Richard Martin. Normal, IL: Dalkey Archive Press: 192–213.

Mehlman, Jeffrey. "How to Read Freud on Jokes: The Critic as Schadchen." *New Literary History* 6(2) (Winter 1975): 439–61.
Miller, David M. (1983). *Modern Fiction Studies* 29(2): 353–56.
Morton, Brian. (1984). Glimpse into the Future Tense. *Times Higher Education Supplement* (October).
Motte, Jr., Warren F., ed. (1986). *Oulipo: A Primer of Potential Literature*. Lincoln: University of Nebraska Press.
Moylan, Tom. (2001) "'Look into the Dark': On Dystopia and the *Novum*." In *Learning from Other Worlds: Estrangement, Cognition, and the Politics of Science Fiction and Utopia*. Ed. Patrick Parrinder. Durham: Duke University Press: 51–71.
Nash, Cristopher. (1987). *World Postmodern Fiction: A Guide*. London and New York: Longman.
Nuttall, A. D. (1982). "Really Fantastic." *London Review of Books*. 4 (November 18): 18.
Orlando, Francesco. (2006). *Obsolete Objects in the Literary Imagination: Ruins, Relics, Rarities, Rubbish, Uninhabited Places, and Hidden Treasures*. Trans. Gabriel Pihas and Daniel Seidel. New Haven: Yale University Press.
Ousby, Ian, ed. (1988). *The Cambridge Guide to Literature in English*. Cambridge and New York: Cambridge University Press.
Owen, E. (1983). "Systemic Criticism." *English* 32(142): 95–103.
Parrinder, Patrick. (1983). Review of *A Rhetoric of the Unreal*. *Modern Language Review* 78(2): 417–18.
Perec, Georges. (1994). *A Void*. Trans. Gilbert Adair. London: HarperCollins.
Pratt, Terrence W. (1984). *Programming Languages: Design and Implementation*. 2nd ed. Englewood Cliffs, NJ: Prentice-Hall.
Queneau, Raymond. (1986). "Potential Literature." In *Oulipo: A Primer of Potential Literature*. Ed. W. F. Motte, Jr. Lincoln: University of Nebraska Press: 51–64.
Richardson, Dorothy M. (1979). *Dawn's Left Hand*. In *Pilgrimage*. Vol. 4: 131–267. Urbana: University of Illinois Press.
———. *Oberland*. In *Pilgrimage*. Vol. 4: 9–127. Urbana: University of Illinois Press.
Rimmon-Kenan, Shlomith. (1982). "Ambiguity and Narrative Levels: Christine Brooke-Rose's *Thru*." *Poetics Today* 3(1): 21–32.
Robbe-Grillet, Alain. (1965). *Towards a New Novel*. Trans. Barbara Wright. London: Calder and Boyars.
———. (1967). *In the Labyrinth*. Trans. Christine Brooke-Rose. London: Calder and Boyars.
Rose, Mark. (1984). Review of *A Rhetoric of the Unreal*. *Comparative Literature* 36(2): 169–171.
Rushdie, Salman. (1996). "In Defense of the Novel, Yet Again." *The New Yorker* 24 (24 June and 1 July): 48–55.
Sage, Lorna. (2002). "Interview by Lorna Sage: Subscript." *Invisible Author: Last Essays*. Columbus: The Ohio State University Press: 169–80.
Silverman, Kaja. (1983). *The Subject of Semiotics*. New York: Oxford University Press.
Smith, John Maynard,, and Eörs Szathmáry (1995). *The Major Transitions in Evolution*. Oxford: W. H. Freeman.
Sobchack, Vivian. (1995). "Beating the Meat/Surviving the Text, or How to Get Out of This Century Alive." In *Cyberspace/Cyberbodies/Cyberpunk: Cultures of*

Technological Embodiment. Ed. Mikie Feathers and Roger Burrows. London: Sage Publications: 205–14.
Sontag, Susan. (1971). "The Aesthetics of Silence." In *The Discontinuous Universe: Selected Writings in Contemporary Consciousness*. Ed. Sallie Sears and Georgianna W. Lord. New York: Basic Books: 50–75.
Stein, Gertrude. (1945). *Wars I Have Seen*. New York: Random House.
———. (1969). *Narration: Four Lectures by Gertrude Stein*. Westport: Greenwood.
Stevenson, Randall. (1991). "Postmodernism and Contemporary Fiction in Britain." In *Postmodernism and Contemporary Fiction*. Ed. Edward J. Smyth. London: B. T. Batsford Ltd.
Stewart, Garrett. (1984). *Death Sentences: Styles of Dying in British Fiction*. Cambridge, MA: Harvard University Press.
Stewart, Susan. (1993). *On Longing: Narratives of the Miniature, the Gigantic, the Souvenir, the Collection*. Durham, NC: Duke University Press.
Suleiman, Susan Rubin. (1989). "Living Between, or, the Loveliness of the Alleinstehende Frau." *Review of Contemporary Fiction* 9(3): 124–7.
Terdiman, Richard. (2005). *Body and Story: The Ethics and Practice of Theoretical Conflict*. Baltimore: The Johns Hopkins University Press.
Tongola, Silvia. (1983). "'The Foot': A Pragmalinguistic Analysis." Zurich: Zurich University.
Turner, Jenny. (1990). "Reclaim the Brain: Christine Brooke-Rose Interviewed." *Edinburgh Review* 84: 19–40.
White, Glyn. (2002). "'You are Here': Reading and Representation in Christine Brooke-Rose's *Thru*." *Poetics Today* 23(4): 611–31.
———. (2005). *Reading the Graphic Surface: The Presence of the Book in Prose Fiction*. Manchester, England: Manchester University Press.
Wilde, Alan. (1981). *Horizons of Assent: Modernism, Postmodernism, and the Ironic Imagination*. Baltimore: Johns Hopkins University Press.
Wittig, Monique. (1985). "The Mark of Gender." *Feminist Issues* 5: 1–12.
Wolfe, Gary K. (1982). "Unreal Rhetoric." *Science Fiction Studies* 9(3): 330–31.
Wood, Michael. (2003). *The Road to Delphi: The Life and Afterlife of Oracles*. New York: Farrar, Straus and Giroux.
Woolf, Virginia. (1984). "Jane Austen." In *The Virginia Woolf Reader*. Ed. Mitchell A. Leaska. San Diego: Harcourt Brace Jovanovich: 220–32.
Wordsworth, William. (1982). "Nuns Fret Not at Their Convent's Narrow Room." *The Poetical Works of Wordsworth*. Boston: Houghton-Mifflin Company: 346.

INDEX

abjection, 9, 13, 22, 24, 25, 38, 54, 198
Adair, Gilbert, 21, 219n10
Adorno, Theodor, 108, 109, 112
Agamemnon, 99, 101
aging: Brooke-Rose's, 195–96, 231n11; in *Life, End Of,* 180, 183–84, 185, 186, 188
AI (Spielberg), 225n20
Aka (*Subscript*), 151, 155, 157, 166, 168–70
Amalgamemnon, 99–116; absence of constative sentences in, 20, 104, 105, 122, 226n10; absence of third-person past tense in, 104–5; alternate future in, 104, 107; ambiguity in, 129; and Herodotus, 102, 103, 104, 107; and *Remake,* 179; and *Subscript,* 156, 163, 167, 168; and *Textermination,* 137, 138, 143, 144, 145; and *Xorandor,* 117, 129; "as if," 110–11; code of suffering in, 153; computers in, 101, 102, 107, 111, 113; constraints in, 104–5; criticism of, 207, 209, 226n10, 227n15;

dialogue in, 119, 120; "direlogues" in, 5, 99, 114; emergence in, 110, 112; female central consciousness in, 54–55, 120, 198, 206; "fibstory," 103, 112; "hauntology," 112, 113; language as guard against extinction, 115–16; modal auxiliaries in, 106, 108, 109–110; "nonrealized tenses" in, 15, 23, 106, 107, 108, 109, 113, 114, 229n3; "oblitopia," 102, 112, 113, 153, 226n8; ontology of characters, 113–14, 129, 227n14, 227n15, 228n3; original title, 100, 226n9; possible annihilation of humanity in, 13, 99, 100, 104, 114–15, 153; predictability in, 102, 104, 106, 110, 125; prophecy in, 99, 100, 101–2, 104, 105, 107, 115, 226n8; puns in, 101, 107; redundancy in, 100–1, 111; "technique for living" in, 104, 116; use of first person, 99, 100, 221n11; use of future tense, 104, 105–6, 109, 207; utopia in, 108–9;

243

women in, 103; word play, 113–14; writing of, 215
ambiguity: in *Amalgamemnon*, 129; in *Turn of the Screw*, 130, 131; in *Xorandor*, 120, 125–26, 127–29, 130–31, 133–34, 136
analogy, 41, 43, 68, 72, 121, 122, 183, 214
Ancient Mariner, 116
anomie, 59, 62, 222n5
apocalypse, 105; in *Amalgamemnon*, 99–100, 105, 114; in *Out*, 13, 24, 32, 33, 34, 37, 156; in *Textermination*, 3, 139–40, 141; in *Xorandor*, 132. *See also* death; disaster; oblivion; extinction
Apollo, 72
Armstrong, Nancy, 60
"as if," 110–111, 189
"as such," 52, 214
astrophysics, 41, 43, 47, 49, 195, 200
Attridge, Derek, 220n8
Austen, Jane, 4, 145, 229n4
authorial existence linked with text, 2, 3, 12, 65, 95, 116, 134, 154, 170–71, 179, 185, 195

"Baroque Imagination, The," 27–28, 30–31, 220n5
Ballard, J. G., 16, 96, 128
Bakhtin, Mikhail, 73
Barthes, Roland: and *Between*, 62, 222n4; in *Thru*, 94, on author and reader, 12; on death of the author, 26; popularity of, 79; readerly and writerly texts, 56–58, 87, 221n2; *S/Z*, 56–58, 83, 87, 201, 218
Baudrillard, Jean, 16
Beckett, Samuel: and "Foot, The," 8, and *Out*, 25; and *Textermination*, 137, 142; Brooke-Rose's reviews of, 29, 191, influence on Brooke-Rose's narrative sentence, 29, 31
Benjamin, Walter, 12, 52, 116
Benveniste, Émile, 48, 79
Bergson, Henri, 164, 170
Bernheimer, Charles, 89
Berressem, Hanjo, 80, 83, 84, 224n8
Between, 56–77; activity versus passivity in, 65–67, 77; and Brooke-Rose, 65, 191; and *In Transit* (Brophy), 69, 77, 197; and *Oberland* (Richardson), 60–61; and *Textermination*, 224n23; and *Thru*, 81, 83, 86, 87, 95, 96,

230n4; and *A Void* (Perec), 21–22, 54, 206; and Woolf, Virginia, 60, 69; computers and, 75–76; *deus ex machina* in, 75, 76, 77; dialogue in, 95, 119, 120; "distant brain" in, 59, 61, 68, 75–76, 224n23; female central consciousness in, 56, 59, 60, 74, 75, 191, 198, 205; gender in, 54–55, 65–66, 67, 69–73, 74, 75, 95, 114, 120, 168, 204, 230n4; language of flowers in, 73; limbo in, 55, 58–59, 61, 62, 66; metastory, 59, 60, 66; mimesis in, 59, 119; multilingualism of, 56, 58, 59, 64, 66, 67–68, 69, 71; myths in, 70, 71–72, 73; narratorless sentence in, 56, 73; omission of "to be" in, 20, 206; personal pronouns in, 73–75; possible annihilation of humanity in, 153; 62; postmodernist and modernist, 62, 63, 64, 65, 77, 222n12; poststructuralist, 67–68; prophecy in, 72; publication of, 57; puns in, 213, 223n20; repetition in, 58, 67; sacred in, 223n15; "technique for living" in, 69, 75; title, 223n19; transgressive syntax in, 58, 68, 69, 221n4; translation in, 56, 58, 60, 64, 65, 66, 70, 168, 191, 204; travel in, 56, 58–59, 60, 62, 71, 77; use of cliché, 66, 73; use of prepositions, 69; use of present tense, 58, 62; "vessels of conception," 53, 59, 63, 66, 69, 71, 72, 221n1; World War II in, 13, 61, 62–63, 64, 65, 114, 138; writing of, 40, 204, 205, 209, 212
Bierce, Ambrose, 125
"bifografy," 176, 178
bilingualism. *See* multilingualism
Birch, Sarah, 41, 136, 142, 220n5, 224n8, 224n12
Bishop, Elizabeth, 186
Blair-Hayley, Tess, in *Remake*, 176, 177, 178, 179, 180, 182, 187, 188, 189. *See also* Tess
Blanchot, Maurice, 66–67, 68, 99, 112, 115, 154, 223n18
blindness, 46, 49, 54, 78, 81, 84, 86, 87, 88, 90, 94, 99, 181, 225n13
Bloch, Ernst, 108–9, 110, 112
Bolter, J. David, 124, 126, 227n4
Bovary, Emma, 139, 140, 146
Brooke-Rose, Christine: as critic and author merged, 3, 23, 31, 57, 80–115,

179, 184; as journalist reviewer, 78–79, 190, 207, 209; as medievalist, 213; as poet, 198–99; as teacher, 78, 79, 175, 176, 201, 209; at British Intelligence Service, 65, 176, 191, 213; critical neglect of, 1–2, 20, 21, 116, 139, 154, 209; dreams, 211–12; enlightened by criticism of her work, 207, 226n10; family, 196, 200, 204–5, 208, 211, 212; her own death, 171, 174, 179, 181, 186; herself as subject, 174–75, 176–77, 180, 185, 186; Jungian analysis of, 210–11, 221n12; mother's death, 187, 208, 231n9; notebooks, 136, 202, 217n1; personal archives, 151, 209, 226n9; physical ailments, 180, 181, 182, 186, 194, 199, 208–209, 215, 218n1, 220n3, 231n10; reading, 202, 216, 221n12; retirement, 201
Brooks, Peter, 54
Brophy, Brigid, 69, 77, 87, 197, 222n6
Buchanan, Brad, 94
Burke, Kenneth, 5
Burroughs, William, 99

Calvino, Italo, 139, 143, 219n8
Cameron, Sharon, 218n2
Canepari-Labib, Michela, 41, 48, 210, 211, 227n15
Casaubon, 140
Caserio, Robert: and *Between*, 221n4, 222n11; and Lawrence, vii–viii, 223n17; and *Thru*, 96; on modernism, 226n13; on *Xorandor*, 128–29, 130, 135, 221n4
Cassandra, 23, 55, 99, 100, 101, 103, 104, 106, 107, 113, 116. *See also* Enketei, Mira
Cassar, Stafania, 164
castration, 9, 19, 54, 88, 94, 95, 188
Chaucer, Geoffrey, 213
"Chi parla?" *See* "Who speaks?"
Chomsky, Noam, 79, 177, 179–80, 188
Christ, 37, 38
circularity, 67, 68, 69, 76, 78
Cixous Hélène, 21, 57, 79, 84, 90, 225n16
Clément, Catherine, 79, 91, 225n16
clichés, 39, 66, 73, 100, 104, 110, 124, 125, 227n6
Coetzee, J. M., 38–39, 196, 220n8
Columbia Encyclopedia, 53

computers, 75, 76, 101, 107, 113, 117–24, 186, 231n10; as source of character, 124. *See also* *Xorandor*
Confessions of Zeno, The (Suevo), 2
Consenstein, Peter, 180, 219n9, 231n7
constraints on language, 16, 19, 20, 21, 36, 194, 198, 206, 212, 219n9, 230n4, 231n7; in *Amalgamemnon*, 20, 104, 105–6, 206, 207, 226n9; in *Between*, 20; in *Life, End Of*, 175, 189; in *Next*, 20, 119; in *Out*, 25, 36, 38, 223n22; in *Remake*, 20, 175–80, 187, 215, 231n5; in *Subscript*, 5, 20, 151, 154–55, 158, 168, 172–73; in *Textermination*, 146; in *Thru*, 96; in *Xorandor*, 120, 135, 136. *See also* lipograms; narratorless narrative; pronouns; person; tenses
"corpus crysis," 5, 13, 78, 88, 91, 95, 192
Costello, Elizabeth, 196
cummings, e e, 179
"Custom-House, The" (Hawthorne), 63

Dalkey Archives, 197
Dante, 44
Dasein, 52, 113
David-Ménard, Monique, 90, 92
de Man, Paul, 78, 80, 224n6
de Rachewiltz, Mary, 205
"dead white male," 37, 39, 40, 52, 198
Dear Deceit, The, 208
death, 132–33; and memory, 228n10; Brooke-Rose's mother's, 176, 187, 231n9; Brigid Brophy's, 197; fiction's link with, 3; in *Amalgamemnon*, 113, 116; in *Between*, 66, 73; in "Foot, The," 12, 15, 199, 200; in *Life, End Of*, 185, 186, 189, 231n8; in "On Terms," 7; in *Out*, 37, 220n3; in *Remake*, 179, 187; in *Subscript*, 151, 152, 153, 160, 162, 170, 193, 198; in *Such*, 23, 37, 39–55, 56, 198, 199; in *Textermination*, 3, 114, 139, 140, 141, 142, 143, 146; in *Thru*, 87, 95, 96; in *Turn of the Screw* (James), 93, 94; in *Xorandor*, 121, 130, 134; instinct, 46, 53, 54; of the archive, 132; of the author, 2, 3, 4, 12, 22, 26, 95, 99, 134, 140, 147, 179, 186, 193, 199, 219n10; of character, 4, 51, 140, 145; of humanism, 23, 38; of languages, 112, 179; of literature, 4, 139, 140, 147, 194; of narrative, 53, 96; of the novel, 4, 52, 99, 134, 140,

147, 194 of realism, 32, 52, 75, 81, 113, 123, 134, 140, 146, 148
Dedalus, Stephen (*Portrait of the Artist as a Young Man*), 89, 181, 231n8
Democritus of Abdera, 88, 224n13
Derrida, Jacques: and Brooke-Rose, 200, 201, 212, 227n8; and *Between*, 223n21; and "Foot, The," 10, 14–15, 19, 199; and *Subscript*, 160; and *Thru*, 79, 81, 85, 224n13, 225n15, 227n8; and *Xorandor*, 130, 131–33, 134, 135, 227n8, 228n10; on language and existence, 3; on memory and death, 228n10; on nuclear war, 131–33, 134, 135; on phallogocentrism, 85; on preserving the archive, 153–54, 160; on translation, 223n21; on writing severed from responsibility, 3, 10
deus ex machina, 75, 76, 77, 123, 142
Dickinson, Emily, 11, 14, 218n2
Diderot, Denis, 86, 217n2
Dimock, Wai Chee, 150
"direlogues," 5, 99, 114
disability: Brooke-Rose's, 180, 194; in *Life, End Of*, 182, 185, 186, 189. *See also* blindness; castration; invalid; self-mutilation
disaster, 67, 115, 188; in *Amalgamemnon*, 100, 115; in the Intercom Quartet, 99, 156; in *Out*, 156; in *Xorandor*, 121, 122, 131, 134. *See also* apocalypse; death; oblivion; extinction
"Discussion with Christine Brooke-Rose, A," 157, 193–216, 221n12
"Dissolution of Character in the Novel, The," characters built by words, 14, 54; death of character by Freud, 51–52; on poetry, 113; on computers, 73, 75–76, 123–24, 227n6; on effects of literary criticism, 139; on textermination, 140; on women portrayed as objects, 76
Disgrace (Coetzee), 38–39, 220n8. *See also* Coetzee, J. M.
Donne, John, 30–31, 179
dreams: Brooke-Rose's, 211–12, 221n12; in *Amalgamemnon*, 226n5; in *Between*, 59; in *Out*, 33, 37, 38; in *Subscript*, 168; in *Such*, 44, 47, 48–50, 52, 210, 211, 221n12; in *Textermination*, 144, 146; in *Thru*, 85, 87, 95, 224n11; in *Xorandor*, 124; Freud on, 48, 49, 51, 211

drives. *See* instincts
Duchamp, Marcel, 219n8
"Dynamic Gradients," 220n4

Eliot, George, 140, 202
Eliot, T. S., 59, 63, 74, 89, 96, 140, 223n15
emergence, 110, 157, 158, 164, 165, 177
Emma. *See* Bovary, Emma; Woodhouse, Emma
Enketei, Mira: in *Amalgamemnon*, 99, 100, 102, 103, 104, 107, 110, 111, 112, 118; in *Textermination*, 125, 135, 137, 140, 141, 163; in *Verbivore*, 229n3
Erikson, Erik, 203
ET: The Extraterrestrial (Spielberg), 117, 227n1
"Eximplosions," 61, 222n12
extinction, 13; Brooke-Rose's, 174; in "Foot, The," 8, 10; in *Out*, 37; in *Subscript*, 15, 23, 152, 162, 168, 170, 171, 188; in *Such*, 53, 54; in *Textermination*, 5, 23, 140; in *Xorandor*, 122, 188; of literature, 4, 5, 140. *See also* apocalypse; death; disaster; oblivion; obsolescence
extremity, 13, 181, 182, 187, 218n1
eyes, 225n14; in *Amalgamemnon*, 100; in *Between*, 70; in "Foot, The," 12; in *Jalousie* (Robbe-Grillet), 31, 36; in *Out*, 29, 37; in *Remake*, 186; in *Subscript*, 155, 165, 166, 167, 172; in *Such*, 52, 53; in *Thru*, 82, 83–84, 85, 88–89, 94; in *Textermination*, 145. *See also* blindness

fantasy: in *Between*, 71; in the novel, 147–48; in "On Terms," 7, 8; in *Out*, 24, 32, 42, 44, 47; in *Rhetoric of the Unreal*, 13, 130, 144, 226n5; in *Subscript*, 168, 170; in *Such*, 40, 42; in *Textermination*, 138, 148; in *Turn of the Screw* (James), 17, 128, 130, 191; in *Xorandor*, 123
Farishta, Gibreel, 139, 147
Felman, Shoshana, 18, 84, 93
fetish, 10, 11, 14, 17, 54
"fibstory," 103, 112
Fish, Stanley, 1
"Foot, The," 8–12, 13, 14, 16–17, 193, 199; and *Life, End Of*, 181, 182, 183, 231n11; and *Thru*, 95; as narrative

of abjection, 9, 13, 24, 198; extremity in, 13; fetishism in, 10, 17; ghosts in, 7–8; language as guard against extinction, 8; language as means of extinction, 10–11; loss and desire in, 12, 17; narrator of, 8, 10, 12, 13, 60, 198; phantom limb, 8–11, 13, 14, 17, 35, 54, 153, 198, 217n1; pain in, 8, 9, 11, 13, 153, 183, 191; presages later works, 16–17, 199, 231n11; suffering's imprint in, 153; treble voice in, 199, 202; use of first person, 8, 12; writing of, 200; writing to control pain, 10–11, 14, 17
Fortey, Richard, 161–62
Foucault, Michel, 201
Fourth Ghost Book, The, 8
Frankenstein, 125
free direct discourse, 73–74. *See also* narratorless narrative
Freudian theory: and the death of character, 51; and instincts, 43, 46, 51, 54 151–52, 164, 204; Brooke-Rose's opinion of, 203, 211, 221n12; Brooke-Rose's reading of, 211, 212, 221n10; in *AI*, 225n20; in Brooke-Rose's criticism, 18, 19, 43, 51, 81, 92, 225n15, 228n10; in dreams and jokes, 48–51, 210, 211; in *Subscript*, 151–52; in *Such*, 44, 46, 48–51, 54, 210–11, 212, 221n12; in *Textermination*, 146; in *Thru*, 81, 89, 92; on hysteria, 89, 92; on identity, 203; on topology of the unconscious, 42–43, 203, 212. *See also* psychoanalysis

Gallop, Jane, 71
Garland, Judy, 158
gender: androgyny, 60, 69, 75, 204; formation, 165; in *Amalgamemnon*, 112, 114; in *Between*, 60, 65–66, 69–71, 73, 75; in paradigms, 230n4; in *Subscript*, 230n10; in *Such*, 54–55, in *Thru*, 85, 86, 95; objectification of female, 88; occlusion of women, 81, 84, 103, 186; unmarked by, 119, 120. *See also* feminism; narrators, female; narrators, male; phallocentrism
Genette, Gerard, 33, 79, 80, 105, 160
genres Brooke-Rose employs: allegory, 213; alternative fiction, 226n12; autobiography, 178, 179, 180–81, 230n5; *bildungsroman*, 157, 181, 213; black comedy, 8; captivity narrative, 168; clan tale, 157; classical history, 103, 105; comic novel, 118; creation story, 157; detective story, 170; diary, 187, 231n9; dream diary, 211; elegy, 12; fable, 132; fantasy, 7, 8, 13, 24, 32, 42, 44, 47, 71, 123, 138, 148, 168, 170, 226n5, 230n6; fictional autobiography, 175–76, 187; ghost story, 7–8, 18, 130, 187, 193; historical fiction, 12, 105; horror story, 170; journey narrative, 55, 56–57, 58, 76, 77, 81, 82, 83; memoir, 180, 181, 182, 184, 185; metafiction, 55, 59, 60, 66, 78, 122, 137, 138, 141, 148, 188, 217n2; myth, 45, 70, 71–73, 88, 90, 99–116, 131, 167, 225n20, 226n6; neocosm, 24, 32, 109; nouveau roman, 2, 20, 33, 37; picaresque, 82, 213; realism (mimicked), 59, 83, 84, 90, 91, 101, 106, 140; satire, 32, 208, 210, 211; science fiction, 31, 118, 121, 124, 125, 128–29, 148, 150, 151, 219n13; survival narrative, 96; travel novel, 71. *See also* fantasy; myth; nouveau roman; realism; science fiction
ghosts, 8, 52; Holy, 123; in "Foot, The," 8, 10, 14; in the machine, 75–76, 77, 123; in *Les revenentes* (Perec), 22; in *Textermination*, 3, 54, 139, 141; in *Thru*, 83–84; in *Turn of the Screw* (James), 18–19, 23, 130. *See also deus ex machina*; genres: ghost stories; hauntings; phantoms; specters
Go When You See the Green Man Walking, 7–8, 13, 95, 193
Goethe, Johann Wolfgang von, 66, 139
Grammar of Metaphor, A, 175, 177, 213, 214
Greimas, Algirdas, 79, 82, 86, 91, 103

Harry Potter, 216
hauntings, 2, 5, 14–15, 90, 19, 22, 23, 199; in *Amalgamemnon*, 102, 112, 113; in *Between*, 64; in "Foot, The," 8, 10–11, 17, 217; in *Remake*, 187; in *Subscript*, 169, 170; in *Thru*, 83–84; in *Turn of the Screw* (James), 131. *See also* ghosts; phantoms; specters
Hayles, N. Katherine, 16–17, 135
Harmon, Philippe, 57
Heart of Darkness (Conrad), 46

Heidegger, Martin, 113, 207
"Heredotage," 180, 183
Herodotus, 102, 103, 104, 107, 168
humanism, rejection of, 23, 25, 27, 35, 28, 101, 112, 113
Hume, David, 203
Hutcheon, Linda, 15–16, 62, 146

"Id is, is id?" 42–43, 221n12, 228n10
illness: Brooke-Rose's, 194, 199, 208–9, 215, 220n2; in *Life, End Of*, 183; in *Out*, 22, 24, 26, 28, 32, 35, 101, 156, 163, 220n3, 220n5; in *Such*, 44, 50, 47. *See also* disability; invalid
instincts, 42, 43, 45–46, 51, 53, 157, 163, 164, 203–4; death, 46, 53, 54; life, 151–52; repression of, 44
intertextuality, 2, 78, 137, 138, 141, 143, 146, 148, 225n2, 227n14, 228n3
invalid: Brooke-Rose as, 180, 195–96, 231n11; in *Life, End Of*, 181–82, 184–85, 187, 231n11. *See also* aging; disability; illness
Irigaray, Luce, 79, 84, 90
"Is Self-Reflexivity Mere?" 80
Intercom Quartet, 99, 113, 117, 121, 136, 137, 148, 156, 225n2, 227n14. *See also Amalgamemnon, Textermination, Verbivore, Xorandor*
Invisible Author, 174, 175–76, 179, 209; combines theory and fiction, 4; constraints explained, 20, 21, 26, 105–6, 175, 176, 184; on *Amalgamemnon*, 102, 103, 105–6, 225n15; on criticism, 223n16; on deconstruction, 81; on narratorless narrative, 20, 25, 26–27, 118, 120, 224n22; on the nature of authorship, 2; on *Next* and *Verbivore*, 219n13; on Oulipo, 21–22; on *Remake*, 179; on scientific present tense, 26, 118, 136, 151; on structuralism, 224n5; on *Subscript*, 151, 156, 158, 163, 166, 229n5; on *Such*, 40, 41; on *Thru*, 80, 81, 82, 84, 86, 96; on writing to combat extinction, 154, 174; on *Xorandor*, 120, 136; redressing critical oversight, 21, 116, 154, 171, 174; reveals her intentions, 3; self-examination in 3, 174

Jakobson, Roman, 79, 82, 230n4

James, Henry, 57, 131, 191, 203. *See also Turn of the Screw*
Jameson, Frederic, 32, 91, 111, 226n13
Janek (*Remake*), 176, 178, 187
Jay, Martin, 87, 225n14
"John" (*Remake*), 177–79, 182, 188
John the Baptist, 88
Johnson, B. S., 190
Johnson, Samuel, 30
Jonah, 51, 55, 58–59, 100, 111
Joyce, James, 135, 144, 196, 197; *Finnegans Wake*, 100, 112; *Portrait of the Artist as a Young Man*, 89, 181, 231n8; *Ulysses*, 146, 190, 231n8
Jung, Karl, 210–11, 221n12

King Lear, 88
Kristeva, Julia, 79, 84, 96
Kundera, Milan, 4, 145. *See also* "unbearable lightness of being"

Lacan, Jacques, 201; theories of: Brooke-Rose's reading of, 203, 212, 221n12; in Brooke-Rose's criticism, 18, 19, 76, 80–81, 84, 95; cited by other critics, 84, 92, 93, 96, 224n8; in *Between*, 67, 71; in *Thru*, 79, 81, 82, 83, 84, 90, 96, 225n11; on gender, 70
Lancelot, 213
Languages of Love, The, 208
Laplanche, Jean, 43, 51, 53
Larry (*Such*), 23, 39, 40–47, 48, 49–51, 52, 53, 54, 221n11, 221n12
Lazarus, 38, 40, 47, 51, 51, 54. *See also* Larry
Le Lionnais, François, 219n8
Lecercle, Jean-Jacques, 109–110, 113–14, 207–8, 226n10
Lehmann, John, 29
"Letters from Paris," 79, 191
Life, End Of, 174, 180, 181–87, 188, 189; and *Invisible Author*, 20; and *Remake*, 187; and *Ulysses* (Joyce), 231n8; explaining her method, 154; metastory, 185, 188; on aging, 23, 164, 180, 181, 182–84, 188, 189, 194; on the nature of authorship, 2; on pain, 182–84; on writing to combat extinction, 154, 174, 189; O.P. (Other People), 182, 186, 194; self-confrontation in, 180, 185; T.F. (True Friends), 182, 185; use

of first person, 187; use of narrative sentence, 175, 182, 183
limbo, 55, 58–59, 61, 66
lipograms, 20, 21, 22, 26, 36, 82, 104, 108, 109, 110, 111, 154, 189, 191. *See also* constraints on language
Little, Judy, 197
Locke, John, 203
losses, 4, 5, 15, 193, 198; and longing, 9, 11–12, 108, 112; in *Amalgamemnon*, 103; in *Between*, 59, 60, 62, 69; in "Foot, The," 10, 14, 198; in *Life, End Of*, 182, 183, 186, 187–88; in *Out*, 25, 32; in *Remake*, 179, 188; in *Subscript*, 154–55, 157, 161, 170; in *Textermination*, 138, 141, 142, 144; in *Turn of the Screw* (James), 19; of the human archive, 5; twentieth century, 5, 14, 61; writing counteracts, 11, 191–92, 198. *See also* pain
Love's Body (Brown), 77
Luckacher, Ned, 92
Lukács, Georg, 138

MacCannell, Dean, 61
"Making It New," 191
Mallarmé, Stéphane, 135, 211
"Man with the Blue Guitar" (Stevens), 96
Middlemen, The, 208
Marx, Groucho, 50–51
Marx, Karl, 51, 108
Matthews, Harry, 219n8
McElroy, Joseph, 179–80, 226n9
McFadgeon, Kelly (*Textermination*), 141, 142, 144
McHale, Brian, 227n14, 228n3
Mehlman, Jeffrey, 221n10
memory: computer-like, 224n23, 228n10; in *Amalgamemnon*, 102, 111, 112; in *Between*, 64, 65, 69; in "Foot, The," 10, 13; in Freud, 43; in *Life, End Of*, 181, 183; in *Out*, 29, 32, 35; in *Remake*, 174, 175, 176, 178, 188; in Robbe-Grillet, 28, 36; in *Subscript*, 151, 152, 153, 159, 160, 162, 163, 167; in *Such*, 40, 44, 52; in *Textermination*, 23, 114, 140, 144, 224n23; in *Thru*, 89; in *Xorandor*, 122, 132, 133, 138; selective, 195–96, 231n6, 231n11
Merlin, 123
metafiction. *See* genres Brooke-Rose employs

"Metafiction and Surfiction," 115
metaphor, 65, 213, 229n6; in *Between*, 59, 60, 65, 71, 179, 222n6; in "Foot, The," 9, 217n1; in *Out*, 218n2; in *Remake*, 188; in *Such*, 41, 47, 49–50, 54, 200; Robbe-Grillet opposed to, 27, 30
Métail, Michèle, 218n8
mimesis, 26, 33, 53, 59, 75, 86, 98, 119, 230n6
Mira. *See* Enketei, Mira
mirroring, 19, 40, 80–81, 82, 83–86, 104, 145, 150, 185, 224n8
modern condition, 15, 51, 61–62, 95, 99, 102, 115, 134, 136, 185, 222n6, 226n4
Montaigne, Michel de, 181
Motte, Jr., Warren F., 20–21, 218n7–8
multilingualism, 56, 58, 59, 62, 64, 66, 67–68, 203, 205, 213
myth: gender-marked, 70, 71–73, 167; Greek, 45, 72, 88, 90, 94, 99–116, 225n20, 226n6; of androgyny, 69; of deconstruction, 223n21; of flight, 71; of humanism, 27; of science, 131

naming, 44, 45, 114, 158, 166, 176–77, 179, 203, 209
narrative sentence (NS), 118, 119, 120, 175, 182, 183, 221n9, 223n22
narratorless narrative, 20; in *Between*, 73; in *Life, End Of*, 154, 183, 185; in *Out*, 25, 26–27, 33, 38, 213, 220n5, 221n11; in *Subscript*, 150, 156, 158; in *Such*, 52, 59; in *Textermination*, 141; in *Thru*, 83, 99
narrators: female, 54–55, 56, 59, 60, 74, 75, 87, 90, 120, 141, 151, 166, 191, 198, 204, 205, 206; male, 10, 12, 24, 39–40, 60, 101, 120, 153, 198, 204; multiple, 98, 103, 105, 120, 137–38, 141, 228n2; unreliable, 87, 95, 146; ungendered, 120
Nash, Christopher, 24, 92, 109
Newton, Isaac, 161
Next, 20, 22, 119, 219n13
Non-Existent Knight, 139, 143
nouveau roman: in Beckett, 29; in Brooke-Rose, 2, 20, 33, 37; in Robbe-Grillet, 26, 27, 30, 51; in Sarraute, 28

oblitopia, 102, 112–13, 153, 226n5
oblivion, 45, 114, 115, 143, 144, 145, 153,

181, 188. *See also* apocalypse; disaster; extinction
obsolescence, 5, 7, 22; in *Amalgamemnon*, 13, 100, 101, 107, 112, 206; in "Foot, The," 14; in *Out*, 38; in *Subscript*, 153, 163; in *Thru*, 94, 95. *See also* apocalypse; extinction; oblivion; redundancy
OED (*Oxford English Dictionary*), 40, 203
Oedipus, 88, 94, 101, 225n20
"On Terms," 7–8
Orion: in *Amalgamemnon*, 103, 104, 111, 114; in *Textermination*, 143, 145
Orlando, Francesco, 22, 219n12
Oulipo, 20–22, 180, 218n8, 219n9
Out, 22, 24–26, 28, 29–30, 31–38, 199; absence of pronouns in, 205; absence of third-person past tense in, 105; and *Amalgamemnon*, 112; and Beckett, 29; and *Between*, 56; and *In the Labyrinth* (Robbe-Grillet), 26; and *Life, End Of*, 183; and *Subscript*, 156, 163; and *Such*, 54; and "Foot, The," 8, 35; as science fiction, 31–32; authority figures in, 34; apocalyptic, 13, 24, 33, 34, 37, 153, 156; criticism of, 196; dystopic, 31, 226n12; dead white male in, 37, 39, 40, 52; emotional valence in, 36–37, 38; fictional deaths in, 99; illness in, 26, 220n3, 220n7; male central character in, 24, 60, 101, 120, 153, 198, 204; narratorless narrative in, 25, 26, 28, 32, 119, 155, 221n11, 223n22; opening sentence, 25, 156; pain of absence in, 35–36; passivity in, 24, 25–26, 156; plot uncertain, 33–34, 35, 36, 37; prolepsis in, 37; "psychoscopy," 34–35; race in, 24, 31–33, 34, 35, 198, 213; technical transgressions in, 33–34; "techniques for living" in, 23, 34, 35; title of, 223n19; use of metaphor, 220n6; use of present tense, 32, 33; writing of, 208, 212, 220n3

pain: as companion, 9, 153, 183, 191, 218n1; coded in humanity, 153; emotional, 31, 36, 49, 88, 89, 90, 91, 98, 114, 133, 156, 191, 217, 218n2; and existence, 9, 13, 14, 23, 38, 52; historical, 38, 39, 62; imprinted on the body, 17, 153, 191; of the twentieth century, 5, 13; physical, 8, 23, 53, 54, 90, 153, 163, 169, 170, 182, 186; writing as conversion method for, 5, 10–11, 14, 17, 180. *See also* losses; phantom pain
"Palimpsest History," 148
Paradise Lost (Milton), 133
Perec, Georges, 21–22, 206–7, 218n8
person: first singular, in *Amalgamemnon*, 99; in "Foot, The," 12, 24; in *Life, End Of*, 184, 187; in *Such*, 221n11; in *Subscript*, 165–66; in *Textermination*, 138, 141–42, 143; first plural, 165; second, 74, 75, 184; third, 21, 26, 74, 75, 140, 176, 204
phallocentrism, 75, 76, 81, 86, 95, 96, 97, 227n6
phantom limb, viii, 23; in "Foot, The," 8–11, 13, 14, 17, 35, 54, 153, 198, 217n1
phantom pain, 8–9, 10, 200
phantoms, 4, 193, 198, 210; in "Foot, The," 8, 9, 10; in *Textermination*, 145, 148. *See also* ghosts; hauntings; specters
pharmakon, 129, 201, 228n8
Pinget, Robert, 191
Plato, 227n8
pleasures of technique, 19, 77, 80, 83, 96, 100, 166, 168, 188. *See also* word play
Pontalis, J. B., 43, 51, 53
postmodernism, 2, 3, 4, 15, 75, 217n2; and the body, 16–17; as broken from modernism, 15–16, 62, 92, 146, 222n12; constrained by history, 62, 63; debt to modernism, 63, 190, 222n10, 222n12; in *Between*, 62, 63, 64, 65, 77, 197, 221n1, 222n12; in *Textermination*, 145, 146, 229n4; in *Turn of the Screw* (James), 130; in *Xorandor*, 128; phallocentrism of, 76
poststructuralism, 3, 12; and structuralism, 19, 57, 67, 78, 90, 91, 195, 218n5; Brooke-Rose as teacher of, 79–80, 201; in *Between*, 67–68; in *Thru*, 78, 80, 81, 83, 85, 86, 89, 90, 91, 95; in *Turn of the Screw* (James), 19
Pound, Ezra, 63, 181, 201, 205, 211, 213, 215, 223n14, 223n15, 228n8
Pratt, Terence W., 227n2
prolepsis, 37, 105
pronouns, personal, 165–66; constraints on; 2, 20, 73–75, 120, 154–55, 157,

172–73, 175, 176, 179, 180, 205, 215, 229n5, 231n5; use of, 8–11, 12, 103, 105, 143, 155, 187, 221n11. *See also* person
pronouns, possessive, 20, 39, 155, 166, 176, 180
prophecy, 54–55, 67, 72, 101, 102–9, 115, 128, 135, 148, 169, 170, 226n8
Proust, Marcel, 11, 195
psychoanalysis: Brooke-Rose as a patient, 210–11; in *Between*, 69, 71; in *Out*, 34; in *Such*, 41, 48–49, 52, 210, 211, 212; in *Thru*, 80, 85, 86, 88, 90, 95, 224n11; in *Turn of the Screw* (James), 18–19. *See also* Freudian theory
Pym, Barbara, 197
Pynchon, Thomas, 196

Queneau, Raymond, 20, 21, 218n7–8

Rabaté, Jean-Michel, 195, 208
race, 24, 31–33, 35, 38, 198, 213
real versus unreal, 15, 18, 84, 99, 130–33, 135, 136, 138, 142–44, 145, 148, 170; in twentieth century fiction, 4, 13, 14, 54, 75, 147; in twentieth-century life, 5, 13, 14, 72, 84, 99, 123, 138, 144, 148, 170, 190, 191, 222n6
realism: as dead, 32, 52, 75, 81, 113, 123, 134, 140, 146, 148; defined, 56, 57, 105, 148; eschewed, 4, 105, 124, 128; mimicked, 59, 83, 84, 90, 91, 101, 106; tricks of, 145, 202
redundancy, 60; in *Amalgamemnon*, 100, 101, 102, 106, 111, 112, 117, 206; in *Subscript*, 163; in *Xorandor*, 122. *See also* obsolescence; repetition
reflexivization, 176, 177, 180
Remake, 174, 175, 176–80, 181, 187–89; and *Invisible Author*, 179; as fiction, 212; as fictional autobiography, 174, 175; as "memesis," 174; "bifografy," 176; 178; constraint on first person, 20, 176, 180, 215; diary simulation, 187, 231n9; explaining her method, 180; grammar in, 178–79; impetus for, 180–81; on aging, 23, 179, 180, 187–88; on critical attention, 175; on memory, 175; paradigms replayed in, 230n4; pleasure of writing, 188–89; puns in, 180; reflexivization

in, 177, 180; self-confrontation in, 177, 181; use of first person, 187; use of narrative sentence, 175, 221n11
repetition, 14, 223n15; in *Amalgamemnon*, 100, 106, 110, 112, in *Between*, 58, 67; in *Out*, 32, 34, 37; in *Remake*, 179; in "Squirm of the True, The," 18; in *Such*, 52–53; in *Thru*, 84, 89, 90, 91. *See also* redundancy
"Review of *Jalousie*," 36
Rhetoric of the Unreal, A: on fiction in the twentieth century, 4–5, 13, 115; on herself, 115; on literary theory, 85, 115; on modernity, 61, 84, 130–31, 132, 144, 226n4; on oblitopia, 226n5; on poetry, 123; on real vs. unreal, 130, 132, 144; on realism, 57; on science fiction, 32; on Sontag, Susan, 61; on technical transgressions, 33–34, 37; on *Turn of the Screw* (James), 17–19, 84, 93, 130, 193, 221n12, 224n7; on the unconscious, 81, 92–93, 95; ontology of characters, 141; quoting Felman, Shoshana, 93–94
Richards, I. A., 66
Richardson, Dorothy, 60
Rimmon-Kenan, Shlomith, 128
Robbe-Grillet, Alain, 20, 26–28, 29, 30–31, 33, 36, 183, 191, 209, 213, 221n11
Roubaud, Jacques, 219n8, 231n7
Rousseau, Jean-Jacques, 154
Rushdie, Salman, 139, 147–48

Sage, Lorna, 153, 158, 170, 209
"Samuel Beckett and the Anti-Novel," 29
Sarraute, Nathalie, 26, 28, 190, 195, 220n4
Scheherezade, 86, 97, 142
Schmidt, Albert-Marie, 219n8
Scholes, Robert, 76
science, 13; and character, 51–52, 124; as method of depersonalization, 27–30, 34, 38, 41, 43, 47; as source of hubris, 136; Brooke-Rose's attraction to, 17, 136, 202, 227n2; fictionalized, 151, 159, 160; limitations of, 47, 127, 130–31, 226n4, 226n5; symbolized, 28; theory, 150–51, 156, 157–158, 162. *See also* tenses, scientific present
science fiction, 32, 105, 124, 220n6; as male-centered, 76; Brooke-Rose

differs from, 32, 109, 124, 128, 200; in the Intercom Quartet, 148; in *Out*, 31; in *Subscript*, 150, 151; in *Verbivore*, 219n13; in *Xorandor*, 118, 121, 124, 125, 128–29, 219n13

"Self-Confrontation and the Writer," 177

self-mutilation, 87–88, 94–95, 97, 218n2

semiotics, 57, 74, 82, 86, 91, 93, 96–97, 103, 110

Shakespeare, William, 130, 124, 216; *Hamlet*, 14; *Macbeth*, 127

sickness. *See* illness

signifiers, 68, 70, 83, 84, 86–87, 90, 96, 98, 104, 111, 114

Sobchack, Vivian, 16, 17

Sontag, Susan, 61

"Soon," 100, 226n9

specters, 4, 7, 10, 14–15; Brooke-Rose as, 2; in *Amalgamemnon*, 99; in *Between*, 63; in "Foot, The," 14, 23; in *Textermination*, 142. *See also* ghosts; hauntings; phantoms

Spielberg, Steven, 117, 225n20

Spivak, Gayatri, 220n7

"Squirm of the True I, The," 191

"Squirm of the True II, The," 18

Stein, Gertrude, 105, 112, 148, 226n8

Steiner, George, 147

Stevenson, Randall, 190

Stewart, Garrett, 52, 55

Stewart, Susan, 11–12

Stories, Theories and Things: and *Invisible Author*, 184; as metafiction, 55; combines theory and fiction, 4; "Id is, is id?" appears in, 43, 228n10; on *Between*, 58, 59, 60, 66, 68; on Brooke-Rose as critic and writer, 1, 3, 115–16; on critical attention to her work, 1–2; on "Custom-House, The" (Hawthorne), 63; on the nature of authorship, 2; on *Out*, 39; on scientific language, 41; on *Such*, 40; on *Thru*, 81, 86; on writing to combat extinction, 154; reveals her intentions, 3

Strachey, James, 48

Subscript, 5, 150–73; and "Foot, The," 13; and *Life, End Of*, 188; and *Remake*, 175; art in, 168–70; Brooke-Rose's preparations for, 202; constraints in, 154–55, 157, 158, 168, 172–73; disappearing persons in, 193; evolution in, 150, 151, 152, 157–58, 160, 161–62, 163, 164; evolutionary theory fictionalized, 160, 165, 170; extinction in, 15, final novel, 194; 23, 152, 153, 162, 168, 188; female central consciousness, 151, 166; Figure A, 154, 158, 159, 172–73, 229n5; gender in, 166–69; genetic code, 152–53, 162–63, 164; joyful change, 156–57; language as guard against extinction, 154, 158; language development in, 166–68; life instinct in, 151–52, 157, 163, 164; memory in, 163; narratorless narrative in, 150, 151, 156, 158; objective observation in, 155–56; obsolescence in, 163; personal pronouns in, 20, 154–55, 157, 165–66; prehuman in, 23, 151, 202; sacred cave, 169–70; scientific present tense in, 151; storytelling in, 157, 161–62, 167; suffering's imprint in, 153; time in, 159–62, 169; title, 152; unreal in, 170; visions in, 169–70

Such, 39–55, 210–12; and *Amalgamemnon*, 95; and *Between*, 56; and "Foot, The," 199–200; and Freudian psychoanalysis, 48, 49, 51, 210, 211, 212; and *Thru*, 81, 95; as fiction, 212; critical reception of, 48, 207, 210, 211; astrophysics in, 41, 43, 47, 49, 195, 200; dead white male in, 198; dead protagonist, 23, 39; dialogue in, 119, 120; drives in, 42, 43, 46, 51, 203–4; first sentence of, 39, 204, 231n6; Freudian topology in, 42–43; gender in, 39–40; illness in, 44, 47; language of science in, 41, 43, 44, 47, 49, 200; male central character in, 39–40, 60, 120, 153, 198, 204; personal pronoun in, 221n11; planetary children in, 44–46, 52, 210, 212, 221n11, 221n12; post-humanism in, 13; psychic journey in, 41–46, 44; rebirth in, 37–38, 40, 44, 51, 198; suffering's imprint in, 153; title, 40, 214; word play in, 48–51, 210, 211; writing of, 200, 204, 209, 211, 212

suffering. *See* pain

Suleiman, Susan, 223n16

Sycamore Tree, The, 208

techne of writing, 100, 102, 104, 105, 113, 124, 195

"techniques for living," 4, 190, 191,

213; in *Amalgamemnon*, 104, 116; in *Between*, 69, 75; in *Invisible Author*, 174; in *Life, End Of*, 182, 184, 186; in *Out*, 23, 34, 35, 38; in *Remake*, 174; in *Subscript*, 154; in *Thru*, 80, 87, 96; in *Xorandor*, 126, 133, 134

Tel Quel, 79, 214, 228n8

tenses: in *Between*, 58, 62; in "Foot, The," 11; in *Life, End Of*, 175, 184; in *Out*, 25, 26, 32, 33, 38, 224n22, in *Remake*, 175, 187; in *Subscript*, 150, 158; in *Textermination*, 141; future, 104, 105–6, 107, 206, 207, 226n9; non-realized, 106–10, 113, 114, 229n3; past, 140; present, 231n7; scientific present, 26–27, 30, 52, 104–5, 118, 136, 151. *See also* narrative sentence; narratorless narrative

Terdiman, Richard, 217n2

Tess, in *Life, End Of*, 180, 182, 184. *See also* Blair-Hayley, Tess

textermination, 2, 23, 135, 148, 152, 154, 186; defined, 99; in *Textermination*, 141, 143, 152; language as guard against, 175; of *Subscript*, 154

Textermination, 137–49, "aerobrain" in, 139, 224n23; and World War II, 138, 148; apocalyptic, 3, 139, 141; as fantasy, 138, 148; as metafiction, 3, 137, 138, 141; Brooke-Rose's preparations for, 202; death in, 114, 140–44, 146, 147, 152, 153; *deus ex machina* in, 142; "direlogues" in, 99; disappearances in, 137, 140, 141, 148, 163; female central consciousness in, 55, 141, 198; ghosts in, 3, 4, 54, 139, 141, 193; in the Intercom Quartet, 99, 137; intertextuality of characters, 137, 139–40, 143–44, 145, 146, 149, 226n2, 229n3; language as guard against extinction, 2, 3–4, 5, 139, 142, 144; narratorless narrative in, 99, 141; on criticism's damage to fiction, 139, 144, 146–47; ontology of characters, 23, 54, 139, 140, 141, 142–46, 156; possible annihilation of humanity in, 153, 188; puns in, 141, 145; reader's responsibility in, 142, 146–47; real and unreal in, 138, 142–44, 148; "unbearable lightness of being" in, 3–4, 23, 144–45, 149; unemployment in 112, 139, 163; use of third-person past tense, 140

theory, literary, 78–80, 85, 212; as desire, 80, 91–93; as pursuit of meaning, 93–94, 136; fictionalized, 78, 82, 86, 87, 91, 136, 146; materialized in language, 212; resistance to, 224n6; shortcomings of, 98; tested by fiction, 115–16; used to reveal the unconscious, 81

Thru, 78–97, 98–99; anagrams in, 82, 90, 92; and *Amalgamemnon*, 103, 104, 114; and *Life, End Of*, 185; and *Subscript*, 153, 157; and *Textermination*, 137, 138; and *Xorandor*, 120; as hysterical text, 87, 88–89, 90–91, 98, 104, 153; as metafiction, 12, 23, 78, 81–82, 129, 217n2; as poetry, 96; as survival narrative, 96, 97; Brooke-Rose's opinion of, 81; "corpus crysis," 5, 13, 78, 88, 91, 95; dialogue in, 90, 91, 95, 99, 119; "disc/horse," 55, 82–83; drivers in, 55, 83, 85; female central consciousness in, 54–55, 87, 90; gender in, 84–85, 86, 88–89, 95; intertextuality, 78, 79, 86, 96, 217n2; journeys in, 81–83; language as guard against extinction, 86; mirrors in, 80–81, 82, 83, 84, 85, 86, 95, 224n8; Oedipus and, 88, 94, 101; ontology of characters, 23, 83, 87, 98, 99; paradigms in, 230n4; psychoanalysis in, 80–81, 85, 86, 88, 90, 95, 225n11; puns in, 80, 81, 83, 85, 88; real and unreal in, 83, 84; "techniques for living" in, 80, 87; theory as desire, 80, 91, 93, 96; theory fictionalized, 23, 78–80, 82, 86, 87, 91, 93, 221n3, 228n8; theory's limitations, 80, 98; title, 99, 223n19; typography in, 82, 89, 110; "unbearable lightness of being" in, 95; unreliable narrator, 83, 87, 95; use of first person in, 105; vision metaphors in, 81, 83–85, 86, 87–88, 90, 94, 99; "Who speaks?" 83, 119, 185, 224n11; "youdipeon discourse," 81, 88, 89, 99, 103

Time's Arrow (Amis), 208

TLS (*Times Literary Supplement*), 79, 216

Todorov, Tzvetan, 17–18, 191, 230n4

"Transgressions," 34, 37, 191

translation, 60, 64–67, 78, 87, 109, 154–55, 199, 201, 204, 205, 209, 223n15

Turing, Alan, 124, 126

Turn of the Screw, The (James), 17–19; and

Between, 59; and *Thru*, 80, 84, 224n7; and *Xorandor*, 128; as exemplar of ambiguity, 130, 131; Freudian reading of, 221n12; ghosts in, 23, 130, 193; reader and therapist in, 93. *See also* James, Henry

twentieth-century fiction, 54, 66, 77, 146, 184. *See also* modern condition; real versus unreal

"unbearable lightness of being," 3, 22, 193; Brooke-Rose's own, 3, 171; in *Amalgamemnon*, 113, 114, 133; in *Go When You See the Green Man Walking*, 7; in *Invisible Author*, 4; in *Life, End Of*, 188; in *Stories, Theories and Things*, 4; in *Remake*, 188; in *Subscript*, 152, 170; in *Such*, 53; in *Textermination*, 144, 145, 149; in *Thru*, 95; in *Xorandor*, 135–36. *See also* Kundera, Milan

Unlikely Ghosts, 8

Utterly Other Discourse (Friedman and Fuchs), 106

"Vanishing Author, The," 191

Verbivore, 219n13; and *Amalgamemnon*, 114, 225n2, 228n3; and *Subscript*, 153; in the Intercom Quartet, 99; narratorless narrative in, 114; sequel to *Xorandor*, 128, 219n13, 228n11; use of first person, 221n11

"vessels of conception," 63, 59, 66, 69, 71, 72, 221n1

Webster's dictionary, 109

"Where Do We Go From Here?" 138, 191

White, Glyn, 90, 99

"Who speaks?" 20, 83, 119, 185, 225n11

Wittig, Monique, 70, 74, 75

"Woman as Semiotic Object," 86, 96, 225n16

"Womb of One's Own, A," 76

Wood, Michael, 105, 196, 226n6

Woodhouse, Emma, 4, 139, 140, 145, 146, 149, 229n4

Woolf, Virginia, 60, 69, 197, 220n3, 229n4

word play, 158, 180, 210, 230n6; anagrams, 22, 82, 90, 92, 175; jokes, 48–51, 86, 118, 142, 159, 208, 210, 211, 229n3; onomatopoeia, 158, 159; puns, 13, 40, 50, 81, 82–83, 85, 86, 88, 101, 103, 111, 113, 114, 115, 122, 129, 141, 145, 180, 182, 186, 204, 213, 223n20

Wordsworth, William, 181, 218n6

writerly text, 57, 58, 83, 87

Xorandor, 117–36; accessibility of, 120, 129, 135; ambiguity in, 120, 125–26, 127–29, 130–31, 133–34, 136; and *Amalgamemnon*, 114, 117; and *Textermination*, 138, 153; and *Verbivore*, 219n13, 228n11; apocalypse in, 15, 114, 130, 132, 134, 188; as alternative fiction, 226n12; communication issues in, 121–22, 125, 126–27; computer language in, 118–19, 125, 129, 135; computer logic in, 119, 122, 124–25, 126, 128, 130, 136; computers generally, 15, 23, 113, 117–24; departure from narrative sentence, 221n11; dialogue in, 48, 99, 118, 119, 120, 121, 198, 219n13; gender in, 120, 198, 227n1; in the Intercom Quartet, 99, 113, 117; language as guard against extinction, 134–35; metafiction, 122; narrators ungendered, 120; nonliving nonhuman in, 15, 23, 117; nuclear deterrence in, 121, 125, 127, 131; ontology of character, 126; prophecy in, 135; puns in, 122, 123, 129; real and unreal in, 122, 123, 130–31, 136, 170; self-sacrifice in, 121, 126, 128, 129, 133, 191, 228n11; syntax errors, 126, 127, 128, 130, 134, 153, 191; "techniques for living" in, 126; theory fictionalized, 136; "unbearable lightness of being" in, 133, 135–36; writing of, 227n2, 228n8; Xorandor's name, 127–28; xorandoric, 127, 128, 133, 135, 221n4

Yeats, William Butler, 23, 77, 182, 183, 185–86

"youdipeon discourse," 81, 88, 89, 99, 110

Zavarzadeh, Mas'ud, 138

www.ingramcontent.com/pod-product-compliance
Lightning Source LLC
Chambersburg PA
CBHW030109010526
44116CB00005B/171